SO-ACA-168

ATE DUE

ACCELERATED DEPRECIATION
IN THE UNITED STATES
1954–60

NATIONAL BUREAU OF ECONOMIC RESEARCH

FISCAL STUDIES

1. *Fiscal Planning for Total War*
   WILLIAM LEONARD CRUM, JOHN F. FENNELLY,
   AND LAWRENCE H. SELTZER

2. *Taxable and Business Income*
   DAN THROOP SMITH AND J. KEITH BUTTERS

3. *The Nature and Tax Treatment of
   Capital Gains and Losses*
   LAWRENCE H. SELTZER

4. *Federal Grants and the Business Cycle*
   JAMES A. MAXWELL

5. *The Income-Tax Burden on Stockholders*
   DANIEL M. HOLLAND

6. *Personal Deductions in the Federal
   Income Tax*
   C. HARRY KAHN

7. *Dividends Under the Income Tax*
   DANIEL M. HOLLAND

8. *Business and Professional Income
   Under the Personal Income Tax*
   C. HARRY KAHN

9. *Accelerated Depreciation in the
   United States, 1954–60*
   NORMAN B. TURE

NORMAN B. TURE

ACCELERATED
DEPRECIATION IN THE
UNITED STATES
1954–60

NATIONAL BUREAU OF ECONOMIC RESEARCH

NEW YORK   1967

Distributed by COLUMBIA UNIVERSITY PRESS

NEW YORK AND LONDON

Copyright © 1967 by National Bureau of Economic Research
All Rights Reserved
L.C. Card No. 66-25245

Printed in the United States of America

HJ
4653
D5
T8

NATIONAL BUREAU OF ECONOMIC RESEARCH
1966

OFFICERS

Frank W. Fetter, *Chairman*
Arthur F. Burns, *President*
Theodore O. Yntema, *Vice-President*
Donald B. Woodward, *Treasurer*
Geoffrey H. Moore, *Director of Research*

Douglas H. Eldridge, *Executive Director*
Hal B. Lary, *Associate Director of Research*
Victor R. Fuchs, *Associate Director of Research*

DIRECTORS AT LARGE

Joseph A. Beirne, *Communications Workers of America*
Wallace J. Campbell, *Foundation for Cooperative Housing*
Erwin D. Canham, *Christian Science Monitor*
Solomon Fabricant, *New York University*
Marion B. Folsom, *Eastman Kodak Company*
Crawford H. Greenewalt, *E. I. du Pont de Nemours & Company*
Gabriel Hauge, *Manufacturers Hanover Trust Company*
Walter W. Heller, *University of Minnesota*
Albert J. Hettinger, Jr., *Lazard Frères and Company*
Harry W. Laidler, *League for Industrial Democracy*

Geoffrey H. Moore, *National Bureau of Economic Research*
Charles G. Mortimer, *General Foods Corporation*
J. Wilson Newman, *Dun & Bradstreet, Inc.*
George B. Roberts, *Larchmont, New York*
Robert V. Roosa, *Brown Brothers Harriman & Co.*
Harry Scherman, *Book-of-the-Month Club*
Boris Shishkin, *American Federation of Labor and Congress of Industrial Organizations*
George Soule, *South Kent, Connecticut*
Gus Tyler, *International Ladies' Garment Workers' Union*
Joseph H. Willits, *Langhorne, Pennsylvania*
Donald B. Woodward, *A. W. Jones and Company*

DIRECTORS BY UNIVERSITY APPOINTMENT

V. W. Bladen, *Toronto*
Francis M. Boddy, *Minnesota*
Arthur F. Burns, *Columbia*
Lester V. Chandler, *Princeton*
Melvin G. de Chazeau, *Cornell*
Frank W. Fetter, *Northwestern*
R. A. Gordon, *California*

Harold M. Groves, *Wisconsin*
Gottfried Haberler, *Harvard*
Maurice W. Lee, *North Carolina*
Lloyd G. Reynolds, *Yale*
Paul A. Samuelson, *Massachusetts Institute of Technology*
Theodore W. Schultz, *Chicago*

Willis J. Winn, *Pennsylvania*

DIRECTORS BY APPOINTMENT OF OTHER ORGANIZATIONS

Percival F. Brundage, *American Institute of Certified Public Accountants*
Nathaniel Goldfinger, *American Federation of Labor and Congress of Industrial Organizations*
Harold G. Halcrow, *American Farm Economic Association*
Walter E. Hoadley, *American Finance Association*

Murray Shields, *American Management Association*
Willard L. Thorp, *American Economic Association*
W. Allen Wallis, *American Statistical Association*
Harold F. Williamson, *Economic History Association*

Theodore O. Yntema, *Committee for Economic Development*

DIRECTORS EMERITI

Shepard Morgan, *Norfolk, Connecticut*
Jacob Viner, *Princeton, New Jersey*

RESEARCH STAFF

Moses Abramovitz	Milton Friedman	John W. Kendrick	Ralph L. Nelson
Gary S. Becker	Victor R. Fuchs	Irving B. Kravis	G. Warren Nutter
Gerhard Bry	H. G. Georgiadis	Hal B. Lary	Richard T. Selden
Arthur F. Burns	Raymond W. Goldsmith	Robert E. Lipsey	Lawrence H. Seltzer
Phillip Cagan	Jack M. Guttentag	Ruth P. Mack	Robert P. Shay
Frank G. Dickinson	Challis A. Hall, Jr.	Jacob Mincer	George J. Stigler
James S. Earley	Daniel M. Holland	Ilse Mintz	Norman B. Ture
Richard A. Easterlin	F. Thomas Juster	Geoffrey H. Moore	Victor Zarnowitz
Solomon Fabricant	C. Harry Kahn	Roger F. Murray	

RELATION OF THE DIRECTORS TO THE WORK AND PUBLICATIONS OF THE NATIONAL BUREAU OF ECONOMIC RESEARCH

1. The object of the National Bureau of Economic Research is to ascertain and to present to the public important economic facts and their interpretation in a scientific and impartial manner. The Board of Directors is charged with the responsibility of ensuring that the work of the National Bureau is carried on in strict conformity with this object.
2. To this end the Board of Directors shall appoint one or more Directors of Research.
3. The Director or Directors of Research shall submit to the members of the Board, or to its Executive Committee, for their formal adoption, all specific proposals concerning researches to be instituted.
4. No report shall be published until the Director or Directors of Research shall have submitted to the Board a summary drawing attention to the character of the data and their utilization in the report, the nature and treatment of the problems involved, the main conclusions, and such other information as in their opinion would serve to determine the suitability of the report for publication in accordance with the principles of the National Bureau.
5. A copy of any manuscript proposed for publication shall also be submitted to each member of the Board. For each manuscript to be so submitted a special committee shall be appointed by the President, or at his designation by the Executive Director, consisting of three Directors selected as nearly as may be one from each general division of the Board. The names of the special manuscript committee shall be stated to each Director when the summary and report described in paragraph (4) are sent to him. It shall be the duty of each member of the committee to read the manuscript. If each member of the special committee signifies his approval within thirty days, the manuscript may be published. If each member of the special committee has not signified his approval within thirty days of the transmittal of the report and manuscript, the Director of Research shall then notify each member of the Board, requesting approval or disapproval of publication, and thirty additional days shall be granted for this purpose. The manuscript shall then not be published unless at least a majority of the entire Board and a two-thirds majority of those members of the Board who shall have voted on the proposal within the time fixed for the receipt of votes on the publication proposed shall have approved.
6. No manuscript may be published, though approved by each member of the special committee, until forty-five days have elapsed from the transmittal of the summary and report. The interval is allowed for the receipt of any memorandum of dissent or reservation, together with a brief statement of his reasons, that any member may wish to express; and such memorandum of dissent or reservation shall be published with the manuscript if he so desires. Publication does not, however, imply that each member of the Board has read the manuscript, or that either members of the Board in general, or of the special committee, have passed upon its validity in every detail.
7. A copy of this resolution shall, unless otherwise determined by the Board, be printed in each copy of every National Bureau book.

(Resolution adopted October 25, 1926,
as revised February 6, 1933, and February 24, 1941)

This report is one of a series of studies on tax structure and economic growth aided by grants from the Rockefeller Brothers Fund and the Life Insurance Association of America. These organizations, however, are not responsible for any of the statements made or views expressed.

TAX POLICIES FOR ECONOMIC GROWTH

ADVISORY COMMITTEE

The Advisory Committee on the Study of Tax Policies for Economic Growth has generously assisted in planning and reviewing the work of the staff. Their advice is gratefully acknowledged without, however, implying their concurrence with the views expressed in this report. The members of the committee are:

Carl S. Shoup, Chairman, *Columbia University*
Julian D. Anthony, *Hartford Life Insurance Company*
Walter J. Blum, *University of Chicago*
George T. Conklin, Jr., *Guardian Life Insurance
    Company of America*
John F. Due, *University of Illinois*
Richard B. Goode, *International Monetary Fund*
C. H. Greenewalt, *E. I. du Pont de Nemours and Company*
Albert J. Hettinger, Jr., *Lazard Frères and Company*
E. Gordon Keith, *University of Pennsylvania*
Wesley Lindow, *Irving Trust Company*
Stacy May, *Wellfleet, Massachusetts*
Maurice Moonitz, *University of California at Berkeley*
Richard A. Musgrave, *Harvard University*
James J. O'Leary, *Life Insurance Association of America*
Joseph A. Pechman, *Brookings Institution*
Maurice E. Peloubet, *Price, Waterhouse & Company*
George B. Roberts, *Larchmont, New York*
Lawrence H. Seltzer, *Wayne State University*
Dan T. Smith, *Harvard University*
Stanley S. Surrey, *U.S. Treasury Department*
George Terborgh, *Machinery and Allied Products Institute*
William C. Warren, *Columbia University*
Laurence N. Woodworth, *Joint Committee on
    Internal Revenue Taxation*

CONTENTS

CONTENTS

TABLES

FOREWORD

To improve understanding of the influence of the federal tax structure on economic growth, the National Bureau of Economic Research has organized a series of studies supported by grants from the Rockefeller Brothers Fund and the Life Insurance Association of America. One set of studies, of which the present volume is part, is directed to the effects of the corporation income tax on business decisions affecting the growth of enterprise. Other studies concerned with business income taxation are being prepared by Challis A. Hall, Jr., Yale University, and Thomas M. Stanback, Jr., New York University. A second set of studies focuses on the personal income tax. These are under the direction of Daniel M. Holland, Massachusetts Institute of Technology; C. Harry Kahn, Rutgers University; Roger C. Miller, University of Wisconsin; and Wilbur Lewellen, Purdue University. In addition, the National Bureau, in cooperation with the Brookings Institution, has published the results of two conferences, one on *The Role of Direct and Indirect Taxes in the Federal Revenue System* and the other on *Foreign Tax Policies and Economic Growth*. Finally, a volume summarizing and integrating the findings of these and other research efforts is in preparation.

The treatment accorded recovery of investment in depreciable facilities is widely considered to be an important determinant of the profitability of investment and of a firm's ability to finance capital outlays. In the postwar period, there have been three major revisions of the tax rules governing depreciable assets: (1) the authorization of the use of the declining-balance method, at twice the straight-line rate, and the use of the sum-of-the-years-digits method in the Internal Revenue Code of 1954; (2) the shortening of authorized service lives (i.e., the period of time over which depreciation allowances must be spread) in Revenue Procedure 62-21 issued in July 1962; and (3) the investment tax credit included in the Revenue Act of 1962. Of the three, the first was in sev-

xviv

eral respects the most significant: it was the first, major, generally applicable liberalization of depreciation rules since the restrictive changes made by the Treasury in 1934; it increased the range of acceptable depreciation methods, allowing taxpayers to use not only the two new accelerated methods but also, within certain limits, depreciation systems of their own devising; and its potential effects on revenue were both relatively and absolutely larger than those of the other two. All three revisions, however, represented an explicit endorsement by the government of the desirability of encouraging business investment in depreciable assets.

The effectiveness of such measures in promoting private capital formation depends on several factors, including the impact on the volume of national saving and the conditions of demand for depreciable assets. Irrespective of these factors, however, the extent to which taxpayers do, in fact, change their depreciation practices when permitted to do so is, clearly, what initially delimits the effect on investment of changes in the tax rules. (In the case of the investment tax credit, the taxpayer is required to claim the credit in determining tax liability.)

One purpose of this survey has been to determine to what extent the accelerated methods authorized in the 1954 legislation were put to use during the 1954–60 period. Experience during this period should not, of course, be construed as a definitive measure of the success or failure of these measures. Taxpayers alter their practices over time as their circumstances change and as they become more familiar with the advantages and disadvantages of alternative ways of managing their affairs. But experience during these first seven years does indicate differences in the responses of various groups of taxpayers, and trends in their responses.

Another purpose has been to estimate the effect of the use of accelerated methods on the amount of corporate depreciation, income tax liabilities, and capital outlays. Unfortunately, we were able to prepare such estimates only for the taxable year 1959, and they cannot readily be projected for subsequent years.

The planning and preparation of this study and of the companion studies mentioned above have benefited greatly by the suggestions and criticisms of the Advisory Committee on the Study of Tax Policies for Economic Growth, whose members are separately listed.

At different stages in the preparation of this survey, I have had the able research assistance of Katherine Dolfis Warden, Julia Clones, and Angeles Buenaventura. Helpful comments were received from my National Bureau colleagues Anna Schwartz, Thomas Stanback, Lawrence Seltzer, and Douglas Eldridge, and from other readers, including, in particular, Robert Bangs, Richard Pollack, and George Terborgh. I appreciate the helpful comments of the National Bureau's Directors' Reading Committee: Percival F. Brundage, C. H. Greenewalt, and Harold M. Groves. The assistance provided by the Statistics Division of the Internal Revenue Service is in evidence throughout the study, and I am deeply grateful to the members of that agency for their advice and continuing cooperation. In particular, I am in debt to the late Ernest J. Engquist, Jr., who was chief of the Statistics Division when most of the data upon which this study is based were assembled. My special thanks are due to Daphne Laird, whose patience in typing the manuscript survived repeated revisions of text and tables. Joan Tron's editing was not only capable and efficient but virtually painless to the author.

N. B. T.

ACCELERATED DEPRECIATION
IN THE UNITED STATES
1954–60

1

INTRODUCTION

The Occasion for This Inquiry

Accelerating economic growth has been one of the principal concerns of federal tax policy during much of the postwar era. Widely divergent views have been expressed on the potential of tax policy for affecting the rate of the nation's economic progress and on the elements of tax policy which are consequential in this regard.[1] A substantial consensus has developed, however, that more rapid growth involves the allocation of a larger share of the economy's resources to fixed capital formation. Liberalizing the rules governing the determination of depreciation charges for income tax purposes is deemed by many to be one of the principal measures of tax policy for this purpose.

Three principal approaches to depreciation liberalization have been urged. One is to substitute replacement cost for original cost as the basis for the depreciation deduction. A second is to alter the pattern of the depreciation deductions so that a larger part of the depreciable amount is charged against income in the earlier years of the asset's service life. A third is to shorten the period of time over which the costs of depreciable facilities are to be charged, as depreciation, against income. Of these three, the last two have in fact been provided in 1954 and 1962, respectively. Acceleration [2] of depreciation allowances was incorporated in the Internal Revenue Code of 1954, which expressly authorized taxpayers to use the declining-balance method with an annual depreciation rate twice the straight-line rate, or the sum-of-the-years-

---

[1] See, for example, Joint Committee on the Economic Report, *Federal Tax Policy for Economic Growth and Stability,* Papers Submitted by Panelists Appearing before the Subcommittee on Tax Policy, Joint Committee Print, 84th Congress, 1st Session, November 9, 1955.

[2] As used in this discussion, the term "accelerated" characterizes depreciation methods which allow the taxpayer to charge off more of the depreciable cost of a facility in the early years than under the straight-line method.

digits method, or any other method which in any year in the first two-thirds of the asset's life yields cumulative allowances not in excess of those generated by use of the declining-balance method. Shortening of service lives was effected by administrative action in the Revenue Procedure 62-21 of July 1962.[3] Substitution of replacement cost for historic cost has not yet been adopted in the United States.[4]

A number of countries have made substantial use of depreciation policy to affect the volume and direction of investment in depreciable facilities. The Swedish experiment with so-called "free depreciation," under which corporate taxpayers might write off the full cost of facilities in the first year, is probably the best-known and most widely cited innovation in this policy area during the period before World War II. In the postwar years, a wide variety of special depreciation arrangements, including initial allowances, investment allowances, and price-index adjustments of depreciable basis, have been used in many countries. Authorizing or requiring the use of the so-called declining-balance method of depreciation in lieu of the straight-line method has been a widely adopted change in policy. In many instances, these postwar measures were taken in conjunction with programs aimed at speeding reconstruction or at spurring capital formation in critical or bottleneck

---

[3] Shortened service lives were also provided—but on a selective basis—in the form of five-year amortization allowances on defense and defense-related facilities for which certificates of necessity were issued during World War II and the Korean emergency. Certification of facilities was terminated as of December 31, 1959.

[4] The investment credit, enacted as part of the Revenue Act of 1962, may be deemed to be a limited approximation thereto since it permits, in effect, total capital recovery allowances in excess of the original cost of the facilities for which the credit may be claimed. For a description of the credit as amended by the Revenue Act of 1964, see Senate Report No. 830, on H.R. 8363, Revenue Act of 1964, 88th Congress, 2nd Session, pp. 40–45. Both the Revenue Procedure 62-21 and the investment credit represent important developments in this area of tax policy; they warrant more detailed examination than could be afforded in this study. For a preliminary examination, see Norman B. Ture, "Tax Reform: Depreciation Problems," *The American Economic Review*, May 1963, pp. 334–353; George Terborgh, *New Investment Incentives, The Investment Credit and the New Depreciation System* (Machinery and Allied Products Institute); E. Cary Brown, "Tax Incentives for Investment," *The American Economic Review*, May 1962, pp. 335–345; William H. White, "Illusions in the Marginal Investment Subsidy," *National Tax Journal*, March 1962, pp. 26–31; Sam B. Chase, Jr., "Tax Credits for Investment Spending," *National Tax Journal*, March 1962, pp. 32–52. See also Lawrence Bridge, "New Depreciation Guidelines and the Investment Tax Credit Effect on 1962 Corporate Profits and Taxes," U.S. Department of Commerce, Office of Business Economics, *Survey of Current Business*, July 1963, pp. 3–9.

industries. In any event, the enactment in the United States of the accelerated depreciation provisions in 1954 and of the investment credit provisions in 1962, as well as the administrative shortening of service lives in the latter year, had abundant precedent in other countries.[5]

Although there are significant differences among the various types of depreciation changes they have a number of major effects in common which are widely supposed to contribute to more rapid fixed capital formation.[6] These effects are briefly examined in a later section of this chapter.

Before one turns to measuring the impact of depreciation changes on capital formation, however, it is necessary to determine whether taxpayers change their depreciation practices when permitted to do so by changes in depreciation rules. Whether the increase in the rate of return or in cash flow, or the reduction in risk, or any of the other consequences of using an accelerated method in lieu of straight-line depreciation will lead to a small or large increase in capital outlays depends first of all on the extent to which taxpayers adopt the accelerated method. It is also pertinent to ask whether there are some characteristics which systematically distinguish taxpayers who do take advantage

[5] The role of depreciation policy changes in postwar development policies in several European countries and in Japan is discussed in detail in *Foreign Tax Policies and Economic Growth,* A Conference Report of the National Bureau of Economic Research and the Brookings Institution, New York, National Bureau of Economic Research, 1966.

[6] Although other considerations were adduced by the Administration and the tax-writing committees of the Congress in regard to the depreciation provisions in the Internal Revenue Code of 1954, principal emphasis was given to the effects of the proposed changes in promoting private investment in depreciable facilities. In connection with Revenue Procedure 62-21, the new service lives and the procedures for adjusting them to each taxpayer's replacement pattern were represented as necessary to make depreciation practices more realistic, but at least equal emphasis was given to the effects of these revisions in encouraging modernization of production facilities, increasing productivity in the industrial sector, and improving the competitive position of the United States in international markets. See *Budget Message of the President,* January 21, 1954, p. 719; Statement by the President, August 16, 1954 (reproduced as Exhibit 38 in the 1954 Annual Report of the Secretary of the Treasury, p. 233); Statement by Secretary of the Treasury George M. Humphrey before the Senate Finance Committee, April 7, 1954 (reproduced as Exhibit 35 in the 1954 Annual Report of the Secretary of the Treasury, pp. 227–228); Report of the Committee on Ways and Means on H.R. 8300, House Report No. 1337, 83rd Congress, 2nd Session, March 9, 1954, p. 24; Report of the Committee on Finance on H.R. 8300, Senate Report No. 1622, 83rd Congress, 2nd Session, June 18, 1954, p. 26; Statement by Secretary of the Treasury Douglas Dillon, July 11, 1962; Statement of the President, July 11, 1962.

of depreciation liberalization from those who do not; identification of these characteristics may be essential in evaluating the likely effects of such changes.

The purpose of this study, then, is to examine the extent to which business income taxpayers made use of the accelerated depreciation methods afforded by the Internal Revenue Code of 1954 and to indicate the magnitude of the change in corporations' depreciation allowances and tax liabilities resulting from the use of these methods. In addition, the nature of the effects of depreciation acceleration on investment decision making is briefly discussed in a later section of this chapter. A large number of factors besides tax considerations, of course, enter into this decision making, and it is difficult to isolate the weight of tax variables therein. With this caution in mind, we offer rough estimates of the effects of the use of accelerated depreciation on corporate investment in depreciable facilities in 1959.

Interpretation of these findings should take into account the fact that they are derived from data covering only the first several years of experience with the accelerated depreciation provisions. In the succeeding years, both the extent and character of taxpayer response may have changed.

The Data

The Statistics Division of the Internal Revenue Service has sought to provide some information about the number of companies using each of the principal depreciation methods and the amounts of depreciation generated thereby. For partnerships and sole proprietorships, such data are available only for the taxable year 1959.[7] For corporations, data have been obtained from special samples for each of the taxable years 1954–61. For the taxable years 1954, 1955, 1957, and 1960, data on corporations are taken from large samples, roughly equivalent in 1957 and 1960 to the regular *Statistics of Income* samples of corporate returns and characterized by roughly the same magnitudes in sampling variability. However, since the frequencies are estimated from company returns which showed method of depreciation, and since not all returns include these data, the frequencies will aggregate to less than the respective taxpaying populations. For 1954, 1955, 1957, and 1960, the data

[7] U.S. Treasury Department, Internal Revenue Service, *Statistics of Income, 1959–60, U.S. Business Tax Returns,* pp. 34–41, 90–99.

show numbers of returns and amount of depreciation by method, industrial division, and size of total assets. For the taxable years 1956, 1958, and 1959, the samples are limited to large corporations, cover roughly 1,000 returns, and show only the number of returns and amount of depreciation by method.

The data on partnerships for the taxable year 1959 show number of businesses, amount of depreciation, and amount of depreciable assets by method, industry division, and size of net profits and net receipts. In the case of sole proprietorships for the same period, the number of businesses and amount of depreciation are shown by method, industry, and size of business receipts.

A substantial amount of data about corporations' depreciable property on hand in the taxable year 1959 is provided by the Statistics Division, in a special compilation entitled the "Life of Depreciable Assets," or LDA. These data were taken from the depreciation schedules of 55,000 out of the 163,000 corporation returns in the regular *Statistics of Income* sample. The regular sample was modified initially by outright elimination of life and mutual insurance companies and by a reduced sampling rate for certain special classes of companies. In addition, not all of the returns included in the modified sample contained depreciation schedules sufficiently complete to be usable for the tabulation. For the returns of companies with total assets of $50 million or more, a field follow-up was used to obtain the data missing from the depreciation schedules in the returns. The reduction in the sample size, of course, increases the relative sampling variability. In addition, since not all of the returns in the regular sample yielded usable data, and because neither the nonresponse nor the field follow-up represented random distributions, there are possible biases in the estimates. The 55,000 returns in the study represent an estimated 557,000 corporate returns, about 52 per cent of the total filed for the year. The amount of depreciation of the represented returns was about $12 billion, 59 per cent of the total claimed for the year. The depreciable assets on these 557,000 returns total about $281 billion; this is 71 per cent of the amount shown in the balance sheet statistics derived from the regular *Statistics of Income* sample for 1959–60.

This compilation presents highly detailed information on the amount of depreciable facilities, accumulated depreciation, and current depreciation for assets in taxpayers' accounts for the taxable year 1959, by method, industry, type of asset, assigned service life, and size of total assets. No count of returns is associated with the amount of asset data, however. Moreover, the degree of detail with which the data are presented varies with the cross classification. For example, the cross classifications with method, size class, and service life provide only for nine industry divisions and six asset types.

A more detailed description of these data is provided in Appendix B.[8]

The Depreciation Rules in the
Internal Revenue Code of 1954

The Internal Revenue Code of 1954 specifically authorizes a taxpayer to compute depreciation allowances by use of the straight-line method, the declining-balance method at a rate not to exceed twice the straight-line rate,[9] the sum-of-the-years-digits method, or by any other method which in any year during the first two-thirds of the asset's life yields cumulative allowances not in excess of those generated by use of the declining-balance method.[10] The straight-line method allocates the depreciable basis of the facility—its cost less its estimated salvage value—over its service life in equal annual installments. With a service life of N years, annual depreciation per dollar of depreciable basis is $\frac{1}{N}$. Under the declining-balance method, a fixed depreciation rate, not to exceed $\frac{2}{N}$, is applied to the remaining undepreciated balance in the asset account. The taxpayer may at any time switch from declining-balance to straight-line; it will be advantageous to do so when the latter method, by dividing remaining cost by remaining service life, yields a larger amount than the former. Up to the switch, annual declining-balance depreciation per dollar of asset cost is $\frac{2}{N}$ in the first year (assuming the asset is acquired at the beginning of the year), $\frac{2}{N}\left(1 - \frac{2}{N}\right)$ in the second year, $\frac{2}{N}\left(1 - \frac{2}{N} - \frac{2}{N}\left[1 - \frac{2}{N}\right]\right)$ in the third year, etc. In summary form,

---

[8] For a more detailed discussion of the LDA sample, see also U.S. Treasury Department, Internal Revenue Service, *Statistics of Income, 1959, Supplementary Depreciation Data from Corporation Income Tax Returns*, pp. 1–9.

[9] While not specifically authorized in the statute, the declining-balance method at 150 per cent of the straight-line rate was allowed under prior law.

[10] Section 167(b).

this may be written for any year as $\frac{2}{N}\left(1 - \frac{2}{N}\right)^{M-1}$, where $M = $ the number of years, including the current year, for which depreciation has been deducted. After the switch, annual depreciation is

$$1 - \sum_{M=1}^{S} \frac{2}{N}\left(1 - \frac{2}{N}\right)^{M-1} \div (N - S + 1),$$

where S is the year in which the switch is made. The switch will be made beginning with the year $S = \frac{N}{2} + 2$, where N is an even number, and with the year $S = \frac{N-1}{2} + 2$, where N is an odd number.[11] In the sum-of-the-years-digits method (hereafter referred to as SYD), a continually decreasing ratio is applied to the asset's original cost less estimated salvage. The ratio in any year has as its numerator the number of years of service life remaining (including the present year) and as its denominator, the sum of the numbers representing the successive years in the estimated life of the asset. Thus, the first year's depreciation charge on a five-year asset would be 5/15 (i.e., 5 over the sum of $1 + 2 + 3 + 4 + 5$) and the second year's depreciation would be 4/15 of the asset's cost less salvage. In summary form, the allowance for any year is $\frac{2(N + 1 - M)}{N(N + 1)}$.

[11] The switch will be made when

$$1 - \sum_{M=1}^{S} \frac{2}{N}\left(1 - \frac{2}{N}\right)^{M-1} \div (N - S + 1) = \frac{2}{N}\left(1 - \frac{2}{N}\right)^{S-1}.$$

The summation may be expressed as

$$\frac{2}{N}\left[1 + \left(1 - \frac{2}{N}\right) + \left(1 - \frac{2}{N}\right)^2 + \cdots \left(1 - \frac{2}{N}\right)^{S-1}\right] =$$

$$\frac{2}{N}\left[\frac{\left(1 - \frac{2}{N}\right)^S - 1}{\left(1 - \frac{2}{N}\right) - 1}\right] = 1 - \left(1 - \frac{2}{N}\right)^S.$$

Substituting gives

$$\left(1 - \frac{2}{N}\right)^S = (N - S + 1)\frac{2}{N}\left(1 - \frac{2}{N}\right)^{S-1}, \text{ which becomes } S = \frac{N}{2} + 2.$$

Since the depreciation deduction is for a full year, $S = \frac{N-1}{2} + 2$, where N is an odd number.

The declining-balance method at twice the straight-line rate, the sum-of-the-years-digits method, and any other unspecified but equivalent method are authorized only for property to which a service life of three years or more is assigned. Moreover, these methods can be applied only to property produced after December 31, 1953, and acquired new by the taxpayer after that date.

Prior to the effective date of the 1954 Code, the law did not specify the method which a taxpayer could or could not use in computing annual depreciation charges. Straight-line depreciation, however, was generally employed, although any taxpayer was entitled to use any other method provided that he could justify its use on the basis of his own experience or that of his industry. Such a justification ordinarily required evidence that the pattern of exhaustion of economic serviceability of the asset differed significantly from that described by the straight-line method. Evidence of this sort would not generally be readily available and might require detailed and expensive annual appraisals. Relatively few taxpayers presumably were able to establish that the straight-line method was not the appropriate way in which to spread the cost of a depreciable facility over its useful life.

While criticism of pre-1954 depreciation policy was directed to a number of its features, including the restriction of total depreciation charges to original cost less salvage value and the allegedly excessive length of service lives indicated by Bulletin "F," the major focus of the legislative action in 1953–54 was on the timing of the distribution of depreciation allowances over an asset's service life. Use of the straight-line method, which distributes recovery of an asset's cost in equal amounts per year over its service life, it was claimed, provides an unrealistic measure of the actual pattern of exhaustion of an asset's value to the taxpayer through time.[12] According to this argument, a depreciation pattern which implies a relatively large reduction in the asset's value in the first year of its life and successively smaller increments thereafter more accurately measures the loss of value over time. This pattern is approximated by use of the declining-balance or SYD methods.

[12] One of the most careful and detailed arguments to this effect was presented to the Committee on Ways and Means by George Terborgh for the Machinery and Allied Products Institute. See *General Revenue Revision,* Hearings before the Committee on Ways and Means, House of Representatives, 83d Congress, 1st Session, Part 2, pp. 743–759. See also Terborgh's *Realistic Depreciation Policy,* Machinery and Allied Products Institute, 1954.

Use of either of these methods results in larger depreciation allowances in the early years and smaller allowances in the later years of life of an asset than those produced by use of the straight-line method (total allowances under each of the methods, of course, are virtually the same). In the case of an asset with a ten-year service life, for example, the annual allowance under the declining-balance method will exceed the straight-line allowance for the first four years (disregarding salvage values). Under SYD, annual allowances will be greater than the straight-line charge for the first five years.[13] Although the number of years during which the accelerated allowances exceed the straight-line charge varies directly with the service life of the asset, the fraction of the asset's service life over which accelerated exceed straight-line allowances diminishes with length of the service life. As service life increases, the fraction falls toward one-third, in the case of declining-balance, and toward one-half in the case of SYD.

Allowances under the SYD method exceed those under the straight-line method for a larger fraction of an asset's service life than do those under the declining-balance method.[14] If N equals the asset's service life and M equals the number of years, including the current year, for which the depreciation deduction has been claimed, then the declining-balance allowance will just equal the straight-line deduction when $M = 1 + \dfrac{\log \frac{1}{2}}{\log\left(1 - \dfrac{2}{N}\right)}$. The SYD deduction will just equal the straight-line allowance when $M = \dfrac{N+1}{2}$.[15] For any given N,

$$\frac{N+1}{2} > 1 + \frac{\log \frac{1}{2}}{\log\left(1 - \dfrac{2}{N}\right)}.$$

---

[13] Assuming the asset is acquired at the beginning of a year.

[14] Assuming no salvage value need be taken into account in computing the SYD allowance (see below).

[15] The break-even point is that value of M at which the declining-balance or the SYD allowances just equal the straight-line deduction. The straight-line allowance in any year is $1/N$ times the asset's cost. The declining-balance deduction may be represented as $\dfrac{2}{N}\dfrac{(N-2)^{M-1}}{N}$ times the asset's cost, in any year. Equality between these two gives

$$\frac{2}{N}\frac{(N-2)^{M-1}}{N} = \frac{1}{N}$$

$$\left(1 - \frac{2}{N}\right)^{M-1} = \frac{1}{2}$$

The break-even points for assets of various service lives are shown in the following table, where M equals the year or fraction thereof in which the depreciation allowance computed under the declining-balance or sum-of-the-years-digits method is just equal to that under the straight-line method, assuming that the facility was acquired at the beginning of a taxable year.

Service Life (years)	M, Computed by Declining-Balance	M, Computed by Sum-of-Years-Digits
3	1.6	2.0
4	2.0	2.5
5	2.4	3.0
10	4.1	5.5
15	5.8	8.0
20	7.6	10.5
25	9.3	13.0
33	12.0	17.0

The accumulated excess of accelerated over straight-line allowances in those years in which the declining-balance and SYD allowances are greater than straight-line similarly varies with the service life of the facility. For example, the declining-balance method yields cumulative depreciation allowances 45.8 per cent greater than straight-line during the first 4.1 years, in the case of a 10-year asset, and 43.8 per cent greater than straight-line during the first twelve years, in the case of a facility with a service life of 33 years. The accumulated excess of SYD

$$(M - 1) \log \left(1 - \frac{2}{N} \right) = \log \frac{1}{2}$$

$$M = 1 + \frac{\log \frac{1}{2}}{\log \left(1 - \frac{2}{N} \right)}$$

The SYD allowance in any year is $\frac{2(N + 1 - M)}{N(N + 1)}$. Setting this equal to $\frac{1}{N}$, the straight-line allowance in any year, we have

$$\frac{2(N + 1 - M)}{N(N + 1)} = \frac{1}{N}$$

$$2(N + 1 - M) = N + 1$$

$$M = \frac{N + 1}{2}$$

over straight-line allowances is 40.5 per cent during the first 5.5 years, for a 10-year asset, and 47.0 per cent during the first seventeen years, for a 33-year facility. The proportionate accumulated excesses [16] of declining-balance and of SYD over straight-line allowances (for various service lives) are shown in the following table.

Service Life (years)	Excess as Per Cent of Asset's Cost		Excess as Per Cent of Accumulated Straight-line Allowance	
	Declining-Balance	SYD	Declining-Balance	SYD
3	26.4	16.7	48.5	25.0
4	25.0	17.5	50.0	28.0
5	22.0	20.0	46.6	33.3
10	18.8	22.3	45.8	40.5
15	17.7	23.3	45.3	43.8
20	17.0	23.7	45.0	45.1
25	16.7	24.0	44.8	46.2
33	16.0	24.2	43.8	47.0

Whether or not allowances under the accelerated methods conform more closely than those under the straight-line method with the actual loss of value of an asset year by year, the change in the law to authorize the use of accelerated methods clearly affords benefits to the taxpayers availing themselves of this privilege. If indeed the accelerated depreciation methods correctly represent the actual pattern of loss of value in use, then the de facto constraint in the pre-1954 law to use straight-line depreciation involved understatement of depreciation, overstatement of taxable income, and consequently overpayment of taxes in the early years of an asset's life. During the later years, depreciation was overstated, taxable income was understated, and taxes underpaid. With an unchanging tax rate, of course, the overpayments and underpayments of taxes just cancel out with respect to any one asset. Nevertheless, the overpayments represent a series of interest-free loans by the taxpayer to the government, while the subsequent underpayments represent repayments of the loans by the government to the taxpayer in increas-

[16] Up to the break-even year (see text table above) in which accelerated allowances equal straight-line allowances. In the case of declining-balance, the amount of the excess in the break-even year was determined by straight-line interpolation, which slightly overstates the excess.

ing annual installments. The use of either declining-balance or sum-of-the-years-digits depreciation instead of straight-line, accordingly, reduces or eliminates these interest-free loans. It therefore benefits the taxpayer to the extent determined by the appropriate earnings rate which he can realize on the additional funds released to him during the early years of the asset's use, less the loss of earnings on the extra funds he would realize under straight-line depreciation in the later years of the asset's use.

If, on the other hand, the real pattern of depreciation is best described by use of the straight-line method, the adoption of an accelerated depreciation method involves the government's affording the taxpayer a series of interest-free loans in the early years of the asset's use and the repayment of such loans in increasing annual installments in the later years. In this event, the taxpayer is benefited, again in an amount depending on the rate of earnings he can realize on the advance of funds to him.

The change in the timing of tax liabilities, and therefore of after-tax receipts, over the lifetime of an asset, resulting from using accelerated rather than straight-line depreciation, increases the present value of the depreciation deductions; hence, it increases the value of the net returns which may be realized upon investment in depreciable facilities. The amount of this increase depends on the rate at which the taxpayer discounts future receipts, the length of life of the asset, and the marginal tax rate. Given the tax rate and the discount rate, the increase in the present value of the depreciation deductions will grow with the asset's service life up to a point and then diminish; given the tax rate and service life, the increase in present value grows with the discount rate up to a point beyond which it falls. Table 1 illustrates these relationships, using SYD as the accelerated depreciation method.

An alternative way of expressing the effect of acceleration of depreciation allowances is as the change in the rate of return realizable on a given outlay for depreciable facilities. Table 2 shows both the percentage point and percentage increases in rates of return resulting from using declining-balance or SYD in lieu of straight-line, at selected service lives and at various rates of return under the straight-line method.

It is evident from the table that the increase in internal rate of return resulting from use of either accelerated method in lieu of the straight-line method is quite limited, whether viewed as the absolute percentage point change or as the relative increase. (It does not follow that the investment response to such limited changes is equally constrained; see the discussion below, pp. 17–22.) The table also shows that for assets with relatively short service lives, the declining-balance method is more profitable than SYD, if salvage value is ignored. As noted above, how-

TABLE 1

Present Worth of Depreciation Deductions as Per Cent of Asset Cost

Service Life (years)	SYD Discount Rates of (per cent)			Straight-Line Discount Rates of (per cent)			SYD Minus Straight-Line Discount Rates of (per cent)		
	4	12	20	4	12	20	4	12	20
10	85	66	50	81	55	39	4	11	11
20	75	48	33	68	36	22	7	12	11
30	68	38	25	57	25	15	11	13	10
40	61	31	20	49	20	11	12	11	9
50	56	26	16	43	16	9	13	10	7
100	37	14	9	24	8	5	13	6	4

Source: E. Cary Brown, "The New Depreciation Policy Under the Income Tax: An Economic Analysis," *National Tax Journal*, March 1955, p. 92.

ever, salvage value reduces the depreciable basis of assets for purposes of SYD depreciation computations but not for the declining-balance allowances. The greater the estimated salvage, the longer the service life for which use of declining-balance will be preferable to SYD; alternatively, for any given service life, the greater the salvage value, the greater is the advantage—or the smaller the disadvantage—in using declining-balance in lieu of SYD.[17] The Revenue Act of 1962 provides for disregarding salvage value up to 10 per cent of the facility's cost (or other basis) in computing straight-line and SYD allowances on

[17] For a rigorous statement of this interrelationship, see Sidney Davidson and David F. Drake, "Capital Budgeting and The 'Best' Tax Depreciation Method," *The Journal of Business* of the University of Chicago, October 1961, pp. 442–452.

TABLE 2

Increase in Rate of Return from Use of Accelerated Depreciation

| Service Life (years) | Rate of Return Under Straight-Line Method[a] of | | | | | |
| | 5 Per Cent | | 10 Per Cent | | 15 Per Cent | |
	Declining-Balance	SYD	Declining-Balance	SYD	Declining-Balance	SYD
	Percentage Point Increase in Rate of Return					
5	.71	.70	1.34	1.20	1.89	1.56
10	.66	.79	1.11	1.37	1.50	1.79
20	.55	.79	.90	1.23	1.19	1.46
30	.48	.73	.77	1.02	.95	1.19
50	.41	.59	.59	.72	.69	.83
	Percentage Increase in Rate of Return					
5	14.20	14.00	13.40	12.00	12.60	10.40
10	13.20	15.80	11.10	13.70	10.00	11.93
20	11.00	15.80	9.00	12.30	7.93	9.73
30	9.60	14.60	7.70	10.20	6.33	7.93
50	8.20	11.80	5.90	7.20	4.60	5.53

Source: George Terborgh, *Effect of the New Tax Depreciation Methods on the Earnings of Depreciable Assets,* Machinery and Allied Products Institute, 1956, pp. 13, 17.

[a]Rate of return is that rate at which cash flow (i.e., profits and depreciation after tax) attributable to a facility over its service life must be discounted to be equal to the facility's cost. These computations assume that the investment is financed entirely from equity capital. Somewhat larger increases in rates of return on the equity share of the investment would be realized if the investment were financed in part with debt.

property acquired after October 16, 1962. This tends to favor use of SYD depreciation.[18] On the whole, declining-balance is advantageous for short-lived assets, while SYD is preferable for facilities with long service lives.

Tables 1 and 2 illustrate the fact that a given change in depreciation rules, undifferentiated to take account of differences in discount rates and service lives, is likely to have differing effects among a heteroge-

[18] See Davidson and Drake, "The 'Best' Tax Depreciation Method—1964," *The Journal of Business* of the University of Chicago, July 1964, pp. 258–260.

neous taxpaying population.[19] A neutral depreciation system would alter the effective tax rate on the return allocable to depreciable facilities by the same fraction, irrespective of the differences in discount rates or service lives. A depreciation system which met this test would afford annual allowances equal to the reduction in the capital value of the asset, measured as the present worth of the income stream remaining at the end of the taxable year. As a practical matter, such a depreciation system would be extremely complicated, probably impossibly so. Depreciation systems of the type long in use in the United States and elsewhere, however, are unneutral in this sense.

Changes in depreciation rules, such as those effected by the Internal Revenue Code of 1954, might move in the direction of greater tax neutrality, if use of an accelerated method were to result in a smaller dispersion of effective rates of tax among assets with varying service lives than results when straight-line depreciation is used. Similarly, the change to an accelerated method would be deemed to be a step toward tax neutrality if, at any given service life, the differences in effective rates of tax from one discount rate to another were reduced. Table 3 suggests that, compared with straight-line, the accelerated methods slightly reduce the dispersion in effective rates of tax as among service lives, given the discount rate, and as among differing discount rates at any service life. Within the context illustrated here, however, the movements toward and away from greater neutrality resulting from adoption of the accelerated methods are not substantial.

The impact of these differential changes in effective rates of tax, and hence in rates of return, on the allocation of investment depends on the rate-of-return elasticities of demand for depreciable facilities. These elasticities, in turn, vary with differences in the production methods among taxpayers. The increase in the present value of depreciation deductions can be viewed as a reduction in the cost of the depreciable facilities involved. Other things being equal, this increases the stock of such facilities which the taxpayer wants to use in combination with other agencies of production (this is a "one-shot" effect, i.e., for any given change in depreciation rules there is a once-and-for-all change in the desired stock). The amount of this increase depends on the possi-

[19] Richard A. Musgrave provides a formal statement of the differential effect of a given set of depreciation rules, or changes therein, in *The Theory of Public Finance,* New York, 1959, pp. 336–346.

TABLE 3

Comparison of Effective Tax Rates[a] Using Straight-Line and Accelerated Depreciation Methods

Service Life (years)	Straight-Line, Pretax Rate of Return (per cent)			Sum-of-the-Years-Digits, Pretax Rate of Return (per cent)			Double-Declining-Balance,[b] Pretax Rate of Return (per cent)		
	10	20	30	10	20	30	10	20	30
5	55.3	54.2	53.6	49.3	48.8	48.4	46.8	48.5	47.8
10	55.6	54.1	53.0	48.5	47.7	47.0	50.2	49.0	48.2
20	54.7	52.6	51.5	47.6	46.8	46.7	49.8	48.3	47.7
30	53.6	51.6	50.8	46.9	46.5	46.8	49.2	47.9	47.7
50	52.0	50.6	50.3	46.5	47.0	47.5	48.2	47.8	48.0

Note: I am indebted to George Terborgh for the computations in this table.

[a]Per cent reduction in net rate of return, assuming a marginal tax rate of 50 per cent, no salvage value, and full equity financing.

[b]Switch to straight-line, as indicated above.

bilities of substituting such facilities for other inputs in the production process. The greater the elasticity of substitution, the greater the increase in the desired capital stock.

The use of an accelerated depreciation method instead of the straight-line method also results in a greater flow of internal funds generated with respect to any given amount of depreciable facilities. For any one asset (or assets acquired in any one year), of course, the increase in cash flow (i.e., profits after tax plus depreciation) in the asset's early years over that resulting from the use of straight-line depreciation will be exactly offset by the reduction in cash flow in the later years of the asset's life. Where assets are acquired in more than one year, however, the use of accelerated in lieu of straight-line depreciation will result in an increase in cumulated cash flow, until the taxpayer completely liquidates his depreciable assets accounts. For a taxpayer whose purchases of depreciable assets are growing, the use of an accelerated depreciation method will continue to yield a larger cash flow than straight-line; only when the asset account is stabilized, i.e., when annual acquisitions and retirements leave the gross value of the account unchanged, will the annual cash flow become the same under both methods of depreciation, but annual cash flow under the accelerated method will never fall below that under the straight-line method so long as the total stock of facilities remains stabilized. For the taxpayer who adopts an accelerated method of depreciation for newly acquired assets and who maintains a fixed amount of depreciable assets, annual cash flow will exceed that which would have resulted from use of straight-line depreciation throughout a full replacement cycle and will become just equal to that under straight-line depreciation when all facilities are being written off under the accelerated method. The excess of accelerated over straight-line depreciation realized when the stock was growing will never be fully offset until the last asset has been retired. Where irregular growth in purchases occurs, the accelerated allowance may fall below the straight-line allowance in some years, even after the holdings of depreciable assets have been stabilized, but as before, total allowances under the accelerated methods will continue to exceed those under the straight-line method until all facilities have been retired.[20]

The more rapid the growth in the stock of depreciable facilities, the greater will be the excess of the cash flow under an accelerated as compared with the straight-line method, as shown in the following table. The impetus for rapidly growing, cash-hungry companies to adopt the use of accelerated depreciation techniques should be particularly strong.

	Percentage Excess of Accumulated Declining-Balance Over Accumulated Straight-Line Allowances,[b] *at the End of*		
Growth Rate [a] *(per cent)*	*10 years*	*20 years*	*30 years*
0	16.9	3.5	2.0
5	20.5	7.7	5.7
10	23.6	11.0	9.3

[a] Annual percentage increase in purchases.
[b] Assumes facilities with ten-year service lives and no dispersion of retirements.

As a corollary to the greater cash flow, the use of accelerated depreciation also serves to reduce the risk of investment in depreciable

[20] This discussion assumes, in the case of declining-balance depreciation, that each year's acquisitions of facilities are maintained in a separate account and that each such account is switched to straight-line at the appropriate time, as indicated earlier in this chapter.

facilities. For example, the SYD method on a ten-year asset results in a tax saving about $1\frac{2}{3}$ as great as that from straight-line depreciation at the end of the first three years. At a 50 per cent tax rate, SYD allowances generate a cash flow of about 25 per cent of the asset's cost in the first three years, compared with 15 per cent under straight-line depreciation. For the business taxpayer relying on a short payoff period approach to allow for the riskiness of investment in depreciable assets, the greater cash flow resulting from the use of accelerated depreciation methods means a greater proportion of the asset's cost will be recovered within the payoff period. For a taxpayer who assigns successively higher rates of discount to receipts of successively later years, the use of accelerated depreciation, which in effect transfers cash flow from later years when it would be subject to relatively heavy discounting to earlier years when the applicable discount is relatively slight, serves to reduce the average effective discount for risk. Under these circumstances, the increase in the present value of total depreciation allowances resulting from a switch to accelerated from straight-line depreciation is augmented by the very nature of the discount function.

A change in depreciation methods may also affect the theoretically optimum replacement cycle for depreciable facilities. In the case of a going concern, i.e., one in which there is no finite limit on the time horizon, an existing piece of equipment will be retired when its after-tax quasi-rent (the excess of its gross revenues over all variable costs attributable to it) falls below the interest on the capitalized value of the excess of after-tax quasi-rents over the costs of acquisition of an infinite succession of replacements (ignoring disposal value). Acceleration of depreciation allowances both increases the present value of this excess of quasi-rents over acquisition costs of the replacement facilities and accelerates the rate of decline in the quasi-rents of the existing facility. The condition for replacement, accordingly, will be realized at an earlier point in time than under nonaccelerated depreciation.[21]

[21] With respect to any given facility, acceleration of depreciation involves no change in the total amount of allowances, hence of quasi-rents, merely their redistribution through time. When the accelerated method allowance falls below the straight-line allowance, the quasi-rent on the facility declines below what it would be under straight-line. For a discussion of optimum economic service life, cf. Friedrich and Vera Lutz, *The Theory of Investment of the Firm,* Princeton, 1951, pp. 101 ff., and Edgar O. Edwards, "Depreciation and the Maintenance of Real Capital," in J. L. Meij (ed.), *Depreciation and Replacement Policy,* Amsterdam, 1961, pp. 46–54.

As a practical matter, a taxpayer comparing the cash flow from existing facilities with that which he might expect from replacements is likely to find that the more rapid reduction in an existing facility's cash flow under accelerated depreciation will make replacement worth while at an earlier date. Some taxpayers may view acceleration as reducing the average length of time their funds are "tied up" in a facility or as writing a facility off their books at an earlier date, thereby justifying earlier replacement.

While the replacement cycle for the firm will be shortened, it does not follow that it will be shortened for the economy as a whole. Since the change in depreciation method for tax purposes does not reflect a change in the real productivity of depreciable facilities, there is little reason to believe that such facilities will be *scrapped,* as opposed to *sold,* earlier than before depreciation acceleration. This conclusion would need to be altered if there is no market for secondhand facilities (or only a weak one), i.e., if facilities are typically scrapped upon retirement. The earlier sale for reuse of depreciable facilities, incidentally, should contribute to expanding or improving the market for used capital goods.

On the other hand, a shift to accelerated depreciation methods tends to reduce outlays on maintenance and repairs relative to those for new facilities. It should also reduce outlays for modification of existing facilities compared with those for new ones. Since the accelerated provisions of the 1954 Code were restricted to new, as opposed to secondhand facilities, an obvious bias towards the former was introduced. Both by reducing the impetus for maintaining the quality of existing facilities and by biasing firms against the purchase of used facilities, the acceleration of depreciation allowances might weaken the used capital goods market and reduce the over-all average period of use of depreciable assets.

In all of the respects indicated above, the acceleration of depreciation allowances should increase a firm's demand for depreciable facilities and expand its financial capabilities for acquiring them. While the direction of these effects seems clear a priori, the magnitude of the effect cannot be readily inferred. If short payoff periods and increasing discount functions are ignored, the effect of the accelerated depreciation provisions of the 1954 Code on the rate of return on investment, as indicated in Tables 1 and 2 above, is of a relatively small order of magnitude. For companies in which the demand for depreciable facilities is highly elastic with respect to anticipated profitability, of course, these changes may be adequate to induce a relatively large expansion of planned investment. That is to say, there may be a relatively large volume of capital projects which become attractive and feasible to the company by virtue of a slight increase in the rate of return realizable upon them and/or an increase in the amount of internally available funds. On the other hand, for other companies the increase in rate of return may be deemed to be too small to affect capital programs. The elasticity of demand for depreciable facilities, in turn, depends on the nature of the firm's production function and upon the elasticity of demand for its output. The elasticity of supply of the capital goods used by the firm in its production function will determine the extent to which increases in demand for depreciable facilities result in increases in the real capital stock or increases in the prices of capital goods. For production activities in which factor combinations are relatively fixed in the short run, the adoption of accelerated depreciation will certainly increase the firm's liquidity and may in the near term affect its inventory and dividend policies and its degree of reliance on external sources of funds; accelerated depreciation may very well have little influence on the ratio of the firm's capital to labor inputs until such time as it becomes technically feasible to introduce a new production arrangement or until alternative lines of production activity involving a higher capital-labor ratio become feasible. On the other hand, even with a technically fixed input combination, the effects of accelerating depreciation may induce the firm to attempt to enlarge the scale of its operations beyond that it would deem desirable using the straight-line method.

It is even more difficult to generalize about the impact of depreciation liberalization on aggregate investment in depreciable facilities. The outcome depends on the effect of this tax change on both investment demand and total saving. An increase in the former without an increase in the latter will result in a rise in the price of capital goods but no change in the short run in the rate of real capital formation. Depreciation liberalization will not necessarily augment total saving. If this tax change occurs under circumstances of full employment, there can be no increase in the rate of expansion of real output to generate an increase in the rate of real saving. Under this condition, the rate of real saving could be increased only if the inflationary expansion of aggregate demand in current prices—but not in real terms—resulted in the transfer of income from persons or companies with low to those with high saving propensities. Alternatively, the short-run revenue loss from depreciation liberalization might be offset by tax increases on other components of national income, in order to forestall inflation. Whether there will be an increase in aggregate saving will depend on the relative saving inclinations of the taxpayers who realize tax reduction through depreciation liberalization and those who incur greater tax liabilities. On the other hand, depreciation liberalization might also be used as a vehicle for net tax reduction under conditions of less than full employment. If investment demand responds to this tax reduction, the consequent increase in aggregate demand and in real output will, with unchanged savings predilections, afford an increase in real saving.

In any event, it is clear that the extent to which accelerated depreciation tax provisions can have any of the effects attributed to them depends on the extent of use of these provisions.

A number of constraints may militate against the firm's shifting from straight-line to other depreciation methods. Depreciation accounting under either the declining-balance or SYD method is more complex than under straight-line and involves greater compliance costs. For small companies or those with relatively small amounts of depreciable facilities, the increase in these costs might outweigh the anticipated benefits. Accounting conventions of the firm, moreover, may make it difficult to report income and costs to shareholders on a different basis from that used for tax purposes; in such a case, the reported increase in depreciation and consequent reduction in profits before tax, resulting from the use of an accelerated instead of the straight-line method, might reflect adversely—albeit inaccurately—on the firm's management. Management may initially misunderstand the consequences of using accelerated instead of straight-line depreciation; it may require a number of years before the financial advantages of acceleration become sufficiently understood to induce a change in depreciation practice.

The lower the applicable marginal rate of tax, the less the benefit in using accelerated compared with straight-line depreciation. The inducement to adopt accelerated methods, presumably, would be relatively weak for many unincorporated businesses and small corporations for this reason. In addition, accelerating depreciation deductions might prove disadvantageous if marginal tax rates are expected to rise, since these higher rates (because of the decreasing depreciation deductions) will apply when taxable income generated by a facility is rising. Unincorporated businesses and very small corporations anticipating growth in income, hence in marginal rates, might therefore wish to defer adoption of accelerated methods.

A frequently heard contention is that many small companies, depreciating their facilities under the straight-line method on the basis of service lives and salvage values significantly less than might be justified by their replacement practices, were reluctant to change to an accelerated method lest the resulting increase in the ratio of their depreciation allowances to their new gross facilities alert revenue agents to these practices. If the revenue agent were consequently to insist on the use of longer service lives or greater salvage values, the net effect might be to reduce rather than to increase depreciation allowances and cash flow.

These, and quite possibly other, factors may have limited the extent to which taxpayers availed themselves of the accelerated depreciation methods. In time, however, these constraints may have become less consequential; as we shall see below, some of our measures show a rapid increase in taxpayer response between the taxable years 1954 and 1960, the period covered by our data. The use of these methods very likely has continued to increase thereafter.[22]

[22] On the other hand, a shift toward greater use of the straight-line method occurred in the taxable years 1962–64, as a result of a feature of the Treasury's Revenue Procedure 62-21 (July 11, 1962), which set forth new guidelines for tax depreciation. For purposes of the reserve ratio test provided by the procedure, the taxpayer must include in his guideline accounts all of the depreciable property on hand and all of the depreciation accumulated thereupon. In group or composite accounting under the straight-line method, the depreciation rate is applied to the gross asset account, no matter what the net balance of the account (i.e., gross assets less accumulated depreciation) might be. The addition of overage, fully depreciated assets to the group account, therefore, expands the depreciable basis, hence the annual depreciation deduction. Subsequent retirement of such assets substantially reduces the reserve ratio and facilitates the taxpayer's meeting the "transition" rules in the reserve ratio test. Accordingly, the procedure created a strong impetus for taxpayers to set up guideline accounts under the straight-line method. The same sort of impetus, but to a lesser degree, is afforded by group or composite SYD accounts, since in such cases, too, the depreciation rate is applied to the gross amount of assets. No similar impetus was afforded under declining-balance, in which the annual allowance, as noted above, is computed by applying the depreciation rate to the remaining balance of the account. For a more detailed discussion, cf. Frederick W. Stevenson, "Tax Depreciation and Business Resources," *National Industrial Conference Board Record*, Vol. II, Nos. 7 and 9, and Vol. III, No. 3; and George E. Lent, "Should the Reserve Ratio Test Be Retained," *National Tax Journal*, December 1964, pp. 365–393, especially, pp. 380–381.

2

RESULTS OF THE STUDY

There are a number of alternative measures of the use of the various depreciation methods authorized in the Internal Revenue Code of 1954. One such is the amount of property to which each of the methods is applied. Another is the amount of depreciation generated under each method and the effect of the adoption of acceleration on the total amount of depreciation allowances. A third is the number of taxpayers with business income electing to use each method. In the following discussion, we have attempted to apply these measures with respect to industry groupings, types of assets, size of company, and/or service life of property.

Very briefly, we found that close to half of the total depreciable facilities acquired by corporations since 1953 were in accelerated method accounts in the taxable year 1959. A larger proportion of the property of big corporations than of small ones was being depreciated under the accelerated methods in 1959, more of the facilities in manufacturing than in other industry divisions were being so depreciated, and a somewhat larger proportion of production equipment and of structures than of other types of property was in rapid depreciation accounts (Tables 25, 27, 28). Large manufacturing corporations (those with total assets of $25 million or more) had 66.5 per cent of their post-1953 facilities in accelerated depreciation accounts (Table 30).

Close to 40 per cent of total corporate depreciation allowances in 1960 were accounted for by the accelerated methods (Table 15), a substantial increase over the 7 per cent accounted for by these methods in 1954. On facilities acquired since 1953, a little more than one-half of corporation depreciation allowances was computed by use of the accelerated methods in 1959 (Table 36). Among sole proprietorships in the same year, a much smaller proportion of total allowances was computed by methods other than straight-line. Partnerships, however, were more in line with corporations in this respect (Table 17). It may be assumed that some gain in this proportion had occurred among unincorporated businesses. Taking all businesses together, about 29 per cent of total depreciation charges in 1959 were computed under accelerated methods (Tables 17 and D-6).

In the taxable years 1959 and 1960, a large number of business concerns were using the accelerated depreciation methods, although these companies represented small proportions of their respective populations (Tables 4 and 11). The proportion of corporation income taxpayers using an accelerated method increased markedly between 1954 and 1960 (Table 4), and it is fair to surmise that use of accelerated methods by unincorporated business income taxpayers had also increased during these years. Nevertheless, at least two-thirds of the business income taxpayers in 1959 and 1960 were using only straight-line depreciation for tax purposes (Tables 4 and 11). The proportion of companies using only the straight-line method has very likely continued to shrink since 1959–60. The accelerated methods were used by a larger proportion of corporations than of unincorporated businesses, of big companies than of little companies (no matter the form of organization), and of corporations and partnerships in manufacturing than in other industry groups (Tables 6, 10, 12, 13, A-2, and A-3). About 58 per cent of manufacturing corporations with total assets of $100 million or more were using the declining-balance method, and use of SYD was reported on the returns of about an equal percentage of such companies. Even greater proportions of the returns of the largest companies in other industrial divisions indicated use of the declining-balance method (Table A-1).

Our rough calculations indicate that use of the accelerated depreciation methods—declining-balance and SYD—resulted in total corporate depreciation allowances in the taxable year 1959 about $2.4 billion greater than would have been claimed had these methods not been available. About 66 per cent of this excess is attributable to companies with total assets of $25 million or more. About 55 per cent of the excess is in the manufacturing industry division and about 19 per cent is in public utilities (Table 40).

The additional corporation depreciation allowances generated by the use of accelerated methods resulted in estimated tax savings of $1.3 billion in 1959. We estimate that as a result of these tax savings, corporate investment in depreciable facilities in that year was $1.3 billion to $5.7 billion greater than it would otherwise have been.

In the following discussion, we detail each of these findings. Our initial concern is with the number of business enterprises using either of the accelerated depreciation methods.

Number of Companies Using Accelerated Depreciation Methods

A good deal of information is available concerning the number of corporations using the accelerated depreciation methods in each of the years since these allowances were first authorized. In the case of unincorporated businesses, however, the information is limited to the single taxable year 1959.[1]

CORPORATIONS

Between 1954 and 1960, a substantial increase occurred in the proportion of the incorporated business population using the declining-balance depreciation method. This increase appears among companies of all sizes in all major industrial divisions. As shown in Table 4, this proportion more than tripled between 1954 and 1960, reaching almost 24 per cent in the latter year. In contrast, the proportion of companies using SYD increased only slightly between 1954 and 1955, when close to 7 per cent of corporate returns showed this method, and fell very slightly thereafter. Little change occurred in the proportion of returns on which straight-line depreciation appears; in 1954, over 97 per cent and in 1960 about 94 per cent of corporations used this method.

A comparison of Table 4 data, which were drawn from large samples of the corporate income tax returns for the respective years, with Table 5, based on small samples of returns of the largest corporations, shows that a much larger proportion of the big corporations used declining-balance and SYD. Moreover, the increase in the proportion using declining-balance was less pronounced, and that in the proportion using SYD sharper, among the largest companies than among corporations in general.

This suggests that most of the increase in the proportion of returns

[1] See pp. 6–8 above for a description of the data sources.

TABLE 4

Per Cent of Corporation Income Tax Returns Reporting Various Depreciation Methods, Taxable Years 1954, 1955, 1957, 1960

Depreciation Method	Per Cent of Returns on Which Method Appears			
	1954	1955	1957	1960
Straight-line	97.4	97.3	96.9	94.3
Declining-balance	7.6	11.3	14.6	23.9
Sum-of-the-years-digits	4.8	6.8	6.6	5.9
Units-of-production	0.2	0.2	n.a.	n.a.
Other methods	1.0	1.8	0.6	0.5
Straight-line only[a]	86.4	79.9	78.2	69.7

Source: Taxable years 1954 and 1955, U.S. Treasury Department, Internal Revenue Service, *Statistics of Income, 1959, Supplementary Depreciation Data from Corporation Income Tax Returns,* pp. 103 and 118; taxable years 1957 and 1960, U.S. Treasury Department, Internal Revenue Service, special tabulations.

Note: Details in any year will not add to 100.0 per cent, since more than one method of depreciation may appear on a return.

[a]Since the taxpayer is not limited to the use of only one method, the per cent of returns on which only the straight-line method was used is a minimum estimate, computed by subtracting the sum of the percentage frequencies for the various methods other than straight-line from 100 per cent. In effect, this procedure assumes that on any return in which, say, the declining-balance method appeared, no other method was used. Since this assumption is unrealistic, the resulting estimate understates the percentage of returns on which only straight-line was used.

using the declining-balance method is attributable to the increasing proportion of smaller companies adopting this method.

Additional evidence on this point is afforded by Table 6, showing the percentage change between the taxable years 1954 and 1960 in the proportion of returns, by size of total assets, reporting use of straight-line, declining-balance, and/or SYD. The percentage increase between these years in the proportion of returns showing declining-balance was greatest among corporations with total assets less than $100,000. For companies with total assets of $50 million or more, the increase was much less substantial than in all other size classes. Much more modest

TABLE 5

Per Cent of Returns of Large Corporations Reporting Various Depreciation Methods, Taxable Years 1956, 1958, 1959

Depreciation Method	1956		1958		1959	
	No. of Returns	Per Cent	No. of Returns	Per Cent	No. of Returns	Per Cent
Total	1,017	—	912	—	912	—
Straight-line	987	97.1	892	97.8	892	97.8
Declining-balance	450	44.2	463	50.8	491	53.8
Sum-of-the-years-digits	359	35.3	356	39.0	366	40.1
Units-of-production	83	8.2	92	10.1	96	10.5
Other methods	131	12.9	181	19.8	225	24.7

Source: Taxable year 1956, Joint Economic Committee, *The Federal Revenue System: Facts and Problems 1959,* Joint Committee Print, 86th Congress, 1st session, p. 205; taxable years 1958 and 1959, U.S. Treasury Department, Internal Revenue Service, *Statistics of Income, 1959-60, U.S. Business Tax Returns,* p. 116.

Note: Details will not add to totals because a business may use more than one method in depreciating its assets.

increases in the proportion of returns showing use of SYD appear in each size class; differences in the magnitude of increases among size classes are also much less than in the case of declining-balance.

From one industrial division to another, relatively little difference is seen (see Table 7) in the percentage increase in the proportion of returns using the declining-balance method, compared with the differences among asset size classes. On the other hand, the percentage increase in returns showing SYD varied somewhat more among industry divisions than among size classes. The greatest percentage increases in returns using these methods appears in the agriculture and the finance divisions.

The relative frequency of returns showing use of straight-line depreciation decreased only very moderately between 1954 and 1960, as the proportion of companies using declining-balance increased. There are two principal reasons why this decrease was not more substantial. In the first place, as noted earlier, the Internal Revenue Code of 1954 authorized use of the declining-balance, SYD, or equivalent methods

TABLE 6

Percentage Change, 1954 to 1960, in Proportion of Corporation Income Tax Returns Reporting Selected Methods of Depreciation, by Size of Total Assets

Size of Total Assets (thousand dollars)	Straight-Line			Declining-Balance			Sum-of-the-Years-Digits		
	1954	1960	Per Cent Change	1954	1960	Per Cent Change	1954	1960	Per Cent Change
Under 100	97.4	94.6	−2.9	4.6	16.6	260.9	2.2	2.8	27.3
100–500	97.8	93.6	−4.3	10.0	30.9	209.0	6.4	7.8	21.9
500–1,000	97.7	94.0	−3.4	14.6	38.6	164.4	10.2	12.3	20.6
1,000–5,000	96.7	94.3	−2.5	16.5	40.7	146.7	12.5	16.2	29.6
5,000–10,000	98.2	96.9	−1.3	14.0	37.8	170.0	14.6	19.3	32.2
10,000–50,000	98.5	97.5	−1.0	16.4	37.5	128.6	17.8	21.0	18.0
50,000–100,000	98.0	98.0	0.0	21.9	40.9	86.8	19.3	28.9	49.7
100,000 and over	97.8	97.2	−0.6	24.0	46.7	94.6	28.4	34.8	22.5
Total	97.5	94.3	−3.3	7.8	23.9	206.4	4.9	5.9	20.4

Source: Table A-1.

Note: Frequencies for 1954 differ from those in Table 4, which includes data from all returns including those without balance sheets.

TABLE 7

Percentage Change, 1954 to 1960, in Proportion of Corporation Income Tax Returns Reporting Selected Methods of Depreciation, by Industry Division

Industry Division	Straight-Line			Declining-Balance			Sum-of-the-Years-Digits		
	1954	1960	Per Cent Change	1954	1960	Per Cent Change	1954	1960	Per Cent Change
Agriculture, forestry, and fisheries	97.9	94.7	−3.3	8.3	27.1	226.5	3.6	5.3	47.2
Mining	95.2	94.7	−0.5	11.2	29.5	163.4	5.5	7.1	29.1
Construction	98.3	95.5	−2.8	8.7	26.7	206.9	5.9	6.0	1.7
Manufacturing	98.4	96.6	−1.8	10.0	29.9	199.0	8.6	10.5	22.1
Transportation, communication, electric, gas, and sanitary services	97.2	94.3	−3.0	7.8	23.4	200.0	4.4	5.5	25.0
Trade	97.9	95.6	−2.3	6.8	21.4	214.7	4.3	4.8	11.6
Finance, insurance, and real estate	96.3	91.1	−5.4	7.0	22.3	218.6	2.9	4.4	51.7
Services	97.3	93.4	−4.0	8.1	23.6	191.4	4.4	5.5	25.0
All industries	97.5	94.3	−3.3	7.8	23.9	206.4	4.9	5.9	20.4

Source: Table A-1.

only with respect to new properties newly acquired by the taxpayer after 1953. Companies formed and acquiring depreciable facilities prior to 1954, therefore, were substantially limited to the use of straight-line depreciation. In the taxable year 1959, about 53 per cent of the active corporations filing tax returns had been incorporated prior to 1954. It may be assumed that most of these companies in the taxable year 1960 had some facilities for which the accelerated methods were not available. Moreover, among the companies organized and acquiring assets after 1953, some will have acquired some secondhand assets and will have had them on hand in depreciable asset accounts as late as 1960. Secondly, the use by a taxpayer of one depreciation method for one group of facilities in no wise precludes his simultaneously using another method for another group of assets. It is evident that a very large proportion of the companies incorporated after 1953 did indeed use straight-line for some of their facilities.

For each of the years in question and in both of the samples, between 94 and 98 per cent of the returns show the use of straight-line depreciation. In the sample of large companies there is a slight increase between 1956 and 1958 and no change between 1958 and 1959 in the percentage of returns showing the use of this method.[2] It seems fair to assume that virtually all of these very large companies were in existence prior to 1954 and, in the taxable years 1956, 1958, and 1959, held depreciable facilities acquired before 1954. In this event, of course, they would have to show the use of straight-line depreciation.[3] In the broader samples, on the other hand, the percentage of returns showing the use of straight-line depreciation decreases from 97.4 per cent in 1954 to 94.3 per cent in 1960. These samples almost certainly include a much larger proportion of companies which are new since 1953.[4] Conceivably, each such new company might have chosen to use only the accelerated depreciation methods; indeed, it may appear surprising that

[2] The 1956 sample is not identical with that for the years 1958 and 1959. The differences in the sample population probably account for the increase in this percentage between 1956 and 1958.

[3] Actually, this overstates the constraint since the statute prior to 1954 did not explicitly limit the taxpayer to the use of the straight-line method. The exaggeration is likely to be slight, however.

[4] One indication is the increase in the size of the sample between 1957 and 1960. The increase in sample size between the years 1954 and 1955, and between 1955 and 1957, can be attributed only in much smaller part to the increase in the corporate population; a much larger part of the increase is attributable to changes in the sample.

the decrease in the percentage of returns using the straight-line method was no greater than that shown in Tables 4 and 6. Of course, not all new corporations would choose to use only the accelerated methods.

The proportion of returns showing the straight-line method appears to have decreased at a somewhat faster rate between 1957 and 1960. This suggests that a more rapid decline in this proportion may be developing.

A striking fact revealed in Table 4 is that on a very large proportion of all returns, only straight-line depreciation was used as late as 1960. Since any company may use different depreciation methods for different assets, the data as presented do not permit precise computation of the number of returns on which only one of the various methods was used. By subtracting from the total number of returns the number on which some method other than straight-line is used, however, a minimum estimate of the number using only the straight-line method is obtained. Of course, the actual number using only this method is likely to be larger than indicated by this computation. Making some rough allowance for the use of more than one method on a return, it seems clear that a large proportion, probably between 70 and 75 per cent, of all corporate returns confined the computation of annual depreciation allowances to the straight-line method in the taxable year 1960.

On the other hand, Table 4 also shows that the minimum proportion of returns using only straight-line declined significantly from 86.4 per cent in 1954 to 69.7 per cent in 1960. As Table 8 shows, this decrease occurred in every size class, most sharply among corporations with total assets of $50 million and over. Presumably this trend continued after 1960, suggesting that a considerably smaller proportion of returns would now show the use only of straight-line depreciation.

Table 8 also shows that among big corporations, only a relatively small proportion of companies confined their depreciation computation to the straight-line method. In the case of corporations with total assets of $100 million or more, which accounted for 59.6 per cent of total depreciable facilities of corporations in 1960, the minimum proportion of returns showing only straight-line in that year is 7.6 per cent.

Tables 6 and 8 suggest that use of the accelerated methods is associated with company size. Examination of Table A-1, presenting the relative frequencies of returns for 1954 and 1960 by depreciation method, major industry division, and size of total assets, reveals that

TABLE 8

Percentage Change, 1954 to 1960, in Proportion of Corporation
Returns on Which Only Straight-Line Depreciation Was Used,
by Size of Total Assets

Size of Total Assets (thousand dollars)	Proportion of Returns Using Only Straight-Line		
	1954	1960	Per Cent Change
Under 100	92.3	80.3	− 13.0
100–500	82.4	60.8	− 26.2
500–1,000	73.6	48.4	− 34.2
1,000–5,000	68.5	41.5	− 39.4
5,000–10,000	68.4	40.6	− 40.6
10,000–50,000	61.3	38.1	− 37.8
50,000–100,000	52.5	23.5	− 55.2
100,000 and over	39.0	7.6	− 80.5
Total	86.1	69.7	− 19.0

Source: Table A-1.

there is, indeed, a substantial positive association between size, as measured by total assets, and relative frequency of returns reporting the use of an accelerated method. Taking all industrial divisions together, the rank correlation with respect to 1960 returns between size class and proportion of returns reporting SYD is perfect; for declining-balance, the Kendall coefficient of rank correlation is .64, with a standard error of .38.

The rank correlation between the estimated minimum percentage of returns on which only the straight-line method was used and size of total assets is also perfect, taking all industries together.

There is evident in Table 9 some variability among industries in the association between size and relative frequency of returns on which declining-balance, SYD, or only straight-line depreciation appear. With respect to both SYD and straight-line only, the rank correlations are quite high in almost every industry. In the case of declining-balance, very low coefficients were found in the mining and in the finance, insurance, and real estate divisions, but very high coefficients are obtained in

TABLE 9

Rank Correlation of Size of Total Assets and Percentage of Returns on Which Declining-Balance, SYD, or Only Straight-Line Method is Shown, Corporations, 1960

Industry Division	Declining-Balance		Sum-of-Years-Digits		Straight-Line Only	
	Coefficient of Rank Correlation	Standard Error	Coefficient of Rank Correlation	Standard Error	Coefficient of Rank Correlation	Standard Error
Agriculture	.73	.39	.87	.29	−.87	.29
Mining	.07	.50	.79	.31	−.79	.31
Construction	.90	.23	.90	.23	−.93	.19
Manufacturing	.93	.19	1.00	0	−1.00	0
Transportation, communication, sanitary services	.93	.19	.71	.35	−1.00	0
Trade	.79	.31	1.00	0	−1.00	0
Finance, insurance, real estate	.21	.49	1.00	0	−.93	.19
Service	.79	.31	.93	.19	−.93	.19
All industries	.64	.38	1.00	0	−1.00	0

Note: Coefficients of rank correlation in the case of declining balance in mining and finance, insurance, and real estate are not significant. Those for declining balance in agriculture and in all industries are significant at the 5 per cent level. All others are significant at the 1 per cent level.

all of the other industrial divisions. With these few exceptions, there-fore, use of one or the other of the accelerated methods—as measured by relative frequency of returns—appears to be closely and positively related to company size.

Relatively little variability from one industry division to another in the proportion of returns showing an accelerated method is evident in Table 10. The proportion of returns showing declining-balance ranged from 21.4 per cent in trade to 29.9 per cent in manufacturing. For SYD, the proportion ranged from 4.4 per cent in finance, etc., to 10.5 per cent in manufacturing. The proportion of returns on which only straight-line depreciation was used ranged from 56.4 per cent in mining to 73.4 per cent in trade.

TABLE 10

Per Cent of Corporation Income Tax Returns Reporting Various Depreciation Methods, by Industry Division, 1960

Industry Division	Straight-Line	Declining-Balance	Sum-of-Years-Digits	Other Methods	Straight-Line Only
Agriculture, forestry, and fisheries	94.7	27.1	5.3	0.3	67.4
Mining	94.7	29.5	7.1	7.0	56.4
Construction	95.5	26.7	6.0	0.3	67.0
Manufacturing	96.6	29.9	10.5	0.9	58.7
Transportation, communication, and sanitary services	94.3	23.4	5.5	1.0	70.2
Trade	95.6	21.4	4.8	0.4	73.4
Finance, insurance, and real estate	91.1	22.3	4.4	0.3	72.9
Services	93.4	23.6	5.5	0.5	70.5
Not allocable	92.3	15.2	a	—	a
All industries	94.3	23.9	5.9	0.6	69.7

Source: U.S. Treasury Department, Internal Revenue Service, special tabulation.

Note: Details do not add to 100.0 per cent because frequently a business uses more than one depreciation method.

[a]Sampling variability too high to show separately.

The proportion of returns on which an accelerated method was used in 1960 does not appear to be associated with industry division. If indeed there were such an association, one would expect to find little variation in the ranking of an industry in each size class with respect to the proportion of returns showing an accelerated method. In fact, however, most industry divisions change ranks from one size class to another; no consistent pattern of variability from one industry to another appears within each size class. This is in contrast with the per cent of companies using an accelerated method, which varies quite regularly with asset size class.

UNINCORPORATED BUSINESSES

A relatively small proportion of unincorporated businesses indicated the use of either the declining-balance or the SYD method for the taxable year 1959, the single year for which such data are available. Among the 6,650,560 sole proprietorships showing depreciation methods, only 365,504 (5.5 per cent) used the declining-balance method, and SYD was indicated in the case of only 61,160 (.9 per cent) of sole proprietorships. A larger proportion of the partnerships used these methods; of the 765,428 firms, 81,785 (10.7 per cent) used declining-balance and 15,613 (2.0 per cent) used SYD (Table 11).

These proportions are markedly below those for corporations in 1960. Just as striking, however, is the much lower proportion of unincorporated than of incorporated businesses showing use of the straight-line method. Only 83.9 per cent of the sole proprietorships and 84.6 per cent of the partnerships indicated use of this method, compared with 94.3 per cent of the corporations in the following year.

In discussing the large proportion of corporations using the straight-line method in 1960, it was pointed out that over half of these companies were in existence prior to 1954 and probably still had on hand in the taxable year 1960 some facilities acquired prior to 1954. Such facilities were not eligible for the declining-balance or SYD methods, and by and large would be depreciated under the straight-line method. The noticeably lower proportion of unincorporated companies showing straight-line depreciation in 1959 might suggest, along the same line of reasoning, that a substantially smaller proportion of these companies were organized prior to 1954. No data bearing on this point are available in the case of sole proprietorships, but roughly 42.5 per cent of

TABLE 11

Per Cent of Sole Proprietorships and Partnerships Reporting Use of Various Depreciation Methods, 1959

Depreciation Method	Sole Proprietorships		Partnerships	
	Number	Per Cent	Number	Per Cent
Straight-line	5,582,253	83.9	647,143	84.6
Declining-balance	365,504	5.5	81,785	10.7
Sum-of-the-years-digits	61,160	0.9	15,613	2.0
Other methods	336,050	5.1	124,632	16.3
Method not described	628,437	9.5	34,679	4.5
Straight-line only	5,259,409	79.1	508,719	66.5
Total	6,650,560		765,428	

Source: U.S. Treasury Department, Internal Revenue Service, *Statistics of Income, 1959-60, U.S. Business Tax Returns,* pp. 34, 92-93.

Note: Details do not add to totals because frequently a business uses more than one method in depreciating its assets.

the partnerships were organized before 1954.[5] The difference between the proportion of partnerships and that of corporations reporting use of the straight-line method is nearly the same as the difference between the respective proportions of these companies organized before 1954. This suggests, but of course does not establish, that the difference in the proportion of the respective populations reporting use of straight-line can be explained by the difference in the proportion of companies organized before the accelerated depreciation methods became available.

At least four-fifths of the sole proprietorships and two-thirds of the partnerships were using only the straight-line method in computing depreciation in the taxable year 1959 (Table 11). In the case of the former, this proportion is substantially greater than among corporations, but, surprisingly, a somewhat smaller minimum percentage of partnerships than of corporations used only straight-line. Moreover, in

[5] U.S. Treasury Department, Internal Revenue Service, *Statistics of Income, 1959–60, U.S. Business Tax Returns,* p. 85.

the case of both sole proprietorships and partnerships, the proportion of firms using only straight-line appears to be quite low, in view of the small frequencies of these companies showing use of an accelerated method. The explanation lies in the fact that the estimate is made by subtracting from 100 per cent the proportions for all methods other than straight-line and that relatively large proportions of unincorporated businesses, particularly of partnerships, reported using methods other than straight-line, declining-balance, or SYD (Table 11). No breakdown of these "other methods" is available, but the much larger proportion of sole proprietorships in the mining than in other industry divisions suggests that the principal other method is units-of-production.[6] Among partnerships, similarly, much larger proportions of the companies in mining and in agriculture than in other divisions reported using "other methods," again strongly suggesting that the method used was units-of-production. Even so, however, the proportion of unincorporated companies in each division reporting use of other methods substantially exceeded the corresponding proportions among corporations. Particularly among partnerships, at least 13.6 per cent of the companies in each industry division indicated use of "other methods," and in agriculture and in mining, these proportions were, respectively, 26.2 per cent and 22.6 per cent (Table A-3). In addition, 9.5 per cent of the sole proprietorships and 4.5 per cent of the partnerships indicated depreciation charges without describing the methods used in computing them (Table 11).

Among both sole proprietorships and partnerships, there is a positive association between company size (as measured by amount of business receipts) and proportion of companies using an accelerated method (Tables 12 and 13). Among sole proprietorships, there is perfect rank correlation between size of business receipts and proportions of companies using declining-balance and SYD, taking all industries together. Unfortunately, the data are too thin in several of the industry divisions

---

[6] In the units-of-production depreciation method, the annual depreciation charge is computed by applying to the depreciable cost of the facility the ratio of the number of units of output in the year to the estimated lifetime capacity of the facility. This method is not related to the facility's service life measured in years. It is more extensively used for facilities in extractive industries where the life of a deposit is frequently more meaningfully measured in terms of total potential output than in years. It is also used relatively frequently in connection with timber cutting operations. Accordingly, we should expect the use of this method to be relatively great in the mining and the agriculture divisions.

TABLE 12

Per Cent of Sole Proprietorships Reporting Use of Various Depreciation Methods, by Size of Business Receipts, 1959

Size of Business Receipts (dollars)	Straight-Line	Declining-Balance	Sum-of-Years-Digits	Other Methods	Method Not Described	Straight-Line Only
Under 10,000	84.4	3.1	0.5	4.7	9.1	82.6
10,000 under 20,000	83.8	6.4	1.0	5.0	9.4	78.2
20,000 under 30,000	84.1	7.7	1.1	5.4	10.0	75.8
30,000 under 50,000	83.4	8.8	1.4	5.1	9.9	74.8
50,000 under 100,000	84.0	11.5	2.1	5.7	10.4	70.3
100,000 and over	81.0	15.5	3.2	8.1	11.6	61.6
Receipts not reported	75.8	2.5	0.7	5.1	10.6	81.1
Total	83.9	5.5	0.9	5.1	9.5	79.1

Source: U.S. Treasury Department, Internal Revenue Service, *Statistics of Income, 1959-60, U.S. Business Tax Returns*, p. 34.

Note: Details do not add to 100.0 per cent because frequently a business uses more than one depreciation method.

TABLE 13

Per Cent of Partnerships Reporting Use of Various Depreciation Methods, by Size of Business Receipts, 1959

Size of Business Receipts (thousand dollars)	Straight-Line	Declining-Balance	Sum-of-Years-Digits	Other Methods	Method Not Described	Straight-Line Only
Under 10	84.2	6.7	1.0	14.7	4.0	73.6
10 under 20	83.3	7.6	1.2	15.8	3.9	71.5
20 under 30	83.8	8.5	1.5	15.1	3.8	71.1
30 under 50	84.4	9.5	1.6	15.8	4.1	69.0
50 under 100	86.5	11.8	2.0	15.4	4.2	66.6
100 under 200	84.0	14.3	2.6	16.8	5.5	60.8
200 under 500	82.7	20.0	5.0	22.7	6.3	46.0
500 under 1,000	95.8	32.7	9.1	30.7	9.6	17.9
1,000 under 5,000	85.7	35.8	10.0	27.1	11.7	15.4
5,000 and over	93.3	58.4	19.2	10.3	48.8	a
Receipts not reported	88.4	10.1	4.5	12.7	5.3	67.4
Total	84.6	10.7	2.0	16.3	4.5	66.5

Source: U.S. Treasury Department, Internal Revenue Service, *Statistics of Income, 1959-60, U.S. Business Tax Returns,* pp. 92-93.

Note: Details do not add to 100.0 per cent because frequently a business uses more than one depreciation method.

aSubtracting the sum of the proportions for declining-balance, sum-of-years-digits, other methods, and methods not described from 100 per cent results in a negative proportion.

to permit computation of such coefficients. However, perfect correlations with respect to per cent of companies showing declining-balance and size are found in agriculture, construction, and services, and high coefficients are observable in trade and in transportation, communication, and sanitary services. For SYD, a perfect rank correlation is found in agriculture; coefficients could not be computed or were statistically insignificant in the other industry divisions (Table A-2). Among partnerships, high coefficients are found in every division except transportation, communication, and sanitary services (in the case of declining-balance), and (for SYD) in agriculture and mining (Table 14).

Among the larger partnerships, the relative frequency of firms show-

TABLE 14

Rank Correlation of Size of Business Receipts and Percentage of Returns on Which Declining-Balance or SYD Is Shown, Partnerships, 1959

Industry Division	Declining-Balance		Sum-of-Years-Digits	
	Coefficient of Rank Correlation	Standard Error	Coefficient of Rank Correlation	Standard Error
Agriculture	.96	.13	.36[a]	.47
Mining	1.00	0	.20[a]	.62
Construction	.91	.18	.81	.32
Manufacturing	.91	.18	1.00	0
Transportation, communication, and sanitary services	.51[a]	.38	.80[b]	.38
Trade	1.00	0	1.00	0
Finance, insurance, and real estate	.96	.13	.87	.22
Services	.91	.18	.96	.13
All industries	1.00	0	1.00	0

Source: Table A-3.

[a]Not statistically significant.

[b]Significant at the 5 per cent level. All other coefficients are significant at the 1 per cent level.

ing use of the declining-balance method was even greater than among the largest corporations (granted, there is a lack of strict comparability of the size classifications). On the other hand, even among the largest partnerships, a relatively small proportion of companies used SYD, whereas more nearly the same proportion of large corporations used SYD and declining-balance.

Little difference among industry divisions is evident in the proportions of sole proprietorships and partnerships using declining-balance or SYD (Tables A-2 and A-3). Moreover, within any given size-of-business-receipts class, there is, in general, little variation from one industry division to another in the proportion of companies showing the use of declining-balance or SYD.

The high rank correlations found between company size and proportion of companies using an accelerated method, and the limited variability from one industry division to another, suggests that election to use an accelerated method was associated with size of the business and not with the industrial division in which it chiefly operated. This is the same surmise as in the case of corporations, but the data suggest it is even more strongly based for unincorporated businesses.

Amount of Depreciation

CORPORATIONS

Between the taxable years 1954 and 1960, total corporate depreciation allowances grew from an estimated $11.5 billion to about $22.2 billion (Table 15).[7] Declining-balance allowances increased from about $0.5 billion to about $5.4 billion, and SYD allowances grew from an estimated $0.3 billion to roughly $3.3 billion. In other words, the accelerated methods generated about $7.9 billion of the $10.7 billion increase in corporate allowances during this period.

As implied by these estimates, the accelerated depreciation methods accounted for a rapidly growing proportion of total corporation de-

---

[7] *Statistics of Income* for the taxable year 1954 does not segregate depreciation allowances from amortization allowed on defense and defense-related facilities for which certificates of necessity had been issued. Graphic interpolation on ratio scale between the amount of depreciation reported in *Statistics of Income* for 1953 and that for 1955 yields an estimate of $11.5 billion in depreciation for 1954. See U.S. Treasury Department, Internal Revenue Service, *Statistics of Income, 1960–61, Corporation Income Tax Returns*, p. 303.

preciation allowances between 1954 and 1960. Table 15 shows that the share of total allowances accounted for by declining-balance was more than five times as great in the latter than in the former year, while SYD allowances, as a fraction of the total, were 6.5 times as great in 1960 as in 1954. Together, these methods accounted for 39.0 per cent of total corporate allowances in 1960, compared with 7 per cent in 1954. Straight-line allowances fell from 89 per cent of the total in 1954 to 58 per cent in 1960.

The substantial increase in the share of total depreciation allowances under SYD contrasts sharply with the very small increase in the proportion of returns on which this method was used. Similarly, the large drop in the proportion of total allowances computed by the straight-line method contrasts sharply with the very slight decrease in the proportion of returns on which the straight-line method appears.

Between the taxable years 1954 and 1960, as indicated in Table A-4, the increase in the ratio of accelerated to total depreciation allowances was quite pronounced, and occurred in virtually every size class in every industry. Taking all industries together, the proportion of declining-balance to total allowances rose in every total asset size class, most notably for corporations with total assets of $50 million or more. The ratio of SYD to total allowances also increased in every size class, and by increasing percentages, the larger the asset size class. Taking all size classes together, the increase in the ratio of accelerated to total allowances was greatest in the manufacturing and in the transportation, communication, electric, gas, and sanitary services divisions. In every industry division, there was a substantial increase in the proportion of total allowances computed under declining-balance, most notably in the public utilities. On the other hand, except for manufacturing, the increase in the share of total allowances accounted for by SYD was much more modest. In manufacturing, however, the increase in the ratio of SYD to total allowances was greater than that of declining-balance to the total.

The proportion of total allowances in 1960 computed under the declining-balance method (Table A-4) shows considerably less of the positive association with company size (as measured by total assets) than was found in the case of the proportion of returns on which this method appears (Table A-1). Indeed, aside from the smallest and largest asset size class, this proportion varies narrowly between 25.6

TABLE 15

Amount of Corporate Depreciation Allowances, by Depreciation Method, Taxable Years 1954, 1955, 1957, and 1960

Depreciation Method	1954	1955	1957	1960
Amount (million dollars)[a]				
Straight-line	10,260	10,829	11,912	12,897
Declining-balance	540	1,328	2,630	5,363
Sum-of-the-years-digits	265	832	1,883	3,280
Units-of-production	170	174	n.a.	n.a.
Other methods	265	255	543	620[b]
Total	11,500	13,419	16,968	22,160[b]
Percentage Distribution				
Straight-line	89.2	80.7	70.2	58.2
Declining-balance	4.7	9.9	15.5	24.2
Sum-of-the-years-digits	2.3	6.2	11.1	14.8
Units-of-production	1.5	1.3	n.a.	n.a.
Other methods	2.3	1.9	3.2	2.8
Total	100.0	100.0	100.0	100.0

Source: Taxable years 1954-1955, U.S. Treasury Department, Internal Revenue Service, *Statistics of Income, 1959, Supplementary Depreciation Data for Corporation Income Tax Returns,* pp. 103 and 118; taxable years 1957 and 1960, U.S. Treasury Department, Internal Revenue Service, special tabulations.

Note: Details may not add to totals because of rounding.

[a]Dollar amounts for each method were estimated by applying the proportions shown in the percentage distribution to the *Statistics of Income* totals for the respective years. Since the samples from which the percentage distributions were drawn were not identical with the *Statistics of Income* samples for the respective years, these amounts should be read more as estimates of the orders of magnitude than as precise measures of corporate allowances.

[b]Includes $65 million of so-called "additional first-year depreciation."

per cent and 29.6 per cent of the total. On the other hand, SYD allowances as a share of the total increase consistently with asset size class. The range is substantial, from 2.6 per cent for the smallest companies to 21.0 per cent for the largest. The combined declining-balance and SYD allowances as a fraction of the total also increase with asset size up to the largest class—total assets of $100 million or more—in which a slight decrease in this proportion is seen. For corporations with total assets of $50 million or more, taking all industries together, accelerated allowances were about 44 per cent of the total for such companies.

A more detailed examination of the size distribution within each industry division shows little positive association between company size and proportion of total allowances computed under the accelerated methods. As indicated in Table 16, a statistically significant positive rank correlation between company size and proportion of total allowances under declining-balance is found only in the construction division. The rank correlations are somewhat better in the case of SYD and of declining-balance and SYD combined, but the data hardly support the same sort of assertion about a size-method association as in the case of the relative frequencies of returns on which accelerated methods appear.

Substantially greater variability among industries is found in the taxable year 1960 in the proportion of total allowances computed under the accelerated methods than in the proportion of returns using the accelerated methods (Tables A-1 and A-4). Declining-balance depreciation was as little as 19 per cent of the total in mining and as much as 36 per cent in construction. SYD allowances were only 3.8 per cent and 3.9 per cent of the total in agriculture and mining, respectively, but accounted for 23.3 per cent of total allowances in manufacturing. Straight-line depreciation was about 51 per cent of total allowances in manufacturing and almost 72 per cent in agriculture.

The relatively large proportion of total allowances under SYD in manufacturing, where it exceeded the proportion accounted for by declining-balance, is sharply in contrast with other industries. In every other industry, except trade, SYD allowances were a relatively small fraction of the total allowances even among the largest corporations. In trade, however, companies in the largest asset size classes accounted for a substantial amount of their total allowances by this method—to a greater extent, indeed, than companies of corresponding size in manufacturing.

TABLE 16

Rank Correlation of Size of Total Assets and Proportion of Total Allowances Computed by
Declining-Balance, SYD, and Declining-Balance and SYD Combined, Corporations, 1960

Industry Division	Declining-Balance		Sum-of-Years-Digits		Declining-Balance and SYD	
	Coefficient of Rank Correlation	Standard Error	Coefficient of Rank Correlation	Standard Error	Coefficient of Rank Correlation	Standard Error
Agriculture	.20	.57	.60	.46	.33	.54
Mining	−.21	.49	.29	.48	−.36	.47
Construction	.71[b]	.37	.81[a]	.31	.81[a]	.31
Manufacturing	−.14	.49	1.00[a]	0	1.00[a]	0
Transportation, communication, sanitary services	.36	.47	.36	.47	.50	.43
Trade	−.07	.50	1.00[a]	0	1.00[a]	0
Finance	.07	.50	.93[a]	.19	.21	.49
Services	0	.50	.50	.43	.36	.47
All industries	0	.50	1.00[a]	.00	.93[a]	.19

Source: Table A-4.

[a]Significant at the 1 per cent level.

[b]Significant at the 5 per cent level. All other coefficients are not statistically significant.

As we might expect, a relatively substantial amount of depreciation in the mining division was computed by "other" methods, undoubtedly the units-of-production method.

The proportion of total allowances under declining-balance in the construction industry substantially exceeds that in other industries, although the relative frequency of returns in construction showing this method was not out of line with other industries. In all but the first two asset size classes, declining-balance allowances in construction were more than 40 per cent of the total depreciation claimed, and in the $50 million under $100 million class, they were more than 55 per cent of the total. In no size class in any other industry did either of the accelerated allowances account for nearly so large a share of the total.

The explanation for the extraordinarily large proportion of total allowances under declining-balance in the construction industry is not obvious from these data. Reference to the "Life of Depreciable Assets" study (LDA), however, shows that the mean service life (for purposes of computing depreciation allowances) of facilities in construction is below that in any other industry.[8] Assuming some positive correlation between service life for tax purposes and average age of facilities, a larger proportion of the facilities on hand in construction than in other industries in 1960 would have been eligible for the declining-balance method. Table 30, based on LDA data, shows that the proportion of facilities acquired after 1953 by construction corporations and placed in declining-balance accounts was exceptionally large. Both of these factors—the short service lives and the larger proportion of facilities under the declining-balance method—account for the unusually large proportion of total allowances under declining-balance in construction.

The substantial lack of significant rank correlation between company size and share of total depreciation allowances computed under the accelerated methods within each industry is, as noted, in contrast with the relatively strong correlation between size and proportion of returns showing use of these methods. The share of total allowances under an accelerated method depends on a number of factors, including the proportion of the total facilities under the method, the average service life of the property under the method relative to those under other methods, and the average age of these facilities. There is, therefore, no necessarily

[8] See Table C-2.

close correspondence between the proportion of returns in a class showing the use of an accelerated method and the proportion of total allowances in that class computed under that method.

UNINCORPORATED BUSINESSES

Although data with respect to the amount of depreciation by method for unincorporated companies are limited to the taxable year 1959, it may be presumed that the proportion of total allowances computed under the accelerated methods by these companies had increased since 1954. The share of their total allowances computed under declining-balance or SYD was quite small compared with corporations, particularly in the case of sole proprietorships. These companies used the straight-line method to compute almost three-fourths of their total allowances. Partnerships, on the other hand, used the straight-line method for only 59 per cent of their total allowance, very nearly the

TABLE 17

Amount of Depreciation by Method, Sole Proprietorships and Partnerships, 1959

(dollars in millions)

Depreciation Method	Sole Proprietorships		Partnerships	
	Amount	Per Cent of Total	Amount	Per Cent of Total
Straight-line	5,150	74.5	1,240	59.0
Declining-balance	479	6.9	383	18.2
Sum-of-the-years-digits	70	1.0	56	2.7
Other methods	416[a]	6.0	279[b]	13.3
Method not described	744	10.8	111	5.3
Total	6,914	100.0	2,103	100.0

Source: U.S. Treasury Department, Internal Revenue Service, *Statistics of Income, 1959-60, U.S. Business Tax Returns*, pp. 34, 92-93.

[a]Excludes $54 million of additional first-year depreciation included in total. Details do not, therefore, add to total.

[b]Excludes $34 million of additional first-year depreciation included in total. Details do not, therefore, add to total.

same proportion as corporations (in 1960). Whereas almost 40 per cent of corporation allowances were computed under declining-balance and SYD, only 7.9 per cent of the total claimed by sole proprietorships and 20.9 per cent of the total for partnerships were computed under these methods. On the other hand, very little of the total allowances of corporations were computed under other methods, while in the case of sole proprietorships, other methods, including those not described by the taxpayer, account for about 17 per cent of the total. For partnerships, almost 19 per cent of the total allowances were computed otherwise than by straight-line, declining-balance, or SYD (Table 17).

As in the case of the relative frequencies, the relative amounts of depreciation computed under the accelerated methods by sole proprietorships was greater the larger the business (as measured by size of business receipts). Table 18 indicates perfect rank correlations of company size and the ratios of declining-balance and of SYD allowances to the total, taking all industries together. The data are too thin, however, to sustain the correlation analysis in several of the industry divisions (Table A-5). They do suggest, nevertheless, a positive asso-

TABLE 18

Percentage Distribution of Depreciation of Sole Proprietorships,
by Depreciation Method and Size of Business Receipts, 1959

Size of Business Receipts (thousand dollars)	Straight-Line	Declining-Balance	Sum-of-Years-Digits	Other Methods	Method Not Described
Under 10	81.6	3.1	0.4	4.7	9.6
10-20	78.6	4.6	0.6	4.9	10.4
20-30	76.9	5.2	1.0	5.6	10.6
30-50	73.2	7.7	1.1	5.7	11.2
50-100	69.2	9.9	1.6	6.6	11.8
100 and over	60.2	15.0	2.2	9.7	11.9
No receipts reported	71.4	3.2	0.4	4.7	19.1
Total	74.5	6.9	1.0	6.0	10.8

Source: U.S. Treasury Department, Internal Revenue Service, *Statistics of Income, 1959-60, U.S. Business Tax Returns,* p. 34.

Note: Details do not add to 100 per cent because small amounts of additional first-year depreciation are not included. See Table 17.

ciation between company size and the proportion of total allowances computed under accelerated methods.

Among partnerships, the ratio of accelerated to total allowances tended to increase with company size, but this relationship is not nearly so strong as in the case of the proportion of partnerships electing the use of the declining-balance or SYD methods (Table 19).

TABLE 19

Percentage Distribution of Partnerships' Depreciation,
by Depreciation Method and Size of Business Receipts, 1959

Size of Business Receipts (thousand dollars)	Straight-Line	Declining-Balance	Sum-of-Years-Digits	Other Methods	Method Not Described
Under 10	74.1	13.1	1.3	7.4	2.9
10 - 20	69.8	14.3	2.0	9.5	3.1
20 - 30	66.3	15.6	2.0	10.8	4.2
30 - 50	67.2	15.0	1.2	10.7	4.6
50 - 100	65.2	16.2	2.4	11.1	3.4
100 - 200	60.9	18.3	1.7	13.8	3.4
200 - 500	51.5	21.0	3.0	16.9	6.2
500 - 1,000	53.1	23.3	5.4	12.1	3.3
1,000 - 5,000	44.9	26.4	5.1	16.7	4.8
5,000 and over	18.4	19.1	3.7	27.9	29.4
No receipts reported	56.0	11.6	11.2	6.1	9.1
Total	59.0	18.2	2.7	13.3	5.3

Source: U.S. Treasury Department, Internal Revenue Service, *Statistics of Income, 1959-60, U.S. Business Tax Returns,* pp. 92-93.

Note: Details do not add to 100 per cent because small amounts of additional first-year depreciation are not included. See Table 17.

Taking all industries together, the coefficient of rank correlation of the ratio of declining balance to total allowances with size of partnership receipts is .82 (standard error = .25), and in the case of SYD, the coefficient is .60 (standard error = .36). Among industries, considerable variability in the correlation is found, as seen in Table 20.

Accelerated allowances as a share of the total varied considerably from one industry to another in the unincorporated business sector. Sole proprietorships in mining, for example, computed about one-fifth

TABLE 20

Rank Correlation of Size of Partnership Receipts and Proportion of Total Allowances Computed by Declining-Balance and SYD, 1959

Industry Division	Declining-Balance		Sum-of-Years-Digits	
	Coefficient of Rank Correlation	Standard Error	Coefficient of Rank Correlation	Standard Error
Agriculture	.82[a]	.25	.36	.47
Mining	1.00[a]	.00	.80[b]	.38
Construction	.60[a]	.36	.14	.53
Manufacturing	.64[a]	.34	1.00[a]	.00
Transportation, communication, and sanitary services	−.02	.45	.80[b]	.38
Trade	.78[a]	.28	.93[a]	.19
Finance, insurance, and real estate	.02	.45	.42	.41
Services	.51[b]	.38	.33	.42
All industries	.82[a]	.25	.60[a]	.36

Source: Table A-4.

[a]Significant at the 1 per cent level.

[b]Significant at the 5 per cent level. All other coefficients are not statistically significant.

of their total depreciation charges by use of the declining-balance and SYD methods, another 11.4 per cent by other methods—probably units-of-production, and 23 per cent of the total by methods which were not described by the taxpayer. Sole proprietorships in agriculture, on the other hand, used the declining-balance method for only 3.5 per cent of total allowances and SYD for less than one-half of 1 per cent (Table A-5).

Among partnerships, similarly, there is a substantial range in the proportion of total allowances accounted for under the accelerated methods from one industry to another. In agriculture, about 7.2 per cent of the total depreciation was declining-balance and SYD, although other methods—probably units-of-production—accounted for a fifth of the total. In the finance, insurance, and real estate division, on the other hand, 37 per cent of all depreciation was accelerated, one-third under the declining-balance method (Table A-6).

The real estate subdivision of this industry division, for partnerships, accounted for 93.7 per cent of total depreciation allowances and 97.9 per cent of allowances computed by use of the declining-balance method in the division.[9] The very high proportion of total allowances under the declining-balance method in this subdivision probably reflects the operation of the so-called "real estate tax shelter." The phrase refers to investment, usually by a group of individuals, in the construction or acquisition of new, real property, generally subject to a substantial mortgage. Each of the individuals in the syndicate will take into his own income for tax purposes his pro rata share of the net rental of the property. In the computation of net rental, interest on the indebtedness and depreciation are deducted from the gross rentals. The depreciation deduction, the basis for which is the total cost of the property, not merely the equity share thereof, is likely to be computed by use of one or the other of the accelerated methods, usually the declining-balance method. The interest deduction, too, often follows a declining-balance pattern, if the indebtedness is amortizable. Thus, the combined interest and depreciation deductions in the early years after acquisition of the property are likely to be relatively large, and indeed, if taken in conjunction with other expenses, to exceed the gross income from the property and to reduce, therefore, taxable income from other sources. In any event, the depreciation deduction increases the taxpayer's disposable income by an amount equal to his marginal income tax rate times the deduction, since these deductions go against ordinary income. By virtue of the declining-balance pattern of the interest and depreciation deductions, net rentals become larger in each succeeding year; when net rental becomes positive, it may pay the syndicate to sell the property. Any gain realized, i.e., any excess of sales proceeds over the basis of the property reduced by accumulated depreciation, was treated as a capital gain (during the period covered by this survey), subject to a maximum rate of 25 per cent.[10] In effect, the deduction of deprecia-

[9] *Statistics of Income, 1959–60, U.S. Business Tax Returns*, p. 90.

[10] The Revenue Act of 1964 included a provision restricting the extent to which such gains might be treated as capital gains instead of ordinary income (see Sec. 1250, Internal Revenue Code).

tion, to the extent that it exceeds the actual reduction in the value of the property, converts ordinary income into capital gains. While the tax advantage is available for any income taxpayer, it increases with the taxpayer's bracket rate applicable to his ordinary income. It is, accordingly, more advantageous to a top-bracket individual taxpayer than to a corporate taxpayer.

One might very well expect, therefore, to find that a relatively large proportion of total depreciation allowances in the real estate industry group was computed by use of declining-balance depreciation.[11] Moreover, one should expect to find this proportion to be particularly high among those partnerships which showed no net profit. These are, indeed, the results reported on partnership information returns for the taxable year 1959. As already indicated, one-third of total depreciation allowances in the finance, insurance, and real estate division were declining-balance charges. Among partnerships without net profits in this division, declining-balance was 50.5 per cent of the total allowances, while partnerships with net profits in this industry used declining-balance to determine 24.5 per cent of total depreciation deductions. Among all industries, excluding finance, insurance, and real estate, only 14.2 per cent of total depreciation allowances were declining-balance. Excluding this division, partnerships without net profits used this method for 14.3 per cent of total allowances, while those with net profits computed 14.1 per cent of their total depreciation charges by using this method.[12]

The data do not permit certain identification of the partnerships nor of the properties with respect to which these results in the finance, insurance, and real estate division are derived. The sharp contrast between this industry division and all other divisions with respect to the relative amounts of declining-balance charges among firms without and those with net profits, however, very closely matches what one might anticipate regarding the real estate tax shelter syndicates.

[11] Use of the SYD method is less advantageous, since annual deductions under this method must reflect estimated salvage value of the property. As indicated above, SYD was more advantageous than declining-balance for long-lived property, when the property is held for a period equal to its service life. Since the syndicate disposes of the property long before its service life expires, determination of which method should be used is based on the amount of allowances each generates in the first five years or so. With a 10 per cent salvage value and a service life of thirty-three years, for example, declining-balance allowances will exceed SYD charges during the first five years by almost 8 per cent.

[12] *Statistics of Income, 1959–60, U.S. Business Tax Returns,* pp. 96–99.

The SYD method accounts for a very small proportion of partnerships' depreciation allowances. Manufacturing firms led in this respect, but even in this division, only 4.4 per cent of total allowances were computed with this method. Over all, only 2.7 per cent of all partnership depreciation allowances were SYD (Table A-6).

Amount of Assets

In this survey, we are interested not only in the number of companies using the accelerated methods and the amount of depreciation generated thereby, but also in the amount of property to which these methods have been applied. As we have seen, there is no necessary correspondence between the proportion of firms using a given depreciation method and the proportion of total allowances computed under that method. The proportion of total depreciation allowances computed under the accelerated methods, in turn, is not an infallible indicator of the extent of use of these methods. It need not, for example, accurately indicate the relative amounts of property assigned to accelerated and straight-line accounts, since differences in service lives and in the age of facilities may have a relatively large effect on the proportion of straight-line and accelerated allowances in any year.

Detailed information for corporations in 1959, providing distributions of the amount of property by method, company size, industrial division, service life, type of property, and date of acquisition, is contained in the Treasury Department's "Life of Depreciable Assets" study, to which reference was made earlier. For partnerships for the taxable year 1959, distributions of the amount of assets by method, by size of company, and by industrial division are available.

We briefly discuss the distribution of partnership assets by method in the following section, and reserve for the succeeding section a more extended examination of the detailed data with respect to corporations.

PARTNERSHIPS

For partnerships, Table 21 shows that close to two-thirds of the depreciable facilities on hand in 1959 were in straight-line accounts, 18.4 per cent were in accelerated accounts, while the remainder were being depreciated under other methods (including a small amount— 3.7 per cent—for which the depreciation method was not described).

These proportions understate the response of partnerships to the availability of the accelerated methods, since they are based on all property on hand in 1959, including assets acquired prior to 1954 and therefore ineligible for declining-balance and SYD. Unfortunately, the data on amount of partnership facilities cannot be classified by year of purchase. It nevertheless seems fair to conclude that the proportion of eligible partnership facilities in accelerated-method accounts in 1959 exceeded—possibly by a substantial margin—the 18.4 per cent shown in Table 21.

The proportion of property in straight-line accounts falls as size of business receipts increases, while the proportion of facilities under the accelerated methods tends to increase with company size, taking all industries together. The rank correlation between size of business receipts and proportion of depreciable facilities under declining-balance, however, is considerably better than in the case of SYD. Moreover, when the amount of assets is cross distributed by size and industry, the rank correlations between size and method of depreciation are highly variable, as shown in Table 22.

A significant positive association between size and proportion of assets under declining-balance appears in each of the industry divisions except the services division and transportation, communication, and sanitary services. On the other hand, the relative amount of property under SYD seems to be significantly correlated with company size only in manufacturing and in trade.

Substantial variability in the relative amounts of facilities under the straight-line and declining-balance methods may be seen from one industry to another in Table 23. In view of the fact that the largest proportion of partnership depreciation allowances under declining-balance was in finance, insurance, and real estate, it is not surprising also to find the largest proportion of facilities under this method in this industrial division. Measured in terms of the amount of depreciable facilities, this is also the largest of the partnership industries, accounting for roughly 37 per cent of the depreciable facilities reported by those partnerships which showed the amount of their facilities by method. Partnerships in this division accounted for about 60 per cent of all partnership facilities under the declining-balance method. Among the other large partnership industrial divisions, however, e.g., trade, services, and agriculture, small amounts of property were in declining-balance accounts.

TABLE 21

Distribution of Partnerships' Depreciable Assets,[a] by Size of Business Receipts and by Depreciation Method, 1959

Size of Business Receipts (thousand dollars)	Total	Straight-Line	Declining-Balance	Sum-of-Years-Digits	Other Methods	Method Not Described
Amount (million dollars)						
Under 10	3,195	2,359	341	38	398	59
10 under 20	2,380	1,696	270	48	322	43
20 under 30	1,861	1,348	236	36	210	32
30 under 50	2,615	1,821	333	17	383	61
50 under 100	3,751	2,548	516	107	476	104
100 under 200	3,509	2,228	609	49	546	77
200 under 500	3,858	2,132	787	90	633	217
500 under 1,000	2,098	1,199	404	80	335	81
1,000 under 5,000	1,899	783	573	61	307	175
5,000 and over	506	188	101	22	79	116
Receipts not reported	188	129	33	13	13	b
Total	25,861	16,431	4,202	561	3,702	965
Percentage Distribution						
Under 10	100.0	73.8	10.7	1.2	12.5	1.8
10 under 20	100.0	71.3	11.3	2.0	13.5	1.8
20 under 30	100.0	72.4	12.7	1.9	11.3	1.7
30 under 50	100.0	69.6	12.7	0.7	14.6	2.3
50 under 100	100.0	67.9	13.8	2.9	12.7	2.8
100 under 200	100.0	63.5	17.4	1.4	15.6	2.2
200 under 500	100.0	55.3	20.4	2.3	16.4	5.6
500 under 1,000	100.0	57.1	19.3	3.8	16.0	3.9
1,000 under 5,000	100.0	41.2	30.2	3.2	16.2	9.2
5,000 and over	100.0	37.2	20.0	4.4	15.6	22.9
Receipts not reported	100.0	68.2	17.4	6.8	6.9	b
Total	100.0	63.5	16.3	2.2	14.3	3.7

Source: U.S. Treasury Department, Internal Revenue Service, *Statistics of Income, 1959-60, U.S. Business Tax Returns,* pp. 92-95.

Note: Details will not add to totals because of rounding.

[a]Amounts shown are assets of partnerships reporting the cost of assets under each method.

[b]Sampling variability is too great to show separately but amount is included in the total.

TABLE 22

Rank Correlation of Size of Business Receipts and Proportion of Total Depreciable Facilities Under Straight-Line, Declining-Balance, or SYD Methods, Partnerships, 1959

Industry Division	Straight-Line		Declining-Balance		Sum-of-Years-Digits	
	Coefficient of Rank Correlation	Standard Error	Coefficient of Rank Correlation	Standard Error	Coefficient of Rank Correlation	Standard Error
Agriculture, forestry, and fisheries	-.73[a]	.30	.82[a]	.25	.36	.47
Mining	-.69[a]	.32	.90[a]	.23	.40	.58
Construction	-.82[a]	.25	.69[a]	.32	.33	.50
Manufacturing	-.87[a]	.22	.87[a]	.22	1.00[a]	.00
Transportation, communication, and sanitary services	-.38	.41	.16	.44	.20	.62
Trade	-.64[a]	.34	.64[a]	.34	.57[b]	.41
Finance, insurance, and real estate	-.56[b]	.37	.60[a]	.36	.16	.44
Services	-.51[b]	.38	.29	.42	.42	.40
All industries	-.91[a]	.21	.87[a]	.22	.60[a]	.36

Source: Table A-7.

[a]Significant at the 1 per cent level.
[b]Significant at the 5 per cent level.

TABLE 23

Distribution of Partnership Depreciable Assets[a] by Industry Division and by Depreciation Method, 1959

Industry Division	Total	Straight -Line	Declining -Balance	Sum-of- Years- Digits	Other Methods	Method Not Described
		Amount (million dollars)				
Agriculture, forestry, and fisheries	3,196	2,287	134	18	644	114
Mining	793	341	125	12	212	103
Construction	1,431	741	275	42	267	105
Manufacturing	1,794	1,121	197	59	281	135
Transportation, communication, and sanitary services	548	338	77	14	106	13
Trade	4,905	3,574	358	85	708	180
Finance, insurance, and real estate	9,517	5,577	2,527	243	972	197
Services	3,582	2,380	503	87	498	114
Not allocable	96	70	6	[b]	15	5
All industries	25,861	16,431	4,202	561	3,702	965

(continued)

TABLE 23 (concluded)

Industry Division	Total	Straight-Line	Declining-Balance	Sum-of-Years-Digits	Other Methods	Method Not Described
		Percentage Distribution				
Agriculture, forestry, and fisheries	100.0	71.6	4.2	0.6	20.1	3.6
Mining	100.0	43.1	15.7	1.6	26.7	12.9
Construction	100.0	51.8	19.2	2.9	18.7	7.3
Manufacturing	100.0	62.5	11.0	3.3	15.7	7.5
Transportation, communication, and sanitary services	100.0	61.8	14.1	2.5	19.3	2.4
Trade	100.0	72.9	7.3	1.7	14.4	3.7
Finance, insurance, and real estate	100.0	58.6	26.6	2.6	10.2	2.1
Services	100.0	66.5	14.0	2.4	13.9	3.2
Not allocable	100.0	72.9	6.3	b	15.6	5.2
All industries	100.0	63.5	16.3	2.2	14.3	3.7

Source: U.S. Treasury Department, Internal Revenue Service, *Statistics of Income, 1959-60, U.S. Business Tax Returns*, pp. 92-95.

Note: Details will not add to totals because of rounding.

aAmounts shown are assets of partnerships reporting the cost of assets under each method.

bSampling variability is too great to show separately but amount is included in the total.

On the whole, there appears to be a relatively close correspondence between the proportion of total depreciable assets under each method and the proportion of total depreciation allowances computed by each method.[13] The differences, while not large, nevertheless are indicative of the effectiveness of the accelerated depreciation methods in generating additional depreciation allowances. The comparison in Table 24, for example, shows that whereas the straight-line method accounted for 63.5 per cent of partnerships' depreciable facilities, it accounted for only

TABLE 24

Comparison of Proportion of Partnerships' Facilities and Depreciation Allowances, by Depreciation Method, 1959

Depreciation Method	Proportion of Total	
	Depreciable Facilities	Depreciation Allowances
Straight-line	63.5	59.0
Declining-balance	16.3	18.2
Sum-of-the-years-digits	2.2	2.7
Other methods	14.3	13.3
Method not described	3.7	5.3

Source: Tables 19 and 21.

59 per cent of their depreciation allowances; on the other hand, accelerated method accounts included 18.4 per cent of partnerships' facilities, but 20.9 per cent of allowances were computed under these methods. The same kind of comparison suggests that the other methods used by partnerships were not accelerated; they accounted for 14.3 per cent of the facilities but only 13.3 per cent of the allowances. On the other hand, although 3.7 per cent of the facilities were in accounts for which the method was not described, these methods accounted for 5.3 per cent of total allowances, from which it might be inferred that these were, on the whole, accelerated depreciation techniques. *see next page !*

[13] The number of partnerships showing the amount of facilities by method— 750,484—is slightly smaller than the number showing the amount of depreciation allowances by method—765,428. This difference, roughly 2 per cent, does not account for differences between the proportion of assets under a given method and the proportion of total allowances computed by that method which may appear in any size class or industry division.

These inferences are, of course, subject to an important qualification, since the proportion of total allowances under any method depends not merely on the depreciation pattern through time and the relative amounts of assets but also on the service lives of the facilities and their average age. In comparing Tables 19 and 21, for example, it is seen that in the $5,000,000 and over business receipts class, straight-line method accounts included 37.2 per cent of total depreciable facilities in the class, but accounted for only 18.4 per cent of total allowances; other methods included 15.6 per cent of the facilities on which 27.9 per cent of allowances were generated. These disproportions might be attributable to differences in the average service life of the facilities in the respective accounts, or to the degree of acceleration provided by these unspecified other methods, or indeed, to both of these factors. It is clear, however, that the disproportion itself is not definitely indicative of the degree of acceleration.

CORPORATIONS

A substantial proportion of corporations' eligible facilities were in accelerated method accounts in the taxable year 1959. Of the total depreciable property in corporation tax accounts in that year, about 24 per cent was being depreciated under the declining-balance and SYD methods. A much larger proportion, about 45 per cent, of the total property acquired since the end of 1953 and on hand in 1959, however, was in accelerated method accounts. Moreover, since only new property newly acquired after 1953 is eligible for the use of the fast write-off methods, and since some of the property acquired after 1953 and on hand in 1959 must have been ineligible on this score, the proportion of eligible facilities in declining-balance and SYD accounts in 1959 must have been somewhat greater than 45 per cent (Table 25).[14]

The share of depreciable facilities acquired after 1953 that was held in accelerated method accounts in 1959 increased with company size, when all industries are taken together. This proportion was 28.5 per cent for companies with total assets less than $1 million, 38.1 per cent for corporations with total assets of $1 million up to $25 million, and

---

[14] Most of the estimates in this section were made by applying ratios derived from the LDA to adjusted *Statistics of Income* magnitudes (for the details of these computations, see Appendix D). Where noted, however, reference is made to the LDA data.

TABLE 25

Cost of Corporations' Depreciable Assets, by Method of Depreciation and Size of Total Assets in 1959:

All Assets and Those Acquired After 1953

A. All Assets on Hand in 1959

Size of Total Assets (million dollars)	Straight -Line	Declining -Balance	Sum-of-the- Years-Digits	Other-Life Methods	Units-of- Production	All Methods
			Amount (thousand dollars)			
Under 1	48,045,429	10,902,570	2,611,904	44,202	15,909	61,620,014
1 - 25	43,542,633	11,541,548	3,558,028	104,441	1,601	58,748,251
25 and over	173,823,667	30,351,054	27,190,779	6,306,175	4,756,807	242,428,482
Total	265,411,729	52,795,172	33,360,711	6,454,818	4,774,317	362,796,747
			Percentage Distribution			
Under 1	78.0	17.7	4.2	0.1	a	100.0
1 - 25	74.1	19.6	6.1	0.2	-	100.0
25 and over	71.7	12.5	11.2	2.6	2.0	100.0
Total	73.2	14.6	9.2	1.8	1.3	100.0

(Continued)

TABLE 25 (concluded)

B. Facilities Acquired after 1953

Size of Total Assets (million dollars)	Straight -Line	Declining -Balance	Sum-of-the- Years-Digits	Other-Life Methods	Units-of- Production	All Methods
			Amount (thousand dollars)			
Under 1	32,015,479	10,217,775	2,581,893	43,315	14,835	44,873,297
1-25	22,767,094	10,561,969	3,500,474	67,552	1,576	36,898,665
25 and over	43,887,284	29,322,823	27,048,889	1,681,660	1,420,572	103,361,228
Total	98,669,857	50,102,567	33,131,256	1,792,527	1,436,983	185,133,190
			Percentage Distribution			
Under 1	71.4	22.8	5.8	0.1	a	100.0
1-25	61.7	28.6	9.5	0.2	a	100.0
25 and over	42.5	28.4	26.2	1.6	1.4	100.0
Total	53.3	27.1	17.9	1.0	0.8	100.0

Source: U.S. Treasury Department, Internal Revenue Service, "Life of Depreciable Assets" source book. Dollar amounts were computed by applying ratios derived from the LDA in each size class in each industrial division to corresponding Statistics of Income observations, and then aggregating to totals shown here. See Appendix D.

Note: Included under the declining-balance method in Part A are $2.7 billion of assets acquired before 1954; under sum-of-the-years-digits, there are $0.2 billion of facilities acquired before 1954. Some portion of the pre-1954 declining-balance facilities are those to which the declining-balance method at 150 per cent of the straight-line rate was applied; this method was available under the tax laws prior to the Internal Revenue Code of 1954. The remainder, like the pre-1954 assets under SYD, probably represents an erroneous application by taxpayers of these accelerated methods to ineligible properties.

aLess than 0.05 per cent. Detail may not add to totals because of rounding.

54.5 per cent for companies with assets of $25 million or more. In contrast, very little difference among the three size classes is to be noted in the share of all facilities on hand in 1959 under accelerated depreciation methods. While corporations with total assets of $25 million or more applied accelerated methods to a larger proportion of eligible

TABLE 26

Percentage Distribution of Corporations' Depreciable Facilities, by Size of Total Assets: All Facilities, Facilities Acquired Since 1953, and Facilities in Accelerated Method Accounts, 1959

Size of Total Assets (million dollars)	All Facilities	Facilities Acquired Since 1953	Facilities in Accelerated Method Accounts[a]	Facilities Acquired Since 1953 as Per Cent of All Facilities
Under 1	17.0	24.2	15.4	72.8
1 - 25	16.2	19.9	16.9	62.8
25 and over	66.8	55.8	67.7	42.6
Total	100.0	100.0	100.0	51.0

Source: Table 25.

[a]Includes only facilities acquired after 1953 and in accelerated method accounts in 1959.

property than did smaller companies, a substantially larger share of the large companies' facilities in 1959 had been acquired prior to 1954 and were, therefore, ineligible for the use of the accelerated methods. As Table 26 shows, although corporations with total assets of $25 million or more accounted for 55.8 per cent of all facilities acquired after 1953 (and on hand in 1959), the post-1953 acquisitions of these companies were only 42.6 per cent of their total depreciable facilities. In contrast, companies with total assets less than $1 million had only 24.2 per cent of all post-1953 facilities, but these assets represented 72.8 per cent of their total depreciable facilities on hand in 1959. Thus, while two-thirds of the facilities in accelerated method accounts in 1959 belonged to companies with total assets of $25 million or more, there was little difference among the three size classes in the proportion of all facilities on hand in 1959 under accelerated methods.

Most of the difference among the three size classes in the proportion of post-1953 facilities in accelerated method accounts in 1959 is attributable to differences in the proportions under the SYD method. In the largest size class, nearly equal amounts of facilities were in declining-balance and SYD accounts; smaller companies, on the other hand, had much less of their post-1953 acquisitions under the SYD than under the declining-balance method (Table 25).

Substantial differences from one industrial division to another are found in the share of post-1953 facilities in accelerated method accounts. In manufacturing, which accounted for 38.4 per cent of all facilities acquired after 1953, declining-balance and SYD taken together include 56.8 per cent of the post-1953 facilities in the industry. In the public utilities, which in 1959 held 29.0 per cent of all post-1953 facilities, the corresponding proportion is 42.1 per cent. On the other hand, corporations in agriculture held only 18.7 per cent of their facilities acquired after 1953 in accelerated method accounts. The spread among industrial divisions was less in the case of declining-balance than SYD; the former accounted for 16.8 per cent of post-1953 facilities in the agriculture and trade divisions and for 32.1 per cent in construction, while SYD facilities were only 1.9 per cent of post-1953 facilities in agriculture and 28.7 per cent of those in manufacturing (Table 27).

Taking the accelerated methods together, little variability is apparent when the facilities are distributed by type of asset and method, according to the LDA survey. Six broad property classes were set up; structures, furniture and fixtures, transportation, production equipment, livestock, and not identifiable. Except for livestock, which accounts for an insignificant fraction of the total, the accelerated methods combined account for between 49 per cent and 53 per cent of the total (Table 28).

A distribution of the data by service life and method in the LDA survey reveals no systematic pattern of variation. It was noted above that with a given salvage value and discount rate, use of the declining-balance method becomes less advantageous compared with SYD as service life increases. The proportionate amounts of property at each service life in declining-balance and SYD accounts, however, do not appear to conform with expectations based on such rate-of-return com-

TABLE 27

Cost of Corporations' Depreciable Assets Acquired After 1953, by Industry Division and Method of Depreciation, 1959

Industry Division	Straight-Line	Declining-Balance	Sum-of-the-Years-Digits	Other-Life Methods	Units-of-Production	All Methods
	Amount (thousand dollars)					
Agriculture, forestry, and fisheries	1,097,439	226,448	25,804	1,204	-	1,350,895
Mining	3,812,337	1,561,469	245,994	269,724	565,427	6,454,951
Construction	2,657,083	1,376,373	253,086	532	-	4,287,074
Manufacturing	29,498,917	19,966,965	20,437,323	501,827	774,975	71,180,007
Transportation, communication, electric, gas, and sanitary services	30,024,137	14,799,672	7,767,184	947,489	79,339	53,617,821
Trade	11,913,772	2,791,590	1,892,329	51,327	15,198	16,664,216
Finance, insurance, and real estate	13,176,009	6,517,732	1,559,197	17,906	1,980	21,272,824
Services	6,431,412	2,858,180	949,644	2,316	64	10,241,616
Total	98,669,857	50,102,567	33,131,256	1,792,527	1,436,983	185,133,190

(continued)

TABLE 27 (concluded)

Industry Division	Straight-Line	Declining-Balance	Sum-of-the-Years-Digits	Other-Life Methods	Units-of-Production	All Methods
	Percentage Distribution					
Agriculture, forestry, and fisheries	81.2	16.8	1.9	0.1	-	100.0
Mining	59.1	24.2	3.8	4.2	8.8	100.0
Construction	62.0	32.1	5.9	a	-	100.0
Manufacturing	41.4	28.1	28.7	0.7	1.1	100.0
Transportation, communication, electric, gas, and sanitary services	56.0	27.6	14.5	1.8	0.2	100.0
Trade	71.5	16.8	11.4	0.3	0.1	100.0
Finance, insurance, and real estate	61.9	30.6	7.3	0.1	a	100.0
Services	62.8	27.9	9.3	a	a	100.0
Total	53.3	27.1	17.9	1.0	0.8	100.0

Source: U.S. Treasury Department, Internal Revenue Service, "Life of Depreciable Assets" source book. Also see source note Table 25.

Note: Detail may not add to totals because of rounding. Totals include small amounts of property not allocable to any industry division.

aLess than 0.05 per cent.

TABLE 28

Per Cent of Cost of Corporations' Depreciable Assets,

Acquired After 1953, in Accelerated Method Accounts,

by Major Asset Type, 1959 (LDA Survey)

Type of Asset	Facilities in Accelerated Method Accounts as Per Cent of Total
Structures and leasehold improvements	53.4
Furniture, fixtures, office and store machinery and equipment	48.5
Transportation vehicles and equipment	50.7
Production machinery and equipment	53.4
Livestock, orchards, and vineyards	9.4
Not identifiable or intangible	53.4
All asset types	52.9

Source: U.S. Treasury Department, Internal Revenue Service, "Life of Depreciable Assets" source book.

Note: Ratios presented here were computed directly from LDA survey data and were not adjusted to a *Statistics of Income* basis. As noted in Appendix B, the LDA survey shows different proportions of property in accelerated method accounts than is derived by applying to *Statistics of Income* magnitudes the ratios of accelerated to total property in each size class in each industrial division based on LDA data.

parisons. As Table 29 shows, the proportions of depreciable assets under the declining-balance and the SYD methods change irregularly from one service life to another. Similar irregularities are seen if the proportions under these methods are combined.

At various points in this discussion there have been suggestions that proportionate use of the accelerated methods increased with company size. Unfortunately, our data are grouped into only three very broad size classes, which precludes rigorous statistical testing of that suggestion. Although we have seen in these data an apparent positive relationship between use of accelerated methods and size, the data may in fact reflect a relationship between method of depreciation and some other characteristic, the incidence of which varies from one size class to

TABLE 29

Per Cent of Cost of Corporations' Depreciable Assets,
Acquired After 1953, in Accelerated Method Accounts,
by Service Life, 1959 (LDA Survey)[a]

Service Life (years)	Declining -Balance	Sum-of-the- Years-Digits	Total Accelerated Methods
3-9	27.8	21.8	49.6
10	25.5	15.4	40.9
11-14	40.0	31.1	71.1
15	51.5	18.3	69.8
16-19	21.2	10.8	32.0
20	25.8	32.0	57.8
21-24	37.7	14.5	52.2
25	27.8	29.0	56.8
26-30	45.7	22.9	68.6
31-35	27.4	18.4	45.8
36-40	41.8	31.7	73.5
41-50	23.9	20.6	44.5
51 and over	46.6	23.6	70.2
Total	31.8	21.8	53.6

Source: U.S. Treasury Department, Internal Revenue Service, "Life of Depreciable Assets" source book.

Note: Ratios presented here were computed directly from LDA survey data and were not adjusted to a *Statistics of Income* basis. As noted in Appendix B, the LDA survey shows different proportions of property in accelerated method accounts than is derived by applying to *Statistics of Income* magnitude the ratios of accelerated to total property in each size class in each industrial division based on LDA data.

[a]Excludes property in units-of-production method accounts, since no service life in years is assigned to such facilities.

another. More detailed distributions of the data permit examination of some of the other possible variables with which choice of method might be associated, e.g., industry, type of asset, service life. To carry out this examination, the data were cross distributed by (1) method, size, and industry; (2) method, size, and property type; (3) method, size, and service life; (4) method, industry, and asset type; (5) method, industry, and service life; and (6) method, service life, and asset type.

1. *Method, size, and industry.* Although a positive association between company size and proportion of post-1953 facilities under the accelerated methods is seen when all industries are taken together, considerable variability in this connection is found among industries. As shown in Table 30, the proportion of property of manufacturing companies under each of the accelerated methods, more noticeably in SYD, increases with company size. Taking the accelerated methods together, a similar pattern is found in the trade and services divisions. In the transportation, communications, electric, gas, and sanitary services division, the middle-sized companies applied the accelerated methods to a smaller proportion of their post-1953 properties than did the smallest companies, but the largest firms in this industry used the accelerated methods for a much larger proportion of post-1953 facilities than is shown for either of the other size classes. In mining, the largest companies held relatively large amounts of property in "other" life methods and in units-of-production accounts; declining-balance and SYD properties were a smaller share of the total in this size group than in the others. In the other divisions, no association between size and proportion of property in accelerated depreciation accounts is observable.

2. *Method, size, and asset type.* Close to 85 per cent of the total amount of property acquired after 1953 and on hand in 1959 consisted of structures and leasehold improvements and production machinery and equipment, according to the LDA survey. In both of these asset groups, and in all of the others except for the very small amount of livestock, orchards, and vineyards, the larger the total asset size class, the greater the proportion of the property under combined accelerated accounts. There appears, on the whole, to be little difference among asset size classes in the proportion of facilities under declining-balance. Except in the case of livestock, etc., however, the proportion of facilities of each type under the SYD method is much larger in the case of the largest asset size class than among the other size classes (Table 31).

TABLE 30

Per Cent of Cost of Corporations' Depreciable Assets, Acquired After 1953, in Accelerated Method Accounts, by Industry Division and Size of Total Assets, 1959

Size of Total Assets by Industry Division (million dollars)	*Ave suc Life* (From table C-3)	Declining -Balance	Sum-of-the- Years-Digits	Total Accelerated Methods
All industries	*14.7*	27.1	17.9	45.0
Under 1	*9.3*	22.8	5.8	28.5
1-25	*12.2*	28.6	9.5	38.1
25 and over	*16.9*	28.4	26.2	54.5
Agriculture, forestry, and fisheries	*7.4*	16.8	1.9	18.7
Under 1	*7.2*	16.8	1.9	18.7
1-25	*7.0*	23.9	2.6	26.5
25 and over	*8.3*	-	-	-
Mining	*10.9*	24.2	3.8	28.0
Under 1	*5.4*	27.1	5.7	32.8
1-25	*c.4*	37.1	5.6	42.8
25 and over	*13.3*	13.0	1.6	14.7
Construction	*5.3*	32.1	5.9	38.0
Under 1	*5.1*	21.7	7.0	28.7
1-25	*4.2*	48.5	4.9	53.4
25 and over	*7.3*	47.4	0.7	48.1
Manufacturing	*13.5*	28.1	28.7	56.8
Under 1	*7.4*	22.3	6.9	29.2
1-25	*9.8*	28.2	13.9	42.1
25 and over	*14.3*	29.2	37.3	66.5
Transportation, communication, electric, gas, and sanitary services	*17.6*	27.6	14.5	42.1
Under 1	*6.0*	20.8	6.2	27.0
1-25	*9.4*	12.1	4.6	16.7
25 and over	*20.8*	30.0	16.3	46.4

(continued)

TABLE 30 *(concluded)*

Size of Total Assets by Industry Division (million dollars)	Declining -Balance	Sum-of-the- Years-Digits	Total Accelerated Methods
Trade 8,9	16.8	11.4	28.1
Under 1 2,0	15.7	3.3	19.0
1-25 7,6	21.5	7.9	29.4
25 and over 12,2	14.8	35.4	50.2
Finance, insurance, and real estate 17,5	30.6	7.3	38.0
Under 1 17,9	27.7	6.1	33.8
1-25 20,0	38.4	7.5	46.0
25 and over 14,7	18.9	12.0	31.0
Services 7,8	27.9	9.3	37.2
Under 1 7,5	27.6	7.1	34.7
1-25 7,7	27.2	11.5	38.7
25 and over 8,4	31.2	15.2	46.4

Source: Table D-4. Also see source note, Table 25.

Note: Detail may not add to total because of rounding. Not shown separately but included under "all industries" are small amounts of property not allocable to any industry division.

3. *Method, size, and service life.* Table 32 shows the proportion of facilities of a given service life in each of the size classes under the accelerated methods in the LDA survey. So arranged, a definite positive association between the proportion of property in accelerated method accounts and company size appears. Only in the sixteen-to-nineteen-year service life interval do the proportions decrease as asset size increases; in the eleven-to-fourteen-year interval, the middle-size class proportion is smaller than in the case of companies with less than $1 million in total assets, and in the forty-one-to-fifty-year interval, the proportion in the middle-size class exceeds those in the other two size groupings. In all other intervals, however, the larger the size class, the greater the proportion of property under the accelerated methods.

TABLE 31

Percentage Distribution of the Cost of Corporations' Depreciable Facilities Acquired After 1953, by Major Asset Type, Size of Total Assets, and Method of Depreciation, 1959 (LDA Survey)

Size of Total Assets, by Asset Type (million dollars)	Straight-Line	Declining-Balance	Sum-of-the-Years-Digits	Other-Life Methods	Units-of-Production	All Methods
All asset types	44.4	31.4	21.5	1.5	1.2	100.0
Under 1	67.2	27.1	5.6	0.1	a	100.0
1 - 25	55.2	36.4	8.2	0.2	a	100.0
25 and over	40.2	31.8	24.8	1.8	1.5	100.0
Structures and leasehold improvements	44.4	33.4	20.0	1.6	0.6	100.0
Under 1	65.4	29.3	5.2	0.1	a	100.0
1 - 25	51.6	40.2	8.1	0.1	-	100.0
25 and over	39.7	33.6	23.9	2.0	0.8	100.0
Furniture, fixtures, office and store machinery and equipment	51.4	19.5	29.0	0.1	0.1	100.0
Under 1	75.4	20.3	4.3	a	a	100.0
1 - 25	64.7	27.2	8.1	a	-	100.0
25 and over	43.8	18.7	37.3	0.1	0.1	100.0
Transportation vehicles and equipment	47.0	35.7	15.0	2.1	0.2	100.0
Under 1	70.9	23.1	5.7	0.3	-	100.0
1 - 25	69.1	24.9	6.0	0.1	-	100.0
25 and over	38.1	40.3	18.5	2.8	0.3	100.0

TABLE 31 (concluded)

Size of Total Assets by Asset Type (million dollars)	Straight-Line	Declining-Balance	Sum-of-the-Years-Digits	Other-Life Methods	Units-of-Production	All Methods
Production machinery and equipment	42.8	29.3	24.1	1.5	2.3	100.0
Under 1	65.8	27.3	6.8	0.1	0.1	100.0
1 - 25	54.7	35.0	9.9	0.4	a	100.0
25 and over	40.5	29.3	26.0	1.7	2.6	100.0
Livestock, orchards, and vineyards	90.6	9.0	0.4	a	-	100.0
Under 1	91.5	8.5	a	-	-	100.0
1 - 25	64.3	34.8	0.9	-	-	100.0
25 and over	99.0	0.2	0.8	a	-	100.0
Not identifiable or intangible	46.4	42.8	10.6	a	0.2	100.0
Under 1	77.4	16.2	6.3	a	-	100.0
1 - 25	66.3	24.3	9.4	-	-	100.0
25 and over	42.3	46.4	11.1	a	0.3	100.0

Source: Table A-10.

Note: Detail may not add to totals because of rounding.

aLess than 0.05 per cent.

TABLE 32

Per Cent of Cost of Corporations' Depreciable Assets,

Acquired After 1953, in Accelerated Method Accounts,

by Service Life and Size of Total Assets, 1959

(LDA Survey)

Service Life (years)	Total Assets (million dollars)		
	Under 1	1 Under 25	25 and Over
3-9	31.8	46.2	59.0
10	26.2	36.5	49.1
11-14	35.4	32.4	73.4
15	30.4	42.6	73.6
16-19	49.7	34.9	31.6
20	28.2	39.3	64.0
21-24	30.5	44.8	52.9
25	32.7	44.0	63.7
26-30	45.0	51.9	70.8
31-35	27.6	41.6	48.4
36-40	56.3	59.2	78.4
41-50	34.2	49.4	44.9
51 and over	27.8	48.8	72.4
Total	32.7	44.6	57.4

Source: Table A-11.

4. *Method, industry, and asset type.* As we have seen, there is considerable variability among major industry divisions in the proportion
of assets acquired after 1953 and held in accelerated depreciation accounts in 1959; and relatively little variability in this proportion among
major asset types in the LDA survey. When the data are cross distributed by industry division and asset type, a much wider range from one
asset type to another is found within any industry in the proportion of
post-1953 property in accelerated method accounts. This is clearly seen

in Table 33. For example, taking all industries together, the proportion of post-1953 property under accelerated methods ranged only from a low of 48.5 per cent, in the case of furniture and fixtures, to a high of 53.4 per cent in the case of structures and leasehold improvements and production machinery and equipment. A much greater range among asset types is found in each industry division. In agriculture, the range was from a low of 10 per cent for livestock, orchards, and vineyards (not shown in Table 33) to a high of 24 per cent for transportation vehicles and equipment, while in the public utilities division the range was from a low of about 21 per cent, in the case of furniture and fixtures, to a high of 57 per cent in the case of structures and leasehold improvements. It is interesting to find in Table A-12 that in each major industry division except services and agriculture, the proportion of property in accelerated method accounts is greatest in the case of those asset types accounting for the largest proportion of the industry's total post-1953 facilities.

If industry were an important characteristic determining the extent to which accelerated depreciation methods were used, one would expect little dispersion from one asset type to another around the mean proportion of post-1953 facilities held in accelerated method accounts. Moreover, one would also expect industry rankings to vary little if at all from one asset type to another. Inspection of Table 33, however, reveals considerable variation in industry rankings, suggesting (with the substantial dispersions around the means already noted) that industry characteristics per se were not a major factor in determining the relative amounts of property held under the various methods.

By the same token, if type of asset figured prominently in the decision about which method of depreciation to use, one would expect to find the proportions of a given type of property under the accelerated methods in each of the industry divisions closely clustered around the average, taking all industries together. As noted, distributing the data by industry as well as by asset type materially expands the range of the proportion of each type of asset in accelerated method accounts. Too, one would expect to find relatively stable rankings of asset types among industrial divisions. Again by inspection of Table 33, considerable variation in the rankings is seen.

5. *Method, industry, and service life.* The per cent of the cost of post-1953 facilities under accelerated methods at each service life in each

TABLE 33

Per Cent of Cost of Corporations' Depreciable Assets, Acquired After 1953, in Accelerated Method Accounts, by Industry Division and Major Asset Type, 1959 (LDA Survey)

Industry Division	Structures and Leasehold Improvements	Furniture, Fixtures, Office and Store Machinery and Equipment	Transportation Vehicles and Equipment	Production Machinery and Equipment	All Asset Types
Agriculture, forestry, and fisheries [a]	15.3	17.9	23.9	19.4	17.1
Mining	15.2	14.7	28.1	19.7	19.2
Construction	36.4	22.4	29.4	43.5	37.5
Manufacturing	63.4	66.0	54.3	68.3	65.9
Transportation, communication, electric, gas, and sanitary services	57.2	20.5	56.4	28.7	48.2
Trade	31.4	43.6	29.5	39.3	36.8
Finance, insurance, and real estate	40.5	30.2	25.4	38.9	39.3
Services	38.5	30.5	43.0	49.4	41.2
All industries	53.4	48.5	50.7	53.4	52.9

Source: Table A-12.

[a] Not shown but important in this industrial division is the asset type "livestock, orchards, and vineyards." About 10.1 per cent of this type of property acquired after 1953, held by corporations in agriculture, was in accelerated method accounts in 1959. See note to Table A-12.

major industrial division (LDA survey data) is shown in Table 34. Within each industrial division, a high degree of variability from one service life to another is found in the proportion of property in accelerated method accounts. In each service life, too, the proportion of post-1953 facilities under accelerated methods varied considerably from one industrial division to another. Industry rankings based on proportion of property in accelerated method accounts, moreover, varied substantially from one service life to another, except in the case of manufacturing. In addition, in no industry division is there any apparent tendency for the proportion of property in accelerated method accounts to vary with service life. The data so distributed suggest little influence of service life on method choice, and appear to confirm the earlier observation that industry characteristics were not particularly consequential in this respect either.

6. *Method, asset type, and service life.* Table 35 presents the per cent of post-1953 depreciable assets at each service life for each major asset type, according to the LDA survey. This distribution appears to strengthen the impressions reported above that neither service life nor asset type were significant factors in determining the extent of use of the accelerated depreciation methods. The table reveals substantial variability within any asset type in the proportion of property in accelerated method accounts from one service life to another. For any given service life, similarly, there is a broad range among asset types in this proportion. In addition, the asset type rankings on the basis of this proportion are quite variable among service lives, except for production machinery and equipment which displays only limited change in rank. The service life rankings with respect to this proportion also vary substantially from one asset type to another.

In summary, on the basis of the "Life of Depreciable Assets" survey, it appears that the bulk of depreciable facilities acquired by corporations after 1953 were structures and leasehold improvements and production machinery and equipment. These facilities were heavily concentrated in companies with total assets in excess of $25 million in manufacturing and public utilities. Substantial amounts of these properties—well over half—were in accelerated depreciation accounts. The use of the accelerated methods appears to be more closely associated with company size than with industry or property type characteristics. Service life of facilities seems to have had little influence on choice of method.

TABLE 34

Per Cent of Cost of Corporations' Depreciable Assets, Acquired After 1953, in Accelerated Method Accounts, by Service Life and Industry Division, 1959 (LDA Survey)

Service Life (years)	All Industries	Agriculture, Forestry, and Fisheries	Mining	Construction	Manufacturing	Transportation, Communication, Electric, Gas, and Sanitary Services	Trade	Finance, insurance, and Real Estate	Services
3	40.7	20.9	44.9	32.6	37.8	60.8	23.0	46.7	28.6
4	33.3	33.0	29.0	37.6	37.4	26.7	32.4	29.7	33.9
5	51.3	21.2	29.1	33.7	68.7	41.7	33.1	33.2	42.1
6	55.7	10.9	19.5	54.8	67.5	60.5	32.5	38.2	65.6
7	56.0	25.1	16.0	57.3	75.5	50.0	30.0	31.8	33.3
8	58.7	19.5	33.6	46.7	68.8	67.1	28.0	35.9	40.1
9	40.5	2.9	56.5	14.5	51.4	10.9	35.4	21.3	63.8
10	40.9	12.3	23.0	40.5	47.0	51.1	23.6	31.4	44.7
11–14	71.1	14.7	29.4	61.1	68.2	91.5	72.2	37.6	45.9
15	69.8	40.7	14.8	36.8	77.1	82.2	18.0	32.6	37.9
16–19	32.0	19.6	47.8	65.5	61.1	9.6	61.9	49.6	35.5
20	57.8	16.1	4.2	14.1	72.0	53.5	37.9	34.7	37.1
21–24	52.2	5.7	13.1	28.9	59.4	47.9	21.8	25.5	59.0
25	56.8	7.9	17.0	16.1	76.1	47.8	25.2	35.9	36.9
26–29	64.9	13.7	90.0	96.9	63.6	67.6	41.8	26.8	49.3
30	73.6	0.5	1.3	2.8	68.8	86.1	59.0	53.1	30.5
31–35	45.8	14.8	30.2	29.1	61.8	46.8	28.8	30.8	45.9
36–39	78.6	-	66.8	49.6	88.0	75.8	78.1	62.2	59.9
40	70.9	22.3	93.4	52.5	86.7	66.1	67.1	58.3	34.4
41–49	32.8	-	50.2	-	71.5	25.7	82.5	16.6	4.8
50	53.9	0.3	45.5	33.4	65.9	58.1	16.0	45.9	74.4
51 and over	70.2	-	60.0	-	64.9	75.5	-	38.9	-
Total	53.6	17.1	23.3	37.5	67.1	48.3	36.9	39.3	41.2

Source: U.S. Treasury Department, Internal Revenue Service, "Life of Depreciable Assets" source book.

TABLE 35

Per Cent of Cost of Corporations' Depreciable Assets,

Acquired After 1953, in Accelerated Method Accounts,

by Service Life and Major Asset Type, 1959

(LDA Survey)

Service Life (years)	Structures and Leasehold Improvements	Furniture, Fixtures, Office and Store Machinery Equipment	Transportation Vehicles and Equipment	Production Machinery and Equipment	All Asset Types
3	73.9	28.6	22.3	40.4	40.7
4	28.2	45.0	33.3	33.9	33.3
5	31.6	68.3	41.5	48.8	51.3
6	58.7	41.7	60.0	56.9	55.7
7	45.0	33.1	48.0	68.8	56.0
8	43.9	49.9	65.9	61.9	58.7
9	32.7	18.9	8.1	62.6	40.5
10	39.3	30.9	66.9	42.5	40.9
11 - 14	68.9	67.7	83.0	72.2	71.1
15	46.8	32.8	77.7	79.8	69.8
16 - 19	42.0	70.4	39.1	29.4	32.0
20	44.0	60.5	38.3	75.1	57.8
21 - 24	46.6	1.7	61.9	64.2	52.2
25	53.0	70.3	56.0	61.7	56.8
26 - 29	67.6	71.1	63.7	57.7	64.9
30	72.8	55.0	69.0	80.2	73.6
31 - 35	44.3	30.9	66.2	53.9	45.8
36 - 39	79.1	86.8	49.2	72.4	78.6
40	71.4	50.0	83.1	83.2	70.9
41 - 49	32.2	39.4	46.8	38.1	32.8
50	52.3	4.4	86.5	74.4	53.9
51 and over	73.6	1.4	95.7	38.4	70.2
Total	53.8	48.5	50.8	54.7	53.6

Source: U.S. Treasury Department, Internal Revenue Service, "Life of Depreciable Assets" source book.

Developments in depreciation practice since 1959 might require some amendment of these findings. We observed above, when discussing the number of companies using the accelerated methods, that there was an obvious trend toward greater use of the declining-balance method, and certain features of the 1962 Revenue Procedure 62-21 may have induced more extensive use of SYD. Increasing frequencies of companies using the accelerated methods presumably should be associated with increasing amounts of property in accelerated method accounts. The proportion of property in such accounts, therefore, may very well have continued to grow after the taxable year 1959. Moreover, the differences in this proportion among companies of different size may well have diminished.

Effect of Acceleration on Corporations' Depreciation Allowances, Tax Liabilities, and Capital Outlays, 1959

One of our principal concerns in this survey is to determine the effect of the use of accelerated depreciation methods on total depreciation allowances and the distribution of this effect with respect to company size, industry, and asset type. Of course, the data with respect to any one year's depreciation allowances do not afford a definitive basis for such an analysis, since the distribution of allowances in any given year will be materially affected by differences in service lives and in the age distribution of depreciable property, which changes from year to year. The measure of the financial gain to a taxpayer from using acceleration is the increase in the present value of the stream of allowances generated by the accelerated method over that under the straight-line method, with respect to some relevant time period and asset stock. If service life distributions were substantially the same among all taxpayers and if all taxpayers held to substantially the same pattern of asset acquisitions and retirement, any one year's depreciation charges under each method would afford a useful index of the relative efficiency of each method. Since both of these assumptions are manifestly unrealistic, only limited reliance should be placed on inferences which can be drawn from data pertaining to a single year. With this reservation in mind, we provide in the following pages some rough estimates of the effects of the use of accelerated methods on depreciation allowances in 1959.[15]

---

[15] For a description of our estimating procedures, see Appendix D.

In the taxable year 1959, a substantial proportion of corporations' depreciation allowances were computed under the accelerated depreciation methods. About 52 per cent of the estimated $14.1 billion of allowances on facilities acquired after 1953 were computed by use of the accelerated methods. Of the $20.5 billion of total allowances in 1959, 36.6 per cent were declining-balance and SYD (Table 36).

Comparison of the proportionate amounts of property under each method with the corresponding proportionate amounts of depreciation allowances, as shown in Table 37, affords a very rough indication of the relative effectiveness of the various methods in generating depreciation allowances.[16] Taking all companies together, the ratio of straight-line depreciation allowances to the total is noticeably smaller than the proportion of the total straight-line property to the total amount of property. The ratio of declining-balance allowances to the total is substantially greater—5.9 percentage points—than the corresponding proportion of property in such accounts to the total, although the difference in these ratios is only 1.3 percentage points in the case of SYD. For companies with total assets of $25 million or more, however, the spread between the proportion of properties and the proportion of allowances under SYD is about the same as that under declining-balance.

Among companies with total assets of $25 million or more, accounting for 47.9 per cent of total allowances on post-1953 property, the accelerated methods were used to compute 65.1 per cent of their total depreciation charges, compared with 46.9 per cent for the middle-size firms, and 35.4 per cent for the smallest companies (Table 38).

Among the major industrial divisions, manufacturing companies accounted for 43.0 per cent of total allowances on property acquired after 1953, and 63.1 per cent of these depreciation charges were computed under the accelerated methods. Public utilities' depreciation was one-fifth of the total and 50.2 per cent of this amount was accelerated depreciation. Excluding the small amounts of depreciation of corporations in agriculture and of those not allocable to an industrial division, accelerated depreciation amounted to from 38 to 46 per cent of the total in each of the other industrial divisions, except in trade (Table 39).

Total corporate depreciation allowances, as shown in *Statistics of*

[16] Only a .very rough indication, as has been repeatedly suggested in this discussion. Disparities in the respective proportions result not merely from differences in method but also from differences in the average service lives and ages of the properties in the accounts under the various methods.

TABLE 36

Corporations' Depreciation Allowances, by Method of Depreciation, 1959

Depreciation Allowances with Respect to	Straight -Line	Declining -Balance	Sum-of-the-Years-Digits	Other-Life Methods	Units-of-Production	All Methods
Amount (thousand dollars)						
All property on hand in 1959	12,469,218	4,776,176	2,721,996	264,404	261,832	20,493,626
Property acquired after 1953	6,531,027	4,658,657	2,711,801	94,347	108,768	14,104,600
Property acquired before 1954	5,938,191	117,519[a]	10,195[a]	170,057	153,064	6,389,026
Percentage Distribution						
All property on hand in 1959	60.8	23.3	13.3	1.3	1.3	100.0
Property acquired after 1953	46.3	33.0	19.2	0.7	0.8	100.0
Property acquired before 1954	92.9	1.8	0.2	2.7	2.4	100.0

Source: Tables D-6 and D-8.
[a]See note to Table 25.

TABLE 37

Per Cent of Cost of Corporations' Depreciable Assets Acquired After 1953 and of Depreciation Allowances on These Facilities, by Method of Depreciation and Size of Total Assets, 1959

Depreciation Method	Total Asset Size Classes (million dollars)			
	Under 1	1 Under 25	25 and Over	Total
Straight-line:				
Per cent of property	71.4	61.7	42.5	53.3
Per cent of depreciation	64.4	52.9	32.0	46.3
Declining-balance:				
Per cent of property	22.8	28.6	28.4	27.1
Per cent of depreciation	28.9	36.8	33.8	33.0
Sum-of-years-digits:				
Per cent of property	5.8	9.5	26.2	17.9
Per cent of depreciation	6.5	10.1	31.3	19.2
Other-life methods:				
Per cent of property	0.1	0.2	1.6	1.0
Per cent of depreciation	0.1	0.2	1.3	0.7
Units-of-production:				
Per cent of property	a	a	1.4	0.8
Per cent of depreciation	a	a	1.6	0.8

Source: Tables D-4 and D-8.

[a]Less than 0.05 per cent.

Income for 1959, were $20.5 billion. By how much did this total exceed that which would have been claimed had the accelerated methods not been available? [17]

The amount of additional depreciation in any year which is generated by use of the accelerated methods depends on (1) the amount of depreciable property in accelerated method accounts, (2) the service lives

[17] Assuming that the availability of the accelerated methods had no effect on the amount or composition of net capital formation since 1953.

TABLE 38

Corporations' Depreciation Allowances on Assets Acquired After 1953, by Size of Total Assets and Method of Depreciation, 1959

Size of Total Assets (million dollars)	Straight -Line	Declining -Balance	Sum-of-the- Years-Digits	Other-Life Methods	Units-of- Production	All Methods
	Amount (thousand dollars)					
Under 1	2,678,991	1,200,941	271,522	4,338	1,410	4,157,202
1 - 25	1,686,663	1,172,886	322,652	5,502	1,118	3,188,821
25 and over	2,165,373	2,284,830	2,117,627	84,507	106,240	6,758,577
Total	6,531,027	4,658,657	2,711,801	94,347	108,768	14,104,600
	Percentage Distribution					
Under 1	64.4	28.9	6.5	0.1	a	100.0
1 - 25	52.9	36.8	10.1	0.2	a	100.0
25 and over	32.0	33.8	31.3	1.3	1.6	100.0
Total	46.3	33.0	19.2	0.7	0.8	100.0

Source: Table D-8.

aLess than 0.05 per cent.

TABLE 39

Corporations' Depreciation Allowances on Assets Acquired after 1953, by Industry Division and Depreciation Method, 1959

Industry Division	Straight-Line	Declining-Balance	Sum-of-the-Years-Digits	Other-Life Methods	Units-of-Production	All Methods
	Amount (thousand dollars)					
Agriculture, forestry, and fisheries	94,646	34,288	3,422	113	-	132,469
Mining	289,189	188,558	19,525	11,786	36,423	545,481
Construction	315,065	229,807	32,575	71	-	577,518
Manufacturing	2,141,468	2,014,318	1,814,208	38,352	63,272	6,071,618
Transportation, communication, electric, gas, and sanitary services	1,359,760	983,783	428,465	35,245	8,002	2,815,255
Trade	1,054,988	380,565	185,841	7,361	850	1,629,605
Finance, insurance, and real estate	670,797	426,290	116,881	1,262	206	1,215,436
Services	599,339	400,229	110,762	150	15	1,110,495
All industries	6,531,027	4,658,657	2,711,801	94,347	108,768	14,104,600
	Percentage Distribution					
Agriculture, forestry, and fisheries	71.5	25.9	2.6	0.1	-	100.0
Mining	53.0	34.6	3.6	2.2	6.7	100.0
Construction	54.6	39.8	5.6	a	-	100.0
Manufacturing	35.3	33.2	29.9	0.6	1.0	100.0
Transportation, communication, electric, gas, and sanitary services	48.3	35.0	15.2	1.3	0.3	100.0
Trade	64.7	23.4	11.4	0.5	0.1	100.0
Finance, insurance, and real estate	55.2	35.1	9.6	0.1	a	100.0
Services	54.0	36.0	10.0	a	-	100.0
All industries	46.3	33.0	19.2	0.7	0.8	100.0

Source: Table D-8.
Note: Column totals include small amounts of depreciation of companies not allocable to an industry division.
aLess than 0.05 per cent.

of these properties, and (3) their age distribution. With respect to any given amount of facilities of a given average age in accelerated accounts, the excess of accelerated over straight-line depreciation will be relatively greater the longer the service life; given the service life, the excess will be smaller the older the property.[18] All three of these factors determine the actual amount of total depreciation allowances, while factors (1) and (2) alone are sufficient to determine the amount of depreciation that would be claimed under straight-line.

In order to compute the difference between actual allowances under the accelerated methods and the amount that would have been claimed under straight-line, it is necessary to know the service lives of the facilities in the accelerated accounts. The LDA study provides quite a detailed distribution of this nature for the taxable year 1959, permitting measurement of this additional depreciation in total, and as among various types of assets, size of company, and major industrial division (the details of this computation are presented in Appendix D).

We estimate that the $20.493 billion of corporate depreciation allowances shown in *Statistics of Income* for 1959 were $2.433 billion larger than they would have been on the same properties had only the straight-line method of depreciation been used.[19] This represents an increase of about 13.5 per cent over the amount to which total allowances would have aggregated had only the straight-line method been used. It is a much larger percentage increase—49.3 per cent—over the amount of depreciation which would have been allowed under the straight-line method on the property in the accelerated accounts. On the property in these accounts, in other words, the use of the accelerated methods made a very substantial difference in 1959 in the amount of depreciation allowances.

Of this $2.433 billion of additional depreciation, about $1.622 billion (66.6 per cent) is accounted for by the excess of declining-balance, and about $.812 billion (33.4 per cent) is the excess of SYD over estimated straight-line charges.

---

[18] As the average age of the property in the accelerated method accounts increases, the excess of accelerated over straight-line depreciation diminishes and after a point becomes negative. See Chapter 1 above.

[19] The use of other methods resulted in depreciation charges only slightly greater than the amount that would have been allowable under the straight-line method on the properties in these accounts. The effect of the use of other methods on aggregate depreciation allowances, accordingly, has been ignored in this discussion.

| | Additional Depreciation | |
Accelerated Method	Million dollars	Per cent of total
Declining-balance	1,621.6	66.6
Sum-of-years-digits	811.9	33.4
Total	2,433.5	100.0

A large proportion, 65.5 per cent, of the difference between actual and estimated straight-line allowances is accounted for by companies with total assets of $25 million or more, as one might expect from the fact that depreciable facilities in accelerated method accounts were heavily concentrated in this size class.

| | Additional Depreciation | |
Size of Total Assets (million dollars)	Million dollars	Per cent of total
Under 1	396.7	16.3
1 under 25	442.0	18.2
25 and over	1,594.7	65.5
Total	2,433.5	100.0

Again, as one might suppose from the major industrial division distribution of post-1953 facilities in accelerated method accounts, a substantial proportion, 54.8 per cent, of the estimated additional depreciation generated by use of the accelerated methods was accounted for by manufacturing corporations. Public utilities account for an additional 19.1 per cent of the difference between actual allowances and those which would have been claimed under the straight-line method.

| | Additional Depreciation | |
Major Industrial Division	Million dollars	Per cent of total
Agriculture, forestry, and fisheries	10.4	0.4
Mining	17.0	0.7
Construction	28.5	1.2
Manufacturing	1,333.7	54.8
Transportation, communication, and sanitary services	465.8	19.1
Trade	144.5	5.9
Finance, insurance, and real estate	241.1	9.9
Services	192.0	7.9
Total	2,433.5 [20]	100.0

[20] Includes $0.4 million not allocable to a major industrial division.

TABLE 40

Additional Depreciation Generated by Use of Accelerated Depreciation
Methods on Corporations' Depreciable Facilities Acquired After 1953,
by Industry Division and Size of Total Assets, 1959

Industry Division	Total Assets Size Class (million dollars)			
	Under 1	1 Under 25	25 and Over	All Sizes
Agriculture, forestry, and fisheries	5.7	4.7	-	10.4
Mining	2.2	5.4	9.5	17.0
Construction	16.2	12.3	0.1	28.5
Manufacturing	84.6	195.4	1,053.8	1,333.7
Transportation, communication, and sanitary services	23.8	38.8	403.3	465.8
Trade	67.0	30.3	47.2	144.5
Finance, insurance, and real estate	80.8	93.8	66.5	241.1
Services	116.3	61.2	14.5	192.0
All Industries [a]	396.7	442.0	1,594.7	2,433.5
	Percentage Distribution			
Agriculture, forestry, and fisheries	0.2	0.2	-	0.4
Mining	0.1	0.2	0.4	0.7
Construction	0.7	0.5	[b]	1.2
Manufacturing	3.5	8.0	43.3	54.8
Transportation, communication, and sanitary services	1.0	1.6	16.6	19.1
Trade	2.8	1.3	1.9	5.9
Finance, insurance, and real estate	3.3	3.9	2.7	9.9
Services	4.8	2.5	0.6	7.9
All Industries [a]	16.3	18.2	65.5	100.0

Source: Appendix Table D-9

Note: Details may not add to totals due to rounding.

[a] Column totals include small amounts of additional depreciation not allocable to an industrial division.

[b] Less than 0.05 per cent.

A large proportion of the additional corporate depreciation generated in 1959 by use of accelerated methods was accounted for by manufacturing and public utility companies of substantial size, i.e., with total assets of $25 million or more, as Table 40 shows. These major industrial divisions accounted for 73.9 per cent of the additional depreciation, and the corporations in the largest asset size class in these divisions had, respectively, 43.3 per cent and 16.6 per cent of the total additional allowances. In other words, manufacturing and public utility corporations with total assets of $25 million or more accounted for 59.9 per cent of the total additional depreciation arising from use of the accelerated depreciation methods in 1959. These companies held 50.0 per cent of all corporate depreciable facilities acquired after 1953 and 63.2 per cent of corporations' post-1953 facilities in accelerated method accounts in 1959. For these companies, the additional depreciation was about 56.7 per cent of the estimated amount that would have been allowable under the straight-line method on the properties in accelerated method accounts.[21]

The contribution of the accelerated methods to total depreciation allowances varied widely from industry to industry and size class to size class in 1959, as shown in Table 41. The additional depreciation generated by the accelerated methods represented only 0.2 per cent of actual total allowances claimed under all methods and on all properties by construction corporations with total assets of $25 million or more. In contrast, the corresponding proportion for manufacturing companies with total assets of $25 million or more was 16.7 per cent, and for companies with total assets of $1 million but less than $25 million in the finance division, it was 17.8 per cent.

Income tax liabilities of the companies claiming the additional depreciation were roughly $1.265 billion lower than they would otherwise have been.[22] This is about 5.6 per cent of the total corporate income tax

[21] Not all of the corporations in this size class in these industries used the accelerated methods to the same extent or effect, of course. For some companies, use of the accelerated methods generated much larger additions to depreciation allowances in 1959; for others, the additional allowances were much less than indicated here.

[22] A precise calculation cannot be made since the data are not distributed by taxable income classes. This estimate assumes a marginal tax rate of 52 per cent. Use of the 52 per cent rate very likely overstates the reducton in tax liability, since undoubtedly some of the companies claiming accelerated depreciation were not subject to the surtax rate of 22 per cent but only to the 30 per cent normal tax, while some other companies undoubtedly sustained net operating losses which might never be offset against income in excess of the $25,000 surtax exemption.

TABLE 41

Additional Depreciation Generated by Use of Accelerated Depreciation Methods as Per Cent of Actual Total Depreciation Allowances, by Industry Division and Size of Total Assets, 1959

Industry Division	Size of Total Assets (million dollars)			
	Under 1	1 Under 25	25 and Over	All Sizes
Agriculture, forestry, and fisheries	5.4	12.5	-	6.3
Mining	1.4	2.2	3.3	2.5
Construction	4.5	5.7	0.2	4.7
Manufacturing	7.5	11.0	16.7	14.5
Transportation, communication, and sanitary services	5.6	7.5	10.4	9.7
Trade	6.2	6.4	11.3	7.3
Finance, insurance, and real estate	10.0	17.8	15.5	13.7
Services	15.5	16.5	10.5	15.2
All Industries[a]	8.2	10.6	13.9	11.9

Source: Appendix Table D-9, and U.S. Treasury Department, Internal Revenue Service, "Life of Depreciable Assets" source book.

[a]Includes very small amounts not allocable to any industry division.

liability of $22.525 billion for the taxable year 1959, as measured in *Statistics of Income*.[23] It is the equivalent of a 5.3 per cent reduction in liabilities (Table 42). For the companies which realized these tax savings, of course, the equivalent tax reduction is greater.

Use of accelerated depreciation methods in 1959 had a widely varying impact on the tax bills of corporations in the various industries and size classes, as may be seen in Table 42. A very large proportion of the total tax savings were in manufacturing and public utilities and on the account of corporations with total assets of $25 million or more. The industrial divisions and size classes in which the bulk of the tax

[23] *Statistics of Income, 1959–60, Corporation Income Tax Returns*, Table 1, p. 52.

TABLE 42

Tax Savings Resulting from Use of Accelerated Depreciation Methods, by Industry Division and Size of Total Assets, 1959

Industry Division	Size of Total Assets (million dollars)			
	Under 1	1 Under 25	25 and Over	All Sizes
Amount (million dollars)				
Agriculture, forestry, and fisheries	3.0	2.4	-	5.4
Mining	1.1	2.8	4.9	8.9
Construction	8.4	6.4	a	14.8
Manufacturing	44.0	101.6	548.0	693.5
Transportation, communication, and sanitary services	12.4	20.2	209.7	242.2
Trade	34.8	15.8	24.5	75.2
Finance, insurance, and real estate	42.0	48.8	34.6	125.4
Services	60.5	31.8	7.5	99.8
All Industries[b]	206.3	229.9	829.2	1,265.4
Per Cent Reduction in Tax Liabilities [c]				
Agriculture, forestry, and fisheries	10.4	8.6	-	8.0
Mining	4.1	3.4	1.3	1.8
Construction	5.7	4.1	0.1	4.3
Manufacturing	5.6	3.5	5.8	5.3
Transportation, communication, and sanitary services	9.6	6.6	6.3	6.4
Trade	4.1	1.8	2.5	2.8
Finance, insurance, and real estate	8.2	8.6	2.2	4.7
Services	23.6	15.0	6.1	16.9
All Industries[b]	7.5	4.4	5.2	5.3

Source: Appendix Table D-9 and U.S. Treasury Department, Internal Revenue Service, *Statistics of Income, 1959-60, Corporation Income Tax Returns,* pp. 67-101.

[a]Less than $.05 million.

[b]Includes very small amounts not allocable to any industrial division. Details may not add to totals because of rounding.

[c]Tax reduction divided by the sum of the tax reduction and tax liabilities shown in *Statistics of Income.*

savings accrued, however, were not those in which the largest percentage reductions in tax liabilities were realized, as shown in part B of Table 42. Taxes of service corporations with total assets of less than $1,000,000 were reduced by an estimated 23.6 per cent of what they would have amounted to had the accelerated methods not been used; these tax savings were about 4.8 per cent of the total. Public utility corporations in the same size class realized tax savings of about 9.6 per cent; these tax savings were less than 1.0 per cent of the total. On the other hand, manufacturing corporations with total assets of $25,000,000 or more accounted for roughly 43.3 per cent of the total tax savings, but reduced their taxes by only 5.8 per cent through the use of accelerated depreciation. Public utilities with total assets of $25,000,000 or more accounted for another 16.6 per cent of the total tax savings; their taxes saved in 1959 were an estimated 6.3 per cent.[24]

No information is available to indicate whether in the years after 1959 the effects of accelerated depreciation on corporate tax liabilities were materially different from those indicated here. As we cautioned at the beginning of this section, only limited inferences may be drawn from the data pertaining to a single year's experience. These data do show, for the taxable year 1959, that the availability of accelerated depreciation methods made a substantial difference in the total amount of depreciation allowances generated on the property on hand in that year, and for many companies, a substantial difference in tax liabilities. If the trend toward an increasing proportion of companies adopting the accelerated methods which was noted during the period 1954–59 continued thereafter, and if this trend is associated with depreciation of increasing amounts of property under accelerated methods, as seems likely, then accelerated depreciation may have had an even more substantial impact on corporate tax liabilities in recent years. On the other hand, the impact of acceleration on depreciation deductions and tax liabilities depends not only on the amount of property in accelerated method accounts but also on the age of these accounts.[25] The likely increase since 1959 in the amount of property under acceleration may

[24] There were 1,377 manufacturing and public utility corporations with total assets of $25,000,000 or more in 1959. The tax savings in this size class in these industry divisions were 59.9 per cent of the total. These companies accounted for about 53.2 per cent of 1959 corporation income tax liabilities (*ibid.*).

[25] The diminishing effect of acceleration is illustrated above, in Chapter 1.

have been offset in whole or in part by the aging of the accelerated method accounts.[26]

These findings suggest that accelerated depreciation could have had a significant effect on the volume of investment in depreciable facilities but they do not afford the basis for a precise estimate of this effect. The interview studies undertaken by Challis Hall and Thomas Stanback, dealing, respectively, with the impact of various features of the corporation income tax on business growth policies and on modernization investment, suggest that business response to changes in tax depreciation rules is substantial. These studies deal primarily with management's reaction to the tax law changes effected in 1962, but the nature of both the inquiries and replies suggest that the response to the 1954 depreciation changes was no less significant. Both studies also bring out that many factors other than taxes predominate in the investment decision, and point up the difficulty in identifying the contribution of tax changes to changes in the volume of capital formation. Our estimate of the effect of accelerated depreciation on capital outlays implicitly recognizes this constraint.

see p 8 xviii

The estimate of the change in expenditures for depreciable facilities is confined to corporate businesses for the single year 1959. It is assumed that the amount of such facilities acquired by corporations in that year is larger than it would have been had accelerated depreciation not been used and that this additional amount reflects the influence of acceleration both on corporate demand for facilities and on the supply of investable funds to corporations (the nature of these effects is described in Chapter 1). The magnitude of the estimated additional investment included in estimated corporate outlays for depreciable facilities in 1959, moreover, depends on the elasticities of the demand and supply functions for these facilities, given the shift in the functions as a result of the use of accelerated depreciation. While the data we have developed in the preceding discussion afford a basis for estimating the shift in the demand and supply functions, an empirical basis for estimating the respective elasticities, unfortunately, is not available. We have, therefore, estimated the amount of additional corporate outlays (in billion dollars) for 1959 depreciable facilities, assuming a range of elasticities in each function. The results are shown in the following table.

[26] See George Terborgh, *The Fading Boom in Corporate Tax Depreciation,* Machinery and Allied Products Institute, Washington, D.C., 1965.

Elasticity of Supply	*Elasticity of Demand for Depreciable Facilities*		
of Investable Funds	*−.5*	*−1.0*	*−2.5*
.5	1.3	1.8	2.2
1.0	1.3	2.0	2.8
2.5	1.3	2.3	4.0
5.0	1.3	2.5	4.9
10.0	1.4	2.6	5.7

Source: Appendix E.

With a relatively low elasticity of demand (e.g., −.5) for depreciable facilities, the amount of additional outlays included in the corporate total is $1.3 billion, slightly less than the estimated corporate tax savings from the use of accelerated methods in that year. Moreover, this estimate is virtually invariant with changes in the estimated elasticity of supply of investable funds. At a higher elasticity of demand, however, the estimated additional outlays are substantially greater than the tax savings and do vary substantially with the elasticity of supply of investable funds.

Evaluation of these estimates depends in part on one's judgment concerning the appropriate range of these elasticities. In our view, the increase in corporate capital outlays in 1959 as a result of the use of accelerated depreciation was at least equal to the tax savings resulting therefrom and may have been equal to several times that amount, e.g., $5.7 billion.[27]

---

[27] These estimates ignore the secondary effects on corporate capital outlays, which might have been induced by the expansion of economic activity resulting from the primary increase in investment in capital goods. See Appendix E for a more complete discussion of these estimates.

3

SUMMARY AND CONCLUSIONS

Our objective in this survey has been to discover and report the extent of use of the accelerated depreciation methods authorized by the Internal Revenue Code of 1954, and to examine the effects of using these methods on the amount of depreciation, tax liabilities, and capital outlays. In appraising these findings, one should keep in mind the fact that they are based on data pertaining to the first six or seven years of experience with these tax provisions, and that in the period since 1959 and 1960, patterns of taxpayer response different from those reported here may have developed.

In very broad terms, we find that in the period covered by this survey, the response of the business income taxpaying population to the availability of accelerated depreciation methods was substantial. A large proportion of the depreciable facilities acquired by corporations since 1953 and still on hand in 1959 was in accelerated method accounts. These methods generated a rapidly increasing proportion of total depreciation allowances in the years 1954–60. In 1959, use of accelerated depreciation resulted in a substantially larger amount of corporate depreciation allowances than would have been claimed had only the straight-line method been available.

More specifically, our major findings include the following.

1. A substantial proportion—about 45 per cent—of the depreciable property acquired by corporations after 1953 and on hand in 1959 was in accelerated depreciation method accounts in 1959. Since not all of the property acquired after 1953 was eligible for the use of these methods, it must be assumed that an even larger proportion of qualified facilities were held in declining-balance and SYD accounts in 1959. Facilities in accelerated method accounts were almost one-fourth of the total amount of corporate depreciable assets (including those acquired

before 1954) covered by depreciation schedules for the taxable year 1959.

2. Corporations with total assets of $25 million or more (accounting in 1959 for about 56 per cent of all corporate depreciable facilities acquired since 1953) held close to 55 per cent of their post-1953 facilities in accelerated method accounts in 1959. For corporations with total assets under $1 million, about 29 per cent of post-1953 facilities were in declining-balance and SYD accounts, and for companies with total assets greater than $1 million but less than $25 million, the proportion was 38 per cent.

3. Among manufacturing corporations of all sizes, accelerated depreciation methods were applied to about 57 per cent of the depreciable facilities acquired by these companies since 1953. In contrast, corporations in the trade and mining industrial divisions held only about 28 per cent of their post-1953 facilities in accelerated depreciation accounts. Manufacturing companies with total assets of $25 million or more had two-thirds of their post-1953 facilities under the declining-balance and SYD methods.

4. The proportion of corporate facilities in accelerated method accounts in 1959 appears to have been more closely associated with company size than with any other characteristic, e.g., industrial division, type of asset, or service life.

5. Accelerated depreciation methods generated a rapidly increasing share of total allowances between 1954 and 1960. In the earlier year, only 7 per cent of total corporation allowances were computed under these methods. By 1960, corporations' accelerated depreciation allowances had increased to 39 per cent of the total. Between the taxable years 1954 and 1960, the increase in the ratio of accelerated to total corporate allowances was quite pronounced, and occurred in virtually every size class in every industry.

6. Corporations' accelerated depreciation allowances in 1959 were 52 per cent of their allowances on facilities acquired since 1953. These accelerated allowances were about 37 per cent of total allowances on all facilities on hand in 1959. For corporations with total assets of $25 million or more, accelerated allowances were almost two-thirds of the total on post-1953 properties. Manufacturing corporations, which accounted for 43 per cent of all allowances on post-1953 facilities, used

the accelerated methods to compute about 63 per cent of these allowances. Half of the allowances on post-1953 acquisitions of public utility companies were under accelerated methods.

7. Among unincorporated businesses, the use of accelerated depreciation methods resulted in substantially smaller allowances relative to total depreciation in the taxable year 1959. Accelerated allowances were only 8 per cent of the total for sole proprietorships and 21 per cent for partnerships.

8. Use of accelerated depreciation methods by corporations resulted in substantially larger allowances in 1959 than would otherwise have been available. According to our estimates, total corporate depreciation allowances in that year would have been $2.4 billion less than the $20.5 billion actually shown in *Statistics of Income,* had straight-line depreciation been used in lieu of the accelerated methods. The $2.4 billion of additional allowances is almost 50 per cent more than the allowances that would have been available under straight-line on facilities in accelerated method accounts. About two-thirds of this $2.4 billion of additional depreciation was generated by the declining-balance method, and one-third by SYD. Close to two-thirds of the additional allowances were claimed by companies with total assets of $25 million or more, and about 55 per cent were in the manufacturing industries. Almost three-fifths of the additional allowances were in manufacturing and public utility corporations with total assets of $25 million or more; these companies held about 63 per cent of all corporate facilities that were acquired after 1953 and were in accelerated method accounts in 1959. For these companies, additional allowances were about 57 per cent greater than would have been allowed had the straight-line method been applied to the property in accelerated method accounts.

9. Additional depreciation allowances resulting from the use of accelerated methods instead of straight-line represented widely varying proportions of actual total allowances from industry to industry and size class to size class. Additional allowances were only 0.2 per cent of total allowances among construction corporations with total assets of $25 million or more. For manufacturing corporations in that size class, the additional allowances were 16.7 per cent of the total. For companies with total assets of more than $1 million but less than $25 million in the finance, insurance, and real estate division, additional allowances were almost 18 per cent of total allowances.

10. Corporations' income tax liabilities in 1959 were $1.265 billion lower than they would have been without the additional depreciation allowances generated by use of the accelerated methods. These tax savings were about 5.6 per cent of actual liabilities of $22.525 billion in 1959. Use of accelerated methods had a widely varying impact on the tax bills of companies in the various size classes and industries. Taxes of service corporations with total assets less than $1 million were reduced by an estimated 23.6 per cent, while those of construction companies with total assets of $25 million or more were reduced by scarcely 0.1 per cent.

11. Use of accelerated depreciation methods had considerable effect on corporations' outlays for depreciable facilities in 1959. We estimate that the outlays were not less than $1.3 billion, and may have been as much as $5.7 billion, more than they would have been in the absence of accelerated depreciation.

12. There was a sharp increase between 1954 and 1960 in the number and proportion of corporations reporting the use of the declining-balance depreciation method but very little increase in the proportion of corporations using SYD. In the former year, only 7.6 per cent of corporate returns indicated use of declining-balance; by 1960, close to one-fourth showed this method. For SYD, on the other hand, the increase was only from 4.8 per cent to 5.9 per cent. The increase in the proportion of returns on which use of declining-balance was shown was greatest among the smallest corporations. The proportion of returns on which an accelerated method is indicated appears to have been associated with company size. In 1960, almost 47 per cent of the returns of companies with total assets of $100 million or more show the declining-balance method and almost 35 per cent of such returns had SYD allowances. Of the companies with total assets less than $100,000, on the other hand, only 16.6 per cent used declining-balance and 2.8 per cent used SYD. However, differences in industry characteristics do not appear to have been significant in this connection. Declining-balance depreciation appeared on 21.4 per cent of returns of corporations in trade and 29.9 per cent of those in manufacturing; for SYD, the proportion ranged only from a low of 4.4 per cent in finance to a high of 10.5 per cent in manufacturing.

13. While a substantial number of unincorporated businesses used the accelerated depreciation methods in 1959, these were a small pro-

portion of the unincorporated business population. Among sole proprietorships claiming depreciation deductions, about 5.5 per cent indicated use of declining-balance and less than 1 per cent showed SYD. Among partnerships, the corresponding proportions were 10.7 per cent and 2.0 per cent.

14. In 1959, four-fifths or more of the sole proprietorships with depreciation were using only the straight-line method. In that year, not less than two-thirds of the partnerships used the straight-line method exclusively. In 1960, at least 70 per cent of corporations relied solely on the straight-line methods. Among all three types of businesses, the proportion of companies using only straight-line decreases as company size increases. For example, in 1960 at least 80 per cent of the corporations with total assets under $100,000 relied only on this method; for corporations with total assets of $100 million or more, the corresponding proportion is 7.6 per cent.

The data we have examined afford evidence of a learning process which suggests that use of these methods may very well have become more extensive in the years following 1959 and 1960. In particular, the relatively rapid increase in the number of small corporations using the accelerated methods suggests that the tax savings therefrom may have been more widely enjoyed after 1959. Similarly, more widespread use of the accelerated methods after 1959 may have had a stimulating effect on capital formation for an increasing number of firms.

APPENDIX A

TABLE A-1

Per Cent of Number of Corporations Reporting Use of Various Methods of Depreciation, by Industry Division and Size of Total Assets, 1954 and 1960

Size of Total Assets (thousand dollars)	Straight -Line		Declining -Balance		Sum-of-the-Years-Digits		Other Methods	
	1954	1960	1954	1960	1954	1960	1954	1960
All Industries								
Under 100	97.4	94.6	4.6	16.6	2.2	2.8	0.9	0.3
100 - 500	97.8	93.6	10.0	30.9	6.4	7.8	1.2	0.6
500 - 1,000	97.7	94.0	14.6	38.6	10.2	12.3	1.6	0.8
1,000 - 5,000	96.7	94.3	16.5	40.7	12.5	16.2	2.5	1.6
5,000 - 10,000	98.2	96.9	14.0	37.8	14.6	19.3	3.0	2.3
10,000 - 50,000	98.5	97.5	16.4	37.5	17.8	21.0	4.5	3.5
50,000 - 100,000	98.0	98.0	21.9	40.9	19.3	28.9	6.3	6.7
100,000 and over	97.8	97.2	24.0	46.7	28.4	34.8	8.6	11.0
Total	97.5	94.3	7.8	23.9	4.9	5.9	1.2	0.6
Agriculture, Forestry, and Fisheries								
Under 100	97.5	93.9	6.2	23.3	1.2	3.7	0.9	a
100 - 500	98.2	95.5	9.8	30.4	5.7	6.3	1.6	a
500 - 1,000	99.2	96.9	10.1	35.6	7.2	a	-	0.3
1,000 - 5,000	99.5	97.2	16.6	43.1	10.7	11.3	1.1	0.3
5,000 - 10,000	100.0	92.9	25.0	50.0	12.5	25.0	12.5	7.1
10,000 - 50,000	100.0	100.0	57.1	40.0	-	20.0	-	5.0
50,000 - 100,000	100.0	-	-	-	-	-	-	-
100,000 and over	-	-	-	-	-	-	-	-
Total	97.9	94.7	8.3	27.1	3.6	5.3	1.1	0.3
Mining								
Under 100	94.5	94.3	9.9	19.7	2.7	5.2	1.0	a
100 - 500	95.7	95.2	11.1	35.4	7.4	7.4	9.7	5.4
500 - 1,000	99.0	96.4	11.7	40.9	7.3	a	9.9	13.5
1,000 - 5,000	94.2	93.5	13.1	40.2	4.7	13.3	21.5	16.4
5,000 - 10,000	94.9	92.9	18.6	33.9	10.2	8.9	27.1	22.3
10,000 - 50,000	94.6	95.3	20.3	31.8	8.1	13.1	32.4	15.0
50,000 - 100,000	100.0	100.0	22.2	30.8	22.2	30.8	44.4	46.2
100,000 and over	100.0	83.3	-	54.2	14.3	20.8	14.3	58.3
Total	95.2	94.7	11.2	29.5	5.5	7.1	8.4	7.0

(continued)

TABLE A-1 *(continued)*

Size of Total Assets (thousand dollars)	Straight -Line		Declining -Balance		Sum-of-the- Years-Digits		Other Methods	
	1954	1960	1954	1960	1954	1960	1954	1960
Construction								
Under 100	98.1	95.5	4.5	18.5	2.4	3.2	0.7 ⎫	
100 - 500	98.4	95.2	13.0	37.4	10.1	9.7	1.1 ⎬	0.3
500 - 1,000	99.3	95.6	21.4	49.6	12.0	12.1	0.7 ⎭	
1,000 - 5,000	98.8	96.2	21.6	55.0	15.9	17.8	2.3	1.4
5,000 - 10,000	97.6	95.0	24.1	60.8	22.9	22.5	3.6	3.3
10,000 - 50,000	100.0	97.2	30.3	55.6	30.3	20.8	-	2.8
50,000 - 100,000	100.0	100.0	-	75.0	100.0	37.5	100.0	12.5
100,000 and over	100.0	-	-	-	-	-	-	-
Total	98.3	95.5	8.7	26.7	5.9	6.0	0.9	0.3
Manufacturing								
Under 100	97.8	96.4	4.9	18.4	3.1	3.6	1.1	0.6
100 - 500	99.0	96.8	11.4	37.6	9.7	12.2	1.0	0.9
500 - 1,000	99.1	96.8	17.5	42.8	15.9	20.1	1.7	0.8
1,000 - 5,000	99.0	96.5	20.6	49.3	20.9	26.9	2.4	1.7
5,000 - 10,000	99.0	97.4	21.4	47.1	28.2	35.4	4.8	3.6
10,000 - 50,000	98.7	97.1	27.8	51.5	31.4	40.3	8.4	6.6
50,000 - 100,000	97.5	98.9	29.5	56.2	34.4	50.2	9.0	12.8
100,000 and over	93.8	97.1	37.0	57.8	43.8	58.1	19.9	20.9
Total	98.4	96.6	10.0	29.9	8.6	10.5	1.4	0.9
Transportation, Communication, Electric, Gas, and Sanitary Services								
Under 100	96.6	94.7	4.3	17.1	2.5	3.2	1.7	a
100 - 500	98.0	92.9	9.4	31.5	5.5	7.5	1.7	1.0
500 - 1,000	98.9	94.5	16.5	35.0	7.9	9.5	2.8	a
1,000 - 5,000	98.8	95.3	18.4	41.3	13.9	16.1	4.6	4.0
5,000 - 10,000	97.8	95.1	25.9	44.3	5.9	20.5	3.7	4.9
10,000 - 50,000	96.9	94.4	28.6	49.3	13.0	17.2	8.7	6.3
50,000 - 100,000	88.6	92.3	37.1	69.2	-	13.9	17.1	12.3
100,000 and over	100.0	97.3	40.2	65.6	21.8	31.2	9.2	13.7
Total	97.2	94.3	7.8	23.4	4.4	5.5	2.1	1.0

(continued)

TABLE A-1 *(continued)*

Size of Total Assets (thousand dollars)	Straight -Line		Declining -Balance		Sum-of-the- Years-Digits		Other Methods	
	1954	1960	1954	1960	1954	1960	1954	1960
Wholesale and Retail Trade								
Under 100	97.5	95.1	4.2	15.8	2.4	2.4	0.8	0.3
100 - 500	94.3	96.2	8.9	27.4	5.6	6.7	1.0	0.4
500 - 1,000	99.1	96.8	14.9	36.5	9.8	12.0	1.5	a
1,000 - 5,000	99.1	96.7	17.2	41.9	15.2	18.2	2.3	1.4
5,000 - 10,000	99.5	98.1	20.0	42.5	16.6	26.8	4.5	1.4
10,000 - 50,000	97.9	98.8	20.4	46.9	27.1	28.8	5.8	3.4
50,000 - 100,000	96.3	100.0	29.6	38.2	40.7	44.1	3.7	8.8
100,000 and over	100.0	97.8	3.8	52.2	53.8	52.2	11.5	8.7
Total	97.9	95.6	6.8	21.4	4.3	4.8	1.0	0.4
Finance, Insurance, and Real Estate								
Under 100	97.0	92.7	4.1	14.6	1.1	2.2	0.6	0.2
100 - 500	96.1	88.2	8.5	28.1	3.4	5.3	0.9	0.3
500 - 1,000	94.0	89.5	10.8	34.2	4.6	6.3	1.3	a
1,000 - 5,000	93.7	91.5	12.8	31.9	5.4	7.7	1.6	0.9
5,000 - 10,000	98.0	96.9	8.8	31.8	9.0	11.4	1.3	1.0
10,000 - 50,000	98.8	97.8	9.3	30.1	11.6	13.8	1.5	1.2
50,000 - 100,000	99.6	98.2	15.6	28.4	12.6	18.1	1.9	1.6
100,000 and over	99.3	97.7	15.1	34.2	20.4	23.6	1.8	3.7
Total	96.3	91.1	7.0	22.3	2.9	4.4	0.9	0.3
Services								
Under 100	97.5	94.0	6.2	18.0	2.5	3.4	0.9	0.4
100 - 500	97.5	92.1	13.3	37.2	8.4	9.7	1.0	0.4
500 - 1,000	99.5	89.4	13.9	47.5	13.9	15.8	0.8	0.4
1,000 - 5,000	97.2	91.9	18.8	45.1	18.2	17.0	4.8	2.1
5,000 - 10,000	91.9	95.3	22.6	45.6	27.4	28.2	6.4	4.0
10,000 - 50,000	97.4	95.1	38.5	52.4	20.5	20.4	5.1	3.9
50,000 - 100,000	100.0	88.9	25.0	66.7	-	33.4	25.0	-
100,000 and over	66.7	100.0	-	60.0	33.3	40.0	33.3	-
Total	97.3	93.4	8.1	23.6	4.4	5.5	1.0	0.5

(continued)

TABLE A-1 *(concluded)*

Size of Total Assets (thousand dollars)	Straight -Line		Declining -Balance		Sum-of-the- Years-Digits		Other Methods	
	1954	1960	1954	1960	1954	1960	1954	1960
Not Allocable								
Under 100	95.5	91.9	2.8	14.2	2.8	a	0.7	-
100 - 500	93.9	95.5	16.4	a	0.6	a	-	-
500 - 1,000	100.0	a	-	a	-	a	-	-
1,000 - 5,000	100.0	90.0	7.7	5.0	-	a	-	-
5,000 - 10,000	100.0	-	-	-	-	-	-	-
10,000 - 50,000	-	-	-	-	-	-	-	-
50,000 - 100,000	-	-	-	-	-	-	-	-
100,000 and over	-	-	-	-	-	-	-	-
Total	95.4	92.5	4.2	15.2	2.5	a	0.6	-

Source: Taxable year 1954, U.S. Treasury Department, Internal Revenue Service, *Statistics of Income, 1959, Supplementary Depreciation Data from Corporation Income Tax Returns,* pp. 119-122; taxable year 1960, U.S. Treasury Department, Internal Revenue Service, special tabulations.

Note: Frequencies for "all industries" in 1954 differ from those in Table 4, which include data from all returns, including those without balance sheets.

[a]Not shown separately because of high sampling variability. However, the data are included in the totals.

TABLE A-2

Per Cent of Sole Proprietorships Reporting Use of Various Depreciation Methods, by Industry Division and Size of Business Receipts, 1959

Size of Business Receipts (thousand dollars)	Method of Depreciation				
	Straight -Line	Declining -Balance	Sum-of-the-Years -Digits	Other Methods	Method not Described
All Industries					
Under 10	84.4	3.1	0.5	4.7	9.1
10 - 20	83.8	6.4	1.0	5.0	9.4
20 - 30	84.1	7.7	1.1	5.4	10.0
30 - 50	83.4	8.8	1.4	5.1	9.9
50 - 100	84.0	11.5	2.1	5.7	10.4
100 and over	81.0	15.5	3.2	8.1	11.6
No receipts reported	75.8	2.5	0.7	5.1	10.6
Total	83.9	5.5	0.9	5.1	9.5
Agriculture, Forestry, and Fisheries					
Under 10	85.3	2.3	0.3	4.4	9.0
10 - 20	84.4	6.1	0.8	4.8	12.0
20 - 30	83.3	8.4	1.4	5.4	12.2
30 - 50	81.9	10.5 ⎫		6.2	11.4
50 - 100	77.2	13.7 ⎬ 1.8		9.3	16.3
100 and over	79.7	20.6 ⎭		11.4	15.0
No receipts reported	78.8	a	a	5.0	10.5
Total	84.7	3.6	0.5	4.7	9.5
Mining					
Under 10	⎫	⎫	⎫	⎫	⎫
10 - 20	⎬ 66.7	⎬ 12.3	⎬ 1.1	⎬ 13.7	⎬ 19.6
20 - 30					
30 - 50	⎭	⎭	⎭	⎭	⎭
50 - 100	58.7	⎫ 19.4	⎫ 3.8	⎫ 15.8	20.4
100 and over	61.4	⎭	⎭	⎭	
No receipts reported[a]					
Total	65.2	12.6	1.9	13.9	18.5

(continued)

TABLE A-2 (continued)

Size of Business Receipts (thousand dollars)	Method of Depreciation				
	Straight -Line	Declining -Balance	Sum-of- the-Years -Digits	Other Methods	Method not Described
Construction					
Under 10	85.9	3.5		4.8	7.7
10 - 20	84.2	4.3		4.9	8.4
20 - 30	85.8	6.2	0.7	5.1	7.5
30 - 50	88.0	7.4		3.6	8.6
50 - 100	85.4	8.6		7.0	7.4
100 and over	83.3	16.7	4.3	8.6	9.3
No receipts reported[a]					
Total	85.6	5.8	0.9	5.2	8.0
Manufacturing					
Under 10	86.5			4.5	7.8
10 - 20	82.6				
20 - 30	83.3	5.5	2.0		
30 - 50	82.6			5.7	
50 - 100	78.9				15.0
100 and over	81.8	22.1		7.7	11.7
No receipts reported	67.2	-	a	a	a
Total	83.5	7.7	2.0	5.1	9.2
Transportation, Communication, and Sanitary Services					
Under 10	81.8	2.5	0.7	5.3	11.0
10 - 20	82.6	8.7		5.8	8.8
20 - 30	86.0	10.6	3.1		13.9
30 - 50	83.3	8.7		6.1	
50 - 100	79.7	15.6	4.5		
100 and over	81.5	23.8		7.0	15.5
No receipts reported	a	-	-	a	a
Total	82.0	5.4	1.1	5.6	10.7

(continued)

TABLE A-2 *(concluded)*

Size of Business Receipts (thousand dollars)	Method of Depreciation				
	Straight -Line	Declining -Balance	Sum-of-the-Years -Digits	Other Methods	Method not Described
Wholesale and Retail Trade					
Under 10	84.3	4.0	0.5	4.3	9.7
10 - 20	85.0	4.2	0.5	4.3	8.4
20 - 30	85.8	4.2		5.2	8.1
30 - 50	84.5	4.7	0.7	4.1	8.7
50 - 100	84.9	7.9		4.6	9.1
100 and over	81.0	13.2	2.5	7.6	10.9
No receipts reported	70.1	a	a	a	a
Total	86.4	6.2	0.9	5.0	9.4
Finance, Insurance, and Real Estate					
Under 10	81.6	5.9	1.0	5.5	9.7
10 - 20	81.3		2.4	5.3	
20 - 30	74.9			6.8	
30 - 50	73.1	12.8		6.4	12.0
50 - 100	78.6		3.7		
100 and over	76.3			9.2	
No receipts reported	63.5	a	a	a	a
Total	80.4	7.8	1.6	5.7	10.3
Services					
Under 10	83.3	4.1	1.1	5.2	8.7
10 - 20	82.4	8.9		5.9	9.9
20 - 30	77.3	10.8	2.2	5.0	10.1
30 - 50	82.3	15.6		6.5	11.4
50 - 100	87.6	23.3	5.0	5.7	11.4
100 and over	80.6	23.8		9.4	16.1
No receipts reported	78.0	a	a	a	a
Total	83.2	7.8	1.6	5.5	9.6

Source: Internal Revenue Service, *Statistics of Income, 1959-60, U.S. Business Tax Returns*, pp. 34-38.

[a]No reliable estimate of sampling variability can be obtained from the sample. Data, however, are included in the totals. Totals include small frequencies of sole proprietorships which were not allocable to an industrial division.

TABLE A-3

*Per Cent of Partnerships Reporting Use of Various Depreciation
Methods, by Industry Division and Size of Business Receipts, 1959*

Size of Business Receipts (thousand dollars)	Method of Depreciation				
	Straight -Line	Declining -Balance	Sum-of-the- Years-Digits	Other Methods	Method not Described
All Industries					
Under 10	84.2	6.7	1.0	14.7	4.0
10 - 20	83.3	7.6	1.2	15.8	3.9
20 - 30	83.8	8.5	1.5	15.1	3.8
30 - 50	84.4	9.5	1.6	15.8	4.1
50 - 100	86.5	11.8	2.0	15.4	4.2
100 - 200	84.0	14.3	2.6	16.8	5.5
200 - 500	82.7	20.0	5.0	22.7	6.3
500 - 1,000	95.8	32.7	9.1	30.7	9.6
1,000 - 5,000	85.7	35.8	10.0	27.1	11.7
5,000 and over	93.3	58.4	19.2	10.3	48.8
No receipts reported	88.4	10.1	4.5	12.7	5.3
Total	84.6	10.7	2.0	16.3	4.5
Agriculture, Forestry, and Fisheries					
Under 10	84.5	3.5	} 0.5	22.2	5.9
10 - 20	85.2	5.6		26.3	5.2
20 - 30	80.9	6.3	} 1.4	30.1	4.1
30 - 50	79.7	10.0		28.6	5.2
50 - 100	82.9	15.8	1.9	31.1	4.5
100 - 200	82.3	16.9	4.4	31.7	5.3
200 - 500	75.0	20.6	2.6	33.4	7.6
500 - 1,000	95.3	37.6	9.8	55.2	8.8
1,000 - 5,000	86.9	32.0	8.5	31.4	6.5
5,000 and over	100.0	57.1	-	100.0	28.6
No receipts reported	84.7	a	a	15.5	a
Total	83.3	7.2	1.1	26.2	5.3

(continued)

TABLE A-3 *(continued)*

Size of Business Receipts (thousand dollars)	Straight-Line	Declining-Balance	Sum-of-the-Years-Digits	Other Methods	Method not Described
Mining					
Under 10	77.7	4.7	1.8	16.7	5.9
10 - 20	73.5			17.4	
20 - 30	64.3	8.3		29.4	
30 - 50	70.7			35.9	
50 - 100	91.8		3.8	25.9	
100 - 200	88.5	23.6		28.9	
200 - 500	63.8	31.5		35.1	6.1
500 - 1,000	72.2	38.1	8.0	38.1	19.3
1,000 - 5,000	53.2	44.1	7.2	50.5	15.3
5,000 and over	100.0	100.0	11.1	100.0	55.6
No receipts reported	74.1	a	a	a	a
Total	76.4	12.7	2.9	22.6	6.3
Construction					
Under 10	90.2	4.4	1.4	8.2	4.1
10 - 20	88.6	6.5		9.3	2.3
20 - 30	88.7	6.1		10.6	
30 - 50	89.0	8.5	1.5	9.5	4.0
50 - 100	87.3	11.5		13.9	3.0
100 - 200	83.6	17.8	2.5	18.4	5.4
200 - 500	83.7	24.6	4.7	22.9	5.4
500 - 1,000	99.6	37.3	10.1	38.7	11.6
1,000 - 5,000	79.5	47.2	12.2	28.6	15.5
5,000 and over	47.2	37.5	6.9	6.9	45.8
No receipts reported	75.6	a	a	a	-
Total	87.5	11.8	2.3	13.6	4.0

(continued)

TABLE A-3 *(continued)*

Size of Business Receipts (thousand dollars)	Method of Depreciation				
	Straight -Line	Declining -Balance	Sum-of-the- Years-Digits	Other Methods	Method not Described
Manufacturing					
Under 10	84.4	8.3		10.9	
10 - 20	87.3	4.8		15.6	4.3
20 - 30	86.0	8.4	1.2	9.7	
30 - 50	87.6	9.5		16.7	
50 - 100	88.9	16.2		14.0	3.4
100 - 200	83.7	15.2	2.2	18.5	5.3
200 - 500	84.3	24.5	7.8	23.3	7.1
500 - 1,000	100.0	38.3	13.4	30.7	11.4
1,000 - 5,000	88.2	42.9	13.9	26.0	13.1
5,000 and over	100.0	66.2	22.5	7.0	70.4
No receipts reported	99.1	a	-	a	a
Total	86.9	14.9	3.1	16.7	5.1
Transportation, Communication, and Sanitary Services					
Under 10	84.3	8.4		11.5	
10 - 20	85.4	6.7	1.8	11.1	3.4
20 - 30	84.0	13.1		17.5	
30 - 50	79.2	9.7		22.1	
50 - 100	78.9	14.8		27.4	
100 - 200	87.6	19.8	4.5	25.2	4.3
200 - 500	81.3	24.1		27.4	
500 - 1,000	79.8	34.8	8.9	24.7	7.0
1,000 - 5,000	74.3	27.1	5.7	25.7	8.6
5,000 and over	100.0	-	33.3	-	-
No receipts reported[a]					
Total	83.1	11.9	2.6	17.7	3.7

(continued)

TABLE A-3 *(continued)*

Size of Business Receipts (thousand dollars)	Method of Depreciation				
	Straight -Line	Declining -Balance	Sum-of-the- Years-Digits	Other Methods	Method not Described
Trade					
Under 10	87.7	3.8	} 0.8	12.1	2.8
10 - 20	86.9	4.0		12.4	4.4
20 - 30	86.4	4.4	} 0.9	11.7	3.7
30 - 50	87.1	5.8		12.7	3.8
50 - 100	87.8	6.8	1.2	12.4	4.1
100 - 200	85.3	10.1	1.9	14.2	5.6
200 - 500	83.7	16.3	3.9	21.7	6.1
500 - 1,000	94.7	27.7	7.3	28.7	8.6
1,000 - 5,000	86.8	32.5	8.3	27.2	9.8
5,000 and over	100.0	50.8	20.5	7.9	39.4
No receipts reported	91.7	a	a	a	a
Total	86.7	8.9	1.9	14.6	4.8
Finance, Insurance, and Real Estate					
Under 10	83.1	9.1	1.1	13.4	3.5
10 - 20	72.9	14.2	2.4	13.6	3.8
20 - 30	74.2	18.8	2.5	13.0	3.6
30 - 50	73.0	21.2	3.8	15.0	4.9
50 - 100	83.4	21.6	5.5	16.0	4.7
100 - 200	72.3	23.7	6.2	16.0	5.1
200 - 500	74.1	31.2	10.1	18.7	8.8
500 - 1,000	100.0	61.6	24.0	17.4	12.4
1,000 - 5,000	100.0	39.1	19.7	17.6	26.2
5,000 and over	100.0	100.0	19.2	7.7	80.8
No receipts reported	100.0	17.2	4.7	17.7	4.6
Total	79.9	13.1	2.2	13.8	3.9

(continued)

TABLE A-3 *(concluded)*

Size of Business Receipts (thousand dollars)	Method of Depreciation				
	Straight -Line	Declining -Balance	Sum-of-the- Years-Digits	Other Methods	Method not Described
Services					
Under 10	83.9	7.8	1.6	12.2	2.7
10 - 20	86.2	7.7	1.2	12.8	3.0
20 - 30	87.5	9.5	2.2	10.8	3.4
30 - 50	86.3	11.6	2.4	15.2	3.9
50 - 100	85.4	17.7	3.1	15.2	4.3
100 - 200	82.7	23.9	4.0	18.7	5.3
200 - 500	82.8	28.0	7.9	21.8	6.2
500 - 1,000	97.6	47.7	10.5	29.7	10.3
1,000 - 5,000	80.3	30.5	10.6	25.1	14.0
5,000 and over	100.0	90.6	31.3	9.4	56.3
No receipts reported	86.1	a	7.7	5.7	7.7
Total	85.3	12.9	2.6	14.2	3.8

Source: Internal Revenue Service, *Statistics of Income, 1959-60, U.S. Business Tax Returns*, pp. 92-95.

[a]No reliable estimate of sampling variability can be obtained from the sample. Data, however, are included in the totals. Totals include small frequencies of partnerships which were not allocable to an industrial division.

TABLE A-4

Percentage Distribution of Amount of Corporation Depreciation, by

Depreciation Method, Industry Division, and Size

of Total Assets, 1954 and 1960

Size of Total Assets (thousand dollars)	Straight -Line		Declining -Balance		Sum-of-the- Years-Digits-		Other Methods		Declining-Balance plus Sum-of-the- Years-Digits	
	1954	1960	1954	1960	1954	1960	1954	1960	1954	1960
All Industries										
Under 100	93.8	79.7	3.8	16.2	1.4	2.6	1.0	0.4	5.2	18.8
100-500	91.7	67.7	5.2	25.7	2.1	5.0	1.0	0.5	7.3	30.7
500-1,000	89.6	63.0	6.5	29.1	2.5	6.5	1.4	0.6	9.0	35.6
1,000-5,000	88.2	58.6	6.9	29.6	2.6	9.5	2.3	1.8	9.5	39.0
5,000-10,000	89.7	57.3	4.8	25.9	2.9	13.9	2.7	2.7	7.7	39.8
10,000-50,000	88.7	56.9	5.4	25.6	2.3	14.9	3.6	2.5	7.7	40.5
50,000-100,000	92.0	52.2	2.5	26.2	2.9	18.3	2.5	3.3	5.4	44.6
100,000 and over	87.7	52.9	3.7	22.6	2.3	21.0	6.2	3.5	6.0	43.6
Total	89.3	58.2	4.7	24.2	2.3	14.8	3.6	2.5	7.0	39.0
Agriculture, Forestry, and Fisheries										
Under 100	95.3	78.1	4.4	16.8	0.3	3.5	a	b	4.7	20.3
100-500	92.4	72.0	3.4	23.9	1.8	2.9	2.4	b	5.2	26.7
500-1,000	94.2	67.2	3.5	28.1	2.3	b	-	a	5.8	32.8
1,000-5,000	92.6	69.4	4.8	25.9	1.6	4.4	0.9	a	6.4	30.3
5,000-10,000	96.0	37.7	3.2	26.0	0.2	11.5	0.7	4.6	3.4	37.5
10,000-50,000	95.1	75.3	4.9	20.4	-	4.3	-	0.1	4.9	24.7
50,000-100,000	100.0	-	-	-	-	-	-	-	-	-
100,000 and over	-	-	-	-	-	-	-	-	-	-
Total	94.2	71.7	3.8	23.3	1.1	3.8	0.9	0.2	4.9	27.1
Mining										
Under 100	85.6	73.1	11.7	22.2	2.2	1.8	0.5	1.5	13.9	24.0
100-500	88.5	68.5	4.4	23.5	1.7	3.4	5.3	4.0	6.1	26.8
500-1,000	89.7	63.3	4.3	28.2	1.4	b	4.6	4.9	5.7	31.9
1,000-5,000	84.9	59.6	4.4	24.1	0.4	5.1	10.2	11.1	4.8	29.1
5,000-10,000	87.8	59.9	2.9	29.0	0.5	2.2	8.8	8.9	3.4	31.2
10,000-50,000	76.4	62.7	6.9	13.7	0.3	7.7	16.3	15.7	7.2	21.4
50,000-100,000	89.2	66.7	3.7	5.8	a	5.7	7.2	21.9	3.7	11.4
100,000 and over	94.1	53.6	-	15.0	0.3	2.3	5.6	29.1	0.3	17.2
Total	86.2	60.7	4.2	19.3	0.7	3.9	8.8	15.9	4.9	23.2

(continued)

TABLE A-4 *(continued)*

Size of Total Assets (thousand dollars)	Straight -Line		Declining -Balance		Sum-of-the- Years-Digits		Other Methods		Declining- Balance plus Sum-of-the- Years-Digits	
	1954	1960	1954	1960	1954	1960	1954	1960	1954	1960
Construction										
Under 100	91.8	75.7	3.5	20.2	3.8	3.0	0.9 ⎫		7.3	23.3
100 - 500	88.0	63.9	6.5	29.6	4.8	5.5	0.6 ⎬	0.1	11.3	35.1
500 - 1,000	88.2	51.9	8.3	42.5	2.9	4.8	0.6 ⎭		11.2	47.3
1,000 - 5,000	87.2	44.0	8.7	45.9	3.0	8.1	1.1	1.7	11.7	54.0
5,000 - 10,000	83.0	35.6	4.6	51.8	9.9	9.7	2.5	2.9	14.5	61.5
10,000 - 50,000	89.2	49.7	8.8	40.4	2.0	9.6	-	0.2	10.8	50.0
50,000 - 100,000	74.7	30.2	-	55.4	23.9	14.1	1.4	0.3	23.9	69.5
100,000 and over	100.0	-	-	-	-	-	-	-	-	-
Total	88.0	56.3	6.8	36.1	4.3	6.4	0.9	0.7	11.1	42.5
Manufacturing										
Under 100	95.3	77.3	2.8	15.4	1.2	5.0	0.7	0.4	4.0	20.3
100 - 500	93.2	68.6	3.6	23.1	2.4	5.8	0.8	0.4	6.0	28.9
500 - 1,000	93.0	64.2	3.7	24.6	2.6	9.2	0.7	0.7	6.3	33.8
1,000 - 5,000	92.2	59.5	3.6	26.2	2.9	12.4	1.2	1.2	6.5	38.6
5,000 - 10,000	91.7	57.2	3.2	22.8	3.5	17.9	1.5	1.9	6.7	40.7
10,000 - 50,000	90.9	54.8	3.4	23.8	2.8	19.9	2.9	1.5	6.2	43.7
50,000 - 100,000	92.5	50.7	2.3	22.8	3.9	23.7	1.2	2.8	6.2	46.4
100,000 and over	82.5	44.0	5.0	21.3	2.7	29.7	9.7	4.8	7.7	51.0
Total	87.6	50.7	4.1	22.4	2.8	23.3	5.4	3.3	6.9	45.7
Transportation, Communication, Electric, Gas, and Sanitary Services										
Under 100	93.5	74.3	3.1	22.7	1.0	1.8	2.3	b	4.1	24.5
100 - 500	93.4	66.7	3.8	27.3	1.7	4.8	1.1	0.6	5.5	32.1
500 - 1,000	92.0	62.8	5.0	29.9	2.0	5.9	1.0	b	7.0	35.8
1,000 - 5,000	89.1	57.0	4.9	31.4	2.1	9.7	3.9	1.7	7.0	41.1
5,000 - 10,000	89.5	60.9	5.3	27.4	0.6	10.6	4.6	1.1	5.9	38.0
10,000 - 50,000	91.0	59.8	4.6	31.3	0.7	7.4	3.7	1.5	5.3	38.6
50,000 - 100,000	89.1	54.4	3.6	37.7	-	4.1	6.6	3.8	3.6	41.8
100,000 and over	96.6	64.0	2.0	25.6	0.8	9.5	0.6	0.9	2.8	35.1
Total	94.5	63.4	2.8	26.7	0.9	8.7	1.7	1.1	3.7	35.4

(continued)

TABLE A-4 *(concluded)*

Size of Total Assets (thousand dollars)	Straight -Line		Declining -Balance		Sum-of-the-Years-Digits		Other Methods		Declining-Balance plus Sum-of-the-Years-Digits	
	1954	1960	1954	1960	1954	1960	1954	1960	1954	1960
Trade										
Under 100	95.0	80.5	3.2	15.5	1.3	2.0	0.5	0.4	4.5	17.3
100-500	93.5	73.5	3.9	22.1	1.9	3.2	0.8	0.1	5.8	25.3
500-1,000	91.6	67.1	5.5	24.7	2.3	7.0	0.7	0.1	7.8	31.7
1,000-5,000	92.3	66.1	4.1	23.2	2.7	9.2	0.9	0.7	6.8	32.4
5,000-10,000	92.0	62.8	3.4	22.3	2.3	14.2	2.3	0.5	5.7	36.4
10,000-50,000	86.0	59.9	8.5	24.1	3.1	14.8	2.5	1.1	11.6	38.9
50,000-100,000	89.0	54.4	3.0	19.4	6.6	24.3	1.5	2.0	9.6	43.6
100,000 and over	90.1	51.7	0.1	16.1	5.4	30.8	4.3	1.4	5.5	46.9
Total	91.9	67.6	3.9	20.7	2.7	10.4	1.5	0.6	6.6	31.0
Finance, Insurance, and Real Estate										
Under 100	95.0	87.9	3.8	10.1	0.6	1.6	0.6	0.2	4.4	11.7
100-500	90.8	66.1	7.4	28.3	1.0	5.0	0.9	0.2	8.4	33.3
500-1,000	82.1	62.0	14.8	33.6	2.7	4.0	0.4	0.1	17.5	37.6
1,000-5,000	78.2	57.3	18.4	35.9	2.7	5.7	0.8	0.7	21.1	41.6
5,000-10,000	82.9	60.8	13.2	28.5	1.4	7.1	2.5	2.7	14.6	35.6
10,000-50,000	84.7	64.0	13.0	26.6	1.7	8.2	0.5	0.5	14.7	34.8
50,000-100,000	92.8	53.3	2.1	35.3	3.6	10.8	1.5	0.4	5.7	46.1
100,000 and over	89.9	67.1	5.0	15.7	3.4	14.6	1.8	2.5	8.4	30.3
Total	86.3	66.9	10.9	25.5	1.9	6.4	0.9	0.8	12.8	31.9
Services										
Under 100	91.1	75.4	5.2	19.9	1.7	3.0	2.0		6.9	22.9
100-500	87.6	59.9	9.2	30.7	2.5	7.0	0.7	0.9	11.7	37.7
500-1,000	82.4	61.2	6.7	31.9	3.6	6.0	7.3		10.3	37.9
1,000-5,000	77.6	56.8	13.0	31.1	2.6	8.1	6.8	3.9	15.6	39.2
5,000-10,000	84.1	44.4	8.6	25.7	2.6	20.7	4.7	9.1	11.2	46.4
10,000-50,000	79.4	46.8	13.9	33.9	1.8	7.6	4.9	11.7	15.7	41.5
50,000-100,000	99.5	59.8	0.4	22.4	-	17.8	0.1	-	0.4	40.2
100,000 and over	55.1	67.5	-	24.5	44.8	8.0	0.1	-	44.8	32.5
Total	85.1	61.2	8.4	28.4	3.1	7.3	3.4	2.6	11.5	35.7

Source: Taxable year 1954, Internal Revenue Service, *Statistics of Income, 1959, Supplementary Depreciation Data from Corporation Income Tax Returns,* pp. 119-122; taxable year 1960, Internal Revenue Service, special tabulation.

Note: Frequencies for all industries in 1954 differ from those in Table 14 which include data from all returns, including those without balance sheets.

[a]Less than 0.05 per cent.

[b]Not shown separately because of high sampling variability. However, the data are included in the totals.

TABLE A-5

Percentage Distribution of Depreciation of Sole
Proprietorships, by Depreciation Method, Industry
Division, and Size of Business Receipts, 1959

Size of Business Receipts (thousand dollars)	Straight -Line	Declining -Balance	Sum-of-the- Years-Digits	Other Methods	Method not Described
All Industries					
Under 10	81.6	3.1	0.4	4.7	9.6
10 - 20	78.6	4.6	0.6	4.9	10.4
20 - 30	76.9	5.2	1.0	5.6	10.6
30 - 50	73.2	7.7	1.1	5.7	11.2
50 - 100	69.2	9.9	1.6	6.6	11.8
100 and over	60.2	15.0	2.2	9.7	11.9
No receipts reported	71.4	3.2	0.4	4.7	19.1
Total	74.5	6.9	1.0	6.0	10.8
Agriculture, Forestry, and Fisheries					
Under 10	83.6	1.9	0.2	4.1	9.7
10 - 20	80.6	3.3	0.3	4.2	10.6
20 - 30	77.3	3.8	0.7	5.0	12.5
30 - 50	74.2	6.1		5.9	11.6
50 - 100	64.2	7.1	0.8	9.6	17.4
100 and over	58.9	9.4		10.2	19.7
No receipts reported	75.1	a	a	4.2	17.3
Total	78.9	3.5	0.4	5.0	11.4
Mining					
Under 10					
10 - 20	51.7	12.2	1.0	11.2	23.9
20 - 30					
30 - 50					
50 - 100	34.0	16.8	5.0	11.7	22.9
100 and over	38.8				
No receipts reported[a]					
Total	43.5	15.0	4.0	11.4	23.2

(continued)

TABLE A-5 *(continued)*

Size of Business Receipts (thousand dollars)	Straight -Line	Declining -Balance	Sum-of-the- Years-Digits	Other Methods	Method not Described
Construction					
Under 10	77.9	4.7		3.2	16.6
10 - 20	78.6	7.2		4.8	8.4
20 - 30	78.3	6.6	0.7	6.4	8.4
30 - 50	82.3	6.3		3.4	6.4
50 - 100	67.0	15.6		5.5	10.2
100 and over	59.9	19.9	4.1	10.3	5.0
No receipts reported[a]					
Total	71.2	11.9	1.8	6.7	7.9
Manufacturing					
Under 10	81.3				
10 - 20	74.0			6.4	10.1
20 - 30	76.9	7.4			
30 - 50	77.1		1.9	8.3	
50 - 100	58.4				15.3
100 and over	60.1	18.8		7.8	8.6
No receipts reported	74.6	-	a	a	a
Total	66.7	11.7	1.9	7.6	10.9
Transportation, Communication, and Sanitary Services					
Under 10	78.7	3.8	0.8	5.5	10.7
10 - 20	76.0	7.2		6.0	9.3
20 - 30	75.3	9.5	3.5	6.4	8.7
30 - 50	72.5	8.2			
50 - 100	68.0	12.1	2.8		
100 and over	50.3	33.2		8.5	3.5
No receipts reported	a	-	-	a	a
Total	69.0	13.6	2.2	6.7	8.0

(continued)

TABLE A-5 *(concluded)*

Size of Business Receipts (thousand dollars)	Straight -Line	Declining -Balance	Sum-of-the- Years-Digits	Other Methods	Method not Described
Wholesale and Retail Trade					
Under 10	78.3	6.7	0.7	5.1	8.8
10 - 20	80.3	4.5	0.7	5.3	8.6
20 - 30	79.9	3.9	-	5.8	9.5
30 - 50	79.4	6.4 }	1.2	3.4	9.6
50 - 100	77.3	6.6 }		5.1	8.6
100 and over	65.9	11.1	1.4	9.5	11.2
No receipts reported	64.5	a	a	a	a
Total	73.9	7.8	1.1	6.6	9.9
Finance, Insurance, and Real Estate					
Under 10	75.2	7.0	0.8	7.1	9.8
10 - 20	68.5 }		2.4	6.2 }	
20 - 30	65.8 }			5.6	
30 - 50	52.6 }	12.4		5.8 }	20.6
50 - 100	57.6 }		2.6 }	5.8 }	
100 and over	34.7 }				
No receipts reported	52.3	a	a	a	a
Total	65.8	9.9	1.7	6.4	15.7
Services					
Under 10	79.3	4.9 }	1.0	5.6	7.7
10 - 20	74.0	6.4 }		6.2	11.7
20 - 30	75.7	7.1 }	1.5	5.7	9.1
30 - 50	67.1	10.6 }		7.8	12.1
50 - 100	69.7	13.7 }	2.3	4.6	8.5
100 and over	58.3	16.1 }		12.3	10.0
No receipts reported	68.5	a	a	a	a
Total	72.4	8.7	1.5	6.5	10.0

Source: Internal Revenue Service, *Statistics of Income, 1959-60, U. S. Business Tax Returns,* pp. 34-38.

[a]No reliable estimate of sampling variability can be obtained from the sample. Data, however, are included in totals. Totals also include small amounts of additional first-year depreciation and depreciation of sole proprietorships not allocable to an industry division.

TABLE A-6

Percentage Distribution of Partnership Depreciation by Depreciation Method, Industry Division, and Size of Business Receipts, 1959

Size of Business Receipts (thousand dollars)	Straight -Line	Declining -Balance	Sum-of-the- Years-Digits	Other Methods	Method not Described
All Industries					
Under 10	74.1	13.1	1.3	7.4	2.9
10 - 20	69.8	14.3	2.0	9.5	3.1
20 - 30	66.3	15.6	2.0	10.8	4.2
30 - 50	67.2	15.0	1.2	10.7	4.6
50 - 100	65.2	16.2	2.4	11.1	3.4
100 - 200	60.9	18.3	1.7	13.8	3.4
200 - 500	51.5	21.0	3.0	16.9	6.2
500 - 1,000	53.1	23.3	5.4	12.1	3.3
1,000 - 5,000	44.9	26.4	5.1	16.7	4.8
5,000 and over	18.4	19.1	3.7	27.9	29.4
No receipts reported	56.0	11.6	11.2	6.1	9.1
Total	59.0	18.2	2.7	13.3	5.3
Agriculture, Forestry, and Fisheries					
Under 10	80.3	3.8	0.2	14.2	1.2
10 - 20	79.1	3.2		16.3	0.8
20 - 30	73.3	3.5	0.7	19.2	1.9
30 - 50	65.1	5.4		21.8	6.3
50 - 100	62.8	9.7	0.7	22.6	2.6
100 - 200	60.4	7.4	1.2	26.0	3.3
200 - 500	55.7	9.1	0.8	26.5	6.8
500 - 1,000	68.0	12.1	5.9	10.2	1.6
1,000 - 5,000	53.9	13.8	2.6	23.9	3.5
5,000 and over	7.1	56.0	-	3.6	22.6
No receipts reported	79.3	a	a	6.5	a
Total	68.1	6.4	0.8	20.5	3.1

(continued)

TABLE A-6 *(continued)*

Size of Business Receipts (thousand dollars)	Straight -Line	Declining -Balance	Sum-of-the- Years-Digits	Other Methods	Method not Described
Mining					
Under 10	59.1	2.3	0.9	12.7	
10 - 20	62.0		0.9	15.9	
20 - 30	70.3	8.7		14.6	6.4
30 - 50	64.5			26.0	
50 - 100	67.3	12.2	1.4	13.7	
100 - 200	68.2			14.7	
200 - 500	32.8	15.5		30.7	17.2
500 - 1,000	38.4	17.3	1.6	37.5	4.5
1,000 - 5,000	24.4	31.2	3.2	32.7	7.9
5,000 and over	12.1	49.4	3.0	23.4	4.3
No receipts reported	41.6	a	a	a	a
Total	41.4	21.4	1.9	25.4	8.4
Construction					
Under 10	86.2	4.7	1.7	2.1	1.1
10 - 20	81.6	7.0		4.6	1.1
20 - 30	84.0	8.4		4.9	
30 - 50	73.5	14.9	1.6	4.8	2.0
50 - 100	73.5	17.6		4.9	1.1
100 - 200	51.9	25.2	1.2	18.0	2.0
200 - 500	40.8	17.1	4.5	22.9	13.4
500 - 1,000	39.0	24.0	7.9	18.9	7.6
1,000 - 5,000	35.9	49.7	4.6	5.4	2.9
5,000 and over	8.5	13.3	1.5	34.5	42.0
No receipts reported	88.7	a	a	a	a
Total	41.6	20.9	2.9	18.6	14.6

(continued)

TABLE A-6 *(continued)*

Size of Business Receipts (thousand dollars)	Straight -Line	Declining -Balance	Sum-of-the- Years-Digits	Other Methods	Method not Described
Manufacturing					
Under 10	75.9	13.7 ⎫		4.7 ⎫	
10 - 20	75.0	2.4 ⎪		17.8 ⎬	2.7
20 - 30	80.4	5.0 ⎬	1.7	8.7 ⎭	
30 - 50	72.0	10.0 ⎪		13.5 ⎫	
50 - 100	77.3	9.7 ⎭		4.4 ⎬	1.4
100 - 200	63.7	11.6	1.8	15.2	2.9
200 - 500	51.4	14.3	4.4	21.2	5.6
500 - 1,000	60.3	23.9	6.1	3.0	1.1
1,000 - 5,000	42.0	23.5	7.4	21.3	1.6
5,000 and over	54.7	23.6	13.2	2.0	3.5
No receipts reported	63.7	a	-	a	-
Total	59.1	16.0	4.4	13.8	2.8
Transportation, Communication, and Sanitary Services					
Under 10	80.6	12.1 ⎫		1.7 ⎫	
10 - 20	75.2	13.3 ⎬	3.1	5.7 ⎬	2.3
20 - 30	60.8	16.2 ⎪		11.9 ⎭	
30 - 50	59.7	6.9 ⎭		26.9	
50 - 100	60.5	15.2 ⎫		18.9 ⎫	
100 - 200	58.5	12.9 ⎬	2.6	21.0 ⎬	1.0
200 - 500	52.7	24.5 ⎭		19.2 ⎭	
500 - 1,000	49.1	23.3	5.2	18.2	1.3
1,000 - 5,000	41.8	12.7	6.3	34.1	3.5
5,000 and over	75.0	-	25.0	-	-
No receipts reported	a	a	-	-	-
Total	59.0	15.7	3.2	18.5	1.6

(continued)

TABLE A-6 *(continued)*

Size of Business Receipts (thousand dollars)	Straight -Line	Declining -Balance	Sum-of-the- Years-Digits	Other Methods	Method not Described
Trade					
Under 10	73.1	4.6 ⎱	0.8	9.0	8.2
10 - 20	78.8	5.5 ⎰		9.9	1.7
20 - 30	80.7	5.4 ⎱	0.7	7.8	4.0
30 - 50	83.1	5.2 ⎰		7.0	2.1
50 - 100	78.0	7.1	1.1	11.1	1.7
100 - 200	75.3	7.5	1.4	12.5	2.1
200 - 500	63.6	11.7	2.3	18.5	2.4
500 - 1,000	68.0	18.6	3.7	6.4	1.2
1,000 - 5,000	55.0	20.6	4.8	16.0	1.4
5,000 and over	53.9	16.1	11.5	8.9	4.8
No receipts reported	62.7	a	a	a	a
Total	70.4	10.8	2.2	12.7	2.2
Finance, Insurance, and Real Estate					
Under 10	75.7	20.0	1.4	1.6	0.5
10 - 20	63.6	28.5	4.2	2.4	0.7
20 - 30	53.5	35.6	3.3	5.6	1.7
30 - 50	58.0	38.2	1.4	1.1	0.4
50 - 100	54.4	37.9	6.5	0.7	0.2
100 - 200	54.8	38.4	2.8	3.0	0.9
200 - 500	48.5	46.6	3.0	1.4	0.5
500 - 1,000	41.4	30.7	14.6	9.3	2.8
1,000 - 5,000	79.9	7.9	6.9	2.3	0.7
5,000 and over	43.7	8.7	6.7	17.5	5.5
No receipts reported	40.3	20.2	29.6	7.4	1.2
Total	59.1	33.3	3.7	2.4	0.7

(continued)

TABLE A-6 *(concluded)*

Size of Business Receipts (thousand dollars)	Straight -Line	Declining -Balance	Sum-of-the- Years-Digits	Other Methods	Method not Described
		Services			
Under 10	58.6	12.6	2.5	16.1	7.6
10 - 20	60.0	12.5	1.7	10.7	12.2
20 - 30	61.8	10.3	2.4	11.0	13.1
30 - 50	65.4	8.6	1.7	10.5	12.9
50 - 100	59.4	14.4	2.0	11.9	10.2
100 - 200	48.5	24.6	1.4	13.0	9.4
200 - 500	39.1	22.6	5.1	16.3	15.3
500 - 1,000	29.8	40.1	4.4	16.2	6.9
1,000 - 5,000	28.3	26.1	3.0	17.7	23.6
5,000 and over	37.3	22.7	17.6	10.3	11.2
No receipts reported	33.5	a	13.1	7.0	40.3
Total	52.0	18.0	2.7	13.2	12.0

Source: Internal Revenue Service, *Statistics of Income, 1959-60, U. S. Business Tax Returns,* pp. 92-95.

[a]No reliable estimate of the sampling variability can be obtained from the sample. Data, however, are included in totals. Totals also include small amounts of additional first-year depreciation and of depreciation by partnerships not allocable to an industry division.

TABLE A-7

Percentage Distribution of Partnerships' Depreciable Assets,
by Depreciation Method, Industry Division,
and Size of Business Receipts, 1959

Size of Business Receipts (thousand dollars)	Straight -Line	Declining -Balance	Sum-of-the- Years-Digits	Other Methods	Method not Described
All Industries					
Under 10	73.9	10.7	1.2	12.5	1.9
10 - 20	71.3	11.4	2.0	13.5	1.8
20 - 30	72.4	12.7	1.9	11.3	1.7
30 - 50	69.6	12.7	0.7	14.7	2.3
50 - 100	67.9	13.8	2.9	12.7	2.8
100 - 200	63.5	17.4	1.4	15.6	2.2
200 - 500	55.3	20.4	2.3	16.4	5.6
500 - 1,000	57.2	19.3	3.8	16.0	3.8
1,000 - 5,000	41.2	30.2	3.2	16.2	9.2
5,000 and over	37.2	20.0	4.4	15.6	22.9
No receipts reported	68.2	17.4	6.8	6.9	a
Total	63.5	16.3	2.2	14.3	3.7
Agriculture, Forestry, and Fisheries					
Under 10	78.2	2.4	0.2	16.2	3.1
10 - 20	78.5	2.2		17.1	2.1
20 - 30	76.9	2.3	0.4	17.8	2.3
30 - 50	69.1	4.0		22.8	3.8
50 - 100	70.1	5.3	0.6	19.7	4.3
100 - 200	67.7	4.9	1.0	23.4	3.9
200 - 500	61.3	7.8	0.6	25.5	
500 - 1,000	50.1	9.7	2.5	29.4	8.3
1,000 - 5,000	59.8	10.5	1.7	22.2	5.8
5,000 and over	64.1	9.7	-	-	26.1
No receipts reported	82.1	a	a	16.1	a
Total	71.6	4.2	0.6	20.1	3.6

(continued)

TABLE A-7 *(continued)*

Size of Business Receipts (thousand dollars)	Straight -Line	Declining -Balance	Sum-of-the- Years-Digits	Other Methods	Method not Described
Mining					
Under 10	73.9	2.2	1.2	20.0	
10 - 20	75.2			10.5	
20 - 30	60.4	5.5		39.5	2.5
30 - 50	55.9			37.5	
50 - 100	66.4	8.5	1.3	21.5	
100 - 200	69.2			20.6	
200 - 500	37.5	14.2		20.1	25.9
500 - 1,000	44.0	11.7	1.1	34.8	8.4
1,000 - 5,000	28.0	19.2	2.1	28.1	22.6
5,000 and over	15.9	31.8	2.1	34.6	15.6
No receipts reported	47.1	a	a	a	a
Total	43.1	15.7	1.6	26.7	12.9
Construction					
Under 10	82.5	3.7	1.8	9.2	
10 - 20	85.5	5.5		7.5	2.4
20 - 30	84.0	5.1		6.1	
30 - 50	67.7	16.3	1.4	10.3	1.6
50 - 100	71.5	10.6		16.6	
100 - 200	47.4	29.5	1.2	18.8	3.2
200 - 500	52.0	16.7	4.8	24.4	2.2
500 - 1,000	41.4	22.6	5.0	24.5	6.5
1,000 - 5,000	27.4	25.4	3.5	23.0	20.7
5,000 and over	19.4	24.7	4.8	17.1	34.0
No receipts reported	91.5	a	a	a	-
Total	51.8	19.2	2.9	18.7	7.3

(continued)

TABLE A-7 *(continued)*

Size of Business Receipts (thousand dollars)	Straight -Line	Declining -Balance	Sum-of-the- Years-Digits	Other Methods	Method not Described
Manufacturing					
Under 10	80.3	9.1		8.0	
10 - 20	80.0	3.3		15.7	2.6
20 - 30	80.7	4.4	1.0	10.1	
30 - 50	76.0	7.2		15.5	4.6
50 - 100	75.8	6.9		9.2	
100 - 200	70.2	9.2	1.5	15.5	3.7
200 - 500	60.1	10.3	4.0	19.0	6.6
500 - 1,000	59.5	13.5	4.7	15.9	6.5
1,000 - 5,000	45.2	15.8	5.2	19.9	13.8
5,000 and over	53.3	14.5	5.5	0.8	25.9
No receipts reported	72.8	a	-	a	-
Total	62.5	11.0	3.3	15.7	7.5
Transportation, Communication, and Sanitary Services					
Under 10	79.8	9.7		7.7	
10 - 20	76.3	9.8	3.3	8.7	2.6
20 - 30	60.3	14.8		15.1	
30 - 50	68.5	4.5		21.4	
50 - 100	56.0	15.7		25.5	
100 - 200	59.4	12.4	2.0	22.9	1.6
200 - 500	55.9	21.0		20.2	
500 - 1,000	61.3	15.9	3.2	18.4	1.2
1,000 - 5,000	54.4	14.1	2.0	19.9	9.6
5,000 and over	77.9	-	22.1	-	-
No receipts reported	a	a	-	-	-
Total	61.8	14.1	2.5	19.3	2.4

(continued)

TABLE A-7 *(continued)*

Size of Business Receipts (thousand dollars)	Straight-Line	Declining-Balance	Sum-of-the-Years-Digits	Other Methods	Method not Described
Trade					
Under 10	77.4	5.9	2.4	10.5	1.6
10 - 20	82.4	3.5		12.1	
20 - 30	82.4	4.6	0.6	10.8	2.0
30 - 50	82.6	3.8		11.4	1.4
50 - 100	81.9	4.7	1.1	11.1	1.2
100 - 200	79.1	5.3	0.9	12.3	2.5
200 - 500	69.3	8.7	1.7	16.6	3.6
500 - 1,000	62.0	11.3	2.4	20.8	3.5
1,000 - 5,000	57.1	12.7	3.6	19.1	7.4
5,000 and over	44.3	9.0	6.7	6.7	33.4
No receipts reported	92.5	a	a	a	-
Total	72.9	7.3	1.7	14.4	3.7
Finance, Insurance, and Real Estate					
Under 10	72.2	13.5	1.1	11.6	1.6
10 - 20	64.9	17.9	3.4	11.7	2.0
20 - 30	66.2	21.4	2.7	8.6	1.9
30 - 50	61.6	23.2	0.4	12.3	
50 - 100	53.5	28.5	6.5	9.2	2.3
100 - 200	50.6	32.1	2.3	15.0	3.5
200 - 500	40.1	41.9	1.5	10.1	
500 - 1,000	64.8	28.8	3.3	2.9	0.3
1,000 - 5,000	29.7	64.4	1.9	3.4	0.6
5,000 and over	64.2	19.1	3.6	9.2	4.0
No receipts reported	51.9	31.8	12.5	2.7	1.1
Total	58.6	26.6	2.6	10.2	2.1

(continued)

TABLE A-7 *(concluded)*

Size of Business Receipts (thousand dollars)	Straight -Line	Declining -Balance	Sum-of-the- Years-Digits	Other Methods	Method not Described
Services					
Under 10	73.4	10.2	2.0	13.2	1.2
10 - 20	73.8	8.3	1.1	15.5	1.3
20 - 30	76.6	8.9	2.3	11.1	1.1
30 - 50	77.9	6.9	1.0	13.5	0.7
50 - 100	72.8	10.0	1.8	12.0	3.5
100 - 200	59.9	21.2	1.0	14.3	3.5
200 - 500	52.1	19.9	4.8	17.0	6.1
500 - 1,000	42.4	30.6	9.1	14.6	3.4
1,000 - 5,000	43.5	24.3	3.4	20.7	8.1
5,000 and over	65.9	7.8	6.0	1.2	19.1
No receipts reported	61.6	a	14.1	15.5	-
Total	66.5	14.0	2.4	13.9	3.2

Source: U.S. Treasury Department, Internal Revenue Service, *Statistics of Income, 1959-60, U.S. Business Tax Returns,* pp. 92-95.

[a]No reliable estimate of the sampling variability can be obtained from the sample. Data, however, are included in totals.

TABLE A-8

Cost of Corporations' Depreciable Assets, By Year of Purchase, Size of Total Assets, and Method of Depreciation, 1959 (LDA Survey)

A. All Size Classes

Year of Purchase	Straight -Line	Declining- Balance	Sum-of-the- Years-Digits	Other-Life Methods	Units-of- Production	Total
	Amount (thousand dollars)					
1960	252,204	188,190	37,306	-	-	477,700
1959	4,361,355	3,610,581	974,739	59,630	53,513	9,059,818
1958	3,776,817	4,438,624	2,973,504	61,515	34,684	11,285,144
1957	3,680,008	4,783,664	4,520,125	147,578	28,059	13,159,434
1956	3,684,809	3,951,267	2,117,480	399,449	24,020	10,177,025
1955	3,460,309	2,413,173	1,320,151	10,026	68,026	7,271,685
1954	3,032,925	2,526,761	1,207,294	188,035	49,979	7,004,994
Post-1953 (year not stated)	23,407,527	10,330,592	8,965,546	681,891	987,161	44,372,717
Pre-1954, total	109,374,924	1,625,818	113,289	4,249,108	2,975,802	118,338,941
All years	155,030,878	33,868,670	22,229,434	5,797,232	4,221,244	221,147,458
	Percentage Distribution					
1960	52.8	39.4	7.8	-	-	100.0
1959	48.1	39.9	10.8	0.7	0.6	100.0
1958	33.5	39.3	26.4	0.5	0.3	100.0
1957	28.0	36.4	34.4	1.1	0.2	100.0
1956	36.2	38.8	20.8	3.9	0.2	100.0
1955	47.6	33.2	18.2	0.1	0.9	100.0
1954	43.3	36.1	17.2	2.7	0.7	100.0
Post-1953 (year not stated)	52.8	23.3	20.2	1.5	2.2	100.0
Pre-1954, total	92.4	1.4	0.1	3.6	2.5	100.0
All years	70.1	15.3	10.1	2.7	1.9	100.0

(continued)

TABLE A-8 (continued)

B. Total Assets Under $1,000,000

Year of Purchase	Straight-Line	Declining-Balance	Sum-of-the-Years-Digits	Other-Life Methods	Units-of-Production	Total
		Amount (thousand dollars)				
1960	149,917	117,180	9,412	–	–	276,509
1959	2,205,806	1,046,713	122,852	5,366	7	3,380,744
1958	1,818,104	852,113	135,951	6,521	714	2,813,403
1957	1,540,773	658,944	134,125	1,379	573	2,335,794
1956	1,432,649	477,776	145,156	100	11	2,055,692
1955	1,100,507	249,712	123,447	241	295	1,474,202
1954	740,019	222,179	71,110	–	1,597	1,034,905
Post-1953(year not stated)	19,795	2,386	1,223	637	–	24,041
Pre-1954, total	5,482,361	381,976	8,519	331	278	5,873,465
All years	14,489,931	4,008,979	751,795	14,575	3,475	19,268,755
		Percentage Distribution				
1960	54.2	42.4	3.4	–	a	100.0
1959	65.3	31.0	3.6	0.2	a	100.0
1958	64.6	30.3	4.8	0.2	a	100.0
1957	66.0	28.2	5.7	0.1	a	100.0
1956	69.7	23.2	7.1	a	a	100.0
1955	74.7	16.9	8.4	a	a	100.0
1954	71.5	21.5	6.9	–	0.2	100.0
Post-1953(year not stated)	82.3	9.9	5.1	2.7a	–	100.0
Pre-1954 total	93.3	6.5	0.2	a	a	100.0
All years	75.2	20.8	3.9	0.1	a	100.0

(continued)

TABLE A-8 *(continued)*

C. Total Assets of $1,000,000 and Under $25,000,000

Year of Purchase	Straight-Line	Declining-Balance	Sum-of-the-Years-Digits	Other-Life Methods	Units-of-Production	Total
	Amount (thousand dollars)					
1960	19,643	46,325	4,452	-	-	70,420
1959	520,310	411,990	47,558	2,464	208	982,530
1958	558,077	415,556	81,544	2,946	76	1,058,199
1957	464,656	335,395	63,045	430	-	863,526
1956	367,541	220,290	78,793	187	-	666,811
1955	392,548	167,261	79,682	446	-	639,937
1954	300,273	128,838	35,128	192	-	464,431
Post-1953 (year not stated)	19,026	14,351	3,026	801	-	37,204
Pre-1954 total	2,252,406	307,770	5,906	7,897	-	2,573,979
All years	4,894,480	2,047,776	399,134	15,363	284	7,357,037
	Percentage Distribution					
1960	27.9	65.8	6.3	-	-	100.0
1959	53.0	41.9	4.8	0.3	a	100.0
1958	52.7	39.3	7.7	0.3	a	100.0
1957	53.8	38.8	7.3	0.1	-	100.0
1956	55.1	33.0	11.8	a	-	100.0
1955	61.3	26.1	12.5	0.1	-	100.0
1954	64.7	27.7	7.6	a	-	100.0
Post-1953 (year not stated)	51.1	38.6	8.1	2.2	-	100.0
Pre-1954 total	87.5	12.0	0.2	0.3	-	100.0
All years	66.5	27.8	5.4	0.2	a	100.0

(continued)

TABLE A-8 (concluded)

D. Total Assets of $25,000,000 and Over

Year of Purchase	Straight -Line	Declining- Balance	Sum-of-the- Years-Digits	Other-Life Methods	Units-of- Production	Total
			Amount (thousand dollars)			
1960	82,644	24,685	23,442	–	–	130,771
1959	1,635,239	2,151,878	804,329	51,800	53,298	4,696,544
1958	1,400,636	3,170,955	2,756,009	52,048	33,894	7,413,542
1957	1,674,579	3,789,325	4,322,955	145,769	27,486	9,960,114
1956	1,884,619	3,253,201	1,893,531	399,162	24,009	7,454,522
1955	1,967,254	1,996,200	1,117,022	9,339	67,731	5,157,546
1954	1,992,633	2,175,744	1,101,056	187,843	48,382	5,505,658
Post-1953 (year not stated)	23,368,706	10,313,855	8,961,297	680,543	987,161	44,311,472
Pre-1954 total	101,640,157	936,072	98,864	4,240,880	2,975,524	109,891,497
All years	135,646,467	27,811,915	21,078,505	5,767,294	4,217,485	194,521,666
			Percentage Distribution			
1960	63.2	18.9	17.9	–	–	100.0
1959	34.8	45.8	17.1	1.1	1.1	100.0
1958	18.9	42.8	37.2	0.7	0.5	100.0
1957	16.8	38.0	43.4	1.5	0.3	100.0
1956	25.3	43.6	25.4	5.4	0.3	100.0
1955	38.1	38.7	21.7	0.2	1.3	100.0
1954	36.2	39.5	20.0	3.4	0.9	100.0
Post-1953 (year not stated)	52.7	23.3	20.2	1.5	2.2	100.0
Pre-1954 total	92.5	0.9	0.1	3.9	2.7	100.0
All years	69.7	14.3	10.8	3.0	2.2	100.0

Source: Internal Revenue Service, "Life of Depreciable Assets" source book.

aLess than 0.05 per cent.

Note: Detail may not add to totals because of rounding.

TABLE A-9

Cost of Corporations' Depreciable Assets Acquired After 1953,

by Industry Division, Size of Total Assets, and

Method of Depreciation, 1959 (LDA Survey)

(thousand dollars)

Size of Total Assets (million dollars)	Straight -Line	Declining -Balance	Sum-of-the-Years-Digits	Other-Life Methods	Units-of-Production	Total
All Industries						
Under 1	9,007,570	3,627,003	743,276	14,244	3,197	13,395,290
1 - 25	2,642,074	1,740,006	393,228	7,466	284	4,783,058
25 and over	34,006,310	26,875,843	20,979,641	1,526,414	1,241,961	84,630,169
Total	45,655,954	32,242,852	22,116,145	1,548,124	1,245,442	102,808,517
Agriculture, Forestry, and Fisheries						
Under 1	207,570	50,429	4,949	356	-	263,304
1 - 25	16,544	6,340	589	-	-	23,473
25 and over	76,511	-	-	-	-	76,511
Total	300,625	56,769	5,538	356	-	363,288
Mining						
Under 1	152,999	73,651	13,167	-	2,418	242,235
1 - 25	62,928	48,066	6,199	22	-	117,215
25 and over	1,170,636	312,344	33,033	218,402	449,595	2,184,010
Total	1,386,563	434,061	52,399	218,424	452,013	2,543,013
Construction						
Under 1	475,212	170,305	46,725	160	-	692,402
1 - 25	54,345	66,430	5,721	-	-	126,496
25 and over	60,188	64,571	839	-	-	125,598
Total	589,745	301,306	53,285	160	-	944,496
Manufacturing						
Under 1	1,200,411	445,554	117,488	857	757	1,765,067
1 - 25	492,166	282,665	117,920	1,141	76	893,968
25 and over	11,521,926	12,828,890	13,942,970	441,712	705,076	39,440,574
Total	13,214,503	13,557,109	14,178,378	443,710	705,909	42,099,609

(continued)

TABLE A-9 *(concluded)*

Size of Total Assets (million dollars)	Straight -Line	Declining -Balance	Sum-of- the- Years- Digits	Other- Life Methods	Units- of- Production	Total
Transportation, Communication, Electric, Gas, and Sanitary Services						
Under 1	517,815	174,110	44,167	2,636	2	738,730
1 - 25	294,023	50,512	16,435	3,103	-	364,073
25 and over	18,303,739	12,563,014	5,813,853	840,685	74,390	37,595,681
Total	19,115,577	12,787,636	5,874,455	846,424	74,392	38,698,484
Trade						
Under 1	1,755,399	401,245	70,483	3,719	-	2,230,846
1 - 25	175,991	63,076	19,800	410	-	259,277
25 and over	1,163,529	419,236	849,816	25,021	11,651	2,469,253
Total	3,094,919	883,557	940,099	29,150	11,651	4,959,376
Finance, Insurance, and Real Estate						
Under 1	3,626,773	1,786,782	332,555	5,706	-	5,751,816
1 - 25	1,316,487	1,103,849	183,803	2,790	208	2,607,137
25 and over	1,335,418	431,044	232,977	594	1,249	2,001,282
Total	6,278,678	3,321,675	749,335	9,090	1,457	10,360,235
Services						
Under 1	1,050,963	523,523	113,476	719	20	1,688,701
1 - 25	227,031	118,497	42,761	-	-	388,289
25 and over	374,363	256,744	106,153	-	-	737,260
Total	1,652,357	898,764	262,390	719	20	2,814,250

Source: Internal Revenue Service, "Life of Depreciable Assets" source book.
Note: Detail may not add to totals because of rounding.

TABLE A-10

Cost of Corporations' Depreciable Assets Acquired After 1953, by Type of Asset, Size of Total Assets, and Method of Depreciation, 1959 (LDA Survey)

(thousand dollars)

Size of Total Assets (million dollars)	Straight -Line	Declining -Balance	Sum-of- the- Years- Digits	Other- Life Methods	Units- of- Production	Total
All Asset Types						
Under 1	9,007,570	3,627,003	743,276	14,244	3,197	13,395,290
1 - 25	2,642,074	1,740,006	393,228	7,466	284	4,783,058
25 and over	34,006,310	26,875,843	20,979,641	1,526,414	1,241,961	84,630,169
Total	45,655,954	32,242,852	22,116,145	1,548,124	1,245,442	102,808,517
Structures and Leasehold Improvements						
Under 1	4,713,945	2,112,822	374,985	5,945	911	7,208,608
1 - 25	1,498,800	1,167,892	234,695	3,251	-	2,904,638
25 and over	14,669,994	12,431,592	8,823,168	735,591	291,657	36,952,002
Total	20,882,739	15,712,306	9,432,848	744,787	292,568	47,065,248
Furniture, Fixtures, Office and Store Machinery and Equipment						
Under 1	817,364	219,535	47,056	339	2	1,084,296
1 - 25	201,171	84,474	25,239	56	-	310,940
25 and over	1,736,056	739,721	1,478,671	2,989	3,447	3,960,884
Total	2,754,591	1,043,730	1,550,966	3,384	3,449	5,356,120
Transportation Vehicles and Equipment						
Under 1	1,324,946	432,289	105,812	6,462	-	1,869,509
1 - 25	351,547	126,844	30,316	355	-	509,062
25 and over	2,419,921	2,558,358	1,171,388	175,280	19,645	6,344,592
Total	4,096,414	3,117,491	1,307,516	182,092	19,645	8,723,163
Production Machinery and Equipment						
Under 1	2,023,108	841,229	208,956	1,457	2,284	3,077,034
1 - 25	521,802	334,198	94,268	3,804	284	954,365
25 and over	14,627,914	10,576,912	9,370,436	612,442	923,754	36,111,458
Total	17,172,824	11,752,339	9,673,660	617,703	926,322	40,142,848

(continued)

TABLE A-10 *(concluded)*

Size of Total Assets (million dollars)	Straight -Line	Declining -Balance	Sum-of- the- Years- Digits	Other- Life Methods	Units- of- Production	Total
Livestock, Orchards, Vineyards						
Under 1	49,079	4,572	7	-	-	53,658
1 - 25	8,018	4,344	108	-	-	12,470
25 and over	33,574	65	274	8	-	33,921
Total	90,671	8,981	389	8	-	100,049
Not Identifiable or Intangible						
Under 1	79,128	16,556	6,460	41	-	102,185
1 - 25	60,736	22,254	8,602	-	-	91,592
25 and over	518,851	569,195	135,704	104	3,458	1,227,312
Total	658,715	608,005	150,766	145	3,458	1,421,089

Source: Internal Revenue Service, "Life of Depreciable Assets" source book.
Note: Detail may not add to totals because of rounding.

TABLE A-11

Cost of Corporations' Depreciable Assets Acquired After 1953,

by Service Life, Size of Total Assets,

and Method of Depreciation, 1959 (LDA Survey)

A. Total Assets Under $1,000,000

Service Life (years)	Straight -Line	Declining -Balance	Sum-of-the- Years-Digits	Other-Life Methods	Total
		Amount (thousand dollars)			
3	383,130	132,711	18,113	69	534,023
4	707,755	235,085	73,996	891	1,017,727
5	1,028,880	379,382	76,796	1,577	1,486,635
6	193,770	128,908	22,922	261	345,861
7	128,628	53,219	7,321	28	189,196
8	231,534	118,265	17,769	1,315	368,893
9	48,579	5,429	1,322	1,822	57,152
10	1,744,259	498,616	121,610	1,175	2,365,660
11-14	197,361	97,106	11,490	781	306,738
15	286,068	105,431	19,415	71	410,985
16-19	114,187	109,047	3,519	86	226,839
20	864,047	294,688	46,022	971	1,205,728
21-24	63,192	23,700	4,014	68	90,974
25	886,306	355,790	74,854	943	1,317,893
26-29	54,958	15,735	329	59	71,081
30	201,533	147,590	46,313	-	395,436
31-35	1,098,847	344,745	75,985	4,009	1,523,586
36-39	29,645	10,710	1,967	-	42,322
40	385,550	420,319	101,590	42	907,501
41-49	14,895	6,954	92	-	21,941
50	233,406	108,524	13,655	-	355,585
51 and over	17,438	5,822	886	-	24,146
Total	9,007,570	3,627,003	743,276	14,244	13,392,093

(continued)

TABLE A-11 *(continued)*

Part A. (concluded)

Service Life (years)	Straight -Line	Declining -Balance	Sum-of-the- Years-Digits	Other-Life Methods	Total
Percentage Distribution					
3	71.8	24.9	3.4	a	100.0
4	69.5	23.1	7.3	0.1	100.0
5	69.2	25.5	5.2	0.1	100.0
6	56.0	37.3	6.6	0.1	100.0
7	68.0	28.1	3.9	a	100.0
8	62.8	32.1	4.8	0.4	100.0
9	85.0	9.5	2.3	3.2	100.0
10	73.7	21.1	5.1	0.1	100.0
11 - 14	64.3	31.7	3.7	0.3	100.0
15	69.6	25.7	4.7	a	100.0
16 - 19	50.3	48.1	1.6	a	100.0
20	71.7	24.4	3.8	0.1	100.0
21 - 24	69.5	26.1	4.4	0.1	100.0
25	67.3	27.0	5.7	0.1	100.0
26 - 29	77.3	22.1	0.5	0.1	100.0
30	51.0	37.3	11.7	-	100.0
31 - 35	72.1	22.6	5.0	0.3	100.0
36 - 39	70.1	25.3	4.7	-	100.0
40	42.5	46.3	11.2	a	100.0
41 - 49	67.9	31.7	0.4	-	100.0
50	65.6	30.5	3.8	-	100.0
51 and over	72.2	24.1	3.7	-	100.0
Total	67.3	27.1	5.6	0.1	100.0

(continued)

TABLE A-11 *(continued)*

B. Total Assets $1,000,000 and Under $25,000,000

Service Life (years)	Straight -Line	Declining -Balance	Sum-of-the- Years-Digits	Other-Life Methods	Total
		Amount (thousand dollars)			
3	63,694	43,049	4,496	254	111,493
4	79,842	72,892	12,494	38	165,266
5	132,548	117,114	21,639	79	271,380
6	47,892	42,805	8,759	19	99,475
7	66,005	43,749	8,007	55	117,816
8	92,122	48,602	8,353	9	149,086
9	26,945	4,197	1,438	-	32,580
10	347,966	150,038	49,561	214	547,779
11 - 14	137,956	50,037	16,082	10	204,085
15	123,830	73,581	21,452	3,901	222,764
16 - 19	100,637	52,109	1,910	-	154,656
20	255,263	144,498	20,899	218	420,878
21 - 24	48,531	33,198	6,162	13	87,904
25	206,732	141,972	20,458	2	369,164
26 - 29	34,446	15,974	2,705	4	53,129
30	62,935	70,417	16,099	-	149,451
31 - 35	293,669	173,666	37,420	2,642	507,397
36 - 39	13,044	7,502	10,973	-	31,519
40	222,978	244,413	80,033	-	547,424
41 - 49	15,761	636	4,090	-	20,487
50	205,014	170,933	39,767	-	415,714
51 and over	29,881	28,532	-	-	58,413
Total	2,642,074	1,740,006	393,228	7,466	4,782,774

(continued)

TABLE A-11 *(continued)*

Part B. (concluded)

Service Life (years)	Straight -Line	Declining -Balance	Sum-of-the- Years-Digits	Other-Life Methods	Total
Percentage Distribution					
3	57.1	38.6	4.0	0.2	100.0
4	48.3	44.1	7.6	a	100.0
5	48.8	43.2	8.0	a	100.0
6	48.1	43.0	8.8	a	100.0
7	56.0	37.1	6.8	0.1	100.0
8	61.8	32.6	5.6	a	100.0
9	82.7	12.9	4.4	-	100.0
10	63.5	27.4	9.1	a	100.0
11 - 14	67.6	24.5	7.9	a	100.0
15	55.6	33.0	9.6	1.8	100.0
16 - 19	65.1	33.7	1.2	-	100.0
20	60.7	34.3	5.0	0.1	100.0
21 - 24	55.2	37.8	7.0	a	100.0
25	56.0	38.5	5.5	a	100.0
26 - 29	64.8	30.1	5.1	a	100.0
30	42.1	47.1	0.8	-	100.0
31 - 35	57.9	34.2	7.4	0.5	100.0
36 - 39	41.4	23.8	4.8	-	100.0
40	40.7	44.7	14.6	-	100.0
41 - 49	76.9	3.1	20.0	-	100.0
50	49.3	41.1	9.6	-	100.0
51 and over	51.2	48.8	-	-	100.0
Total	55.2	36.4	8.2	0.2	100.0

(continued)

TABLE A-11 *(continued)*

C. Total Assets $25,000,000 and Over

Service Life (years)	Straight -Line	Declining -Balance	Sum-of-the- Years-Digits	Other-Life Methods	Total
	Amount (thousand dollars)				
3	187,992	63,351	174,145	676	426,164
4	462,451	120,926	111,302	6,022	700,701
5	668,788	331,113	1,005,987	2,217	2,008,105
6	415,293	287,671	334,000	705	1,037,669
7	549,047	690,771	162,565	14,029	1,416,412
8	564,428	470,836	602,170	2,683	1,640,117
9	271,331	157,623	110,116	62,928	601,908
10	2,257,500	1,256,263	980,182	55,611	4,549,556
11-14	1,999,588	3,386,675	2,725,594	219,240	8,331,097
15	1,561,598	3,203,901	1,159,552	7,031	5,932,082
16-19	8,520,900	2,594,329	1,393,813	112,622	12,621,664
20	2,359,084	1,809,724	2,718,068	191,474	7,078,350
21-24	1,842,063	1,537,748	602,231	65,435	4,047,477
25	1,298,654	1,428,612	1,915,627	606,526	5,249,419
26-29	1,363,767	1,849,168	805,395	391	4,018,721
30	502,180	1,193,046	777,573	42,757	2,515,556
31-35	5,558,445	3,029,334	2,267,417	86,966	10,942,162
36-39	443,120	534,933	1,218,781	3	2,196,837
40	623,744	1,547,648	687,973	33,449	2,892,814
41-49	1,440,350	336,664	370,117	1,685	2,148,816
50	798,411	547,383	581,427	13,815	1,941,036
51 and over	289,486	492,347	266,175	116	1,048,124
Total	34,006,310	26,875,843	20,979,641	1,526,414	83,388,208

(continued)

TABLE A-11 *(concluded)*

Part C. (concluded)

Service Life (years)	Straight -Line	Declining -Balance	Sum-of-the- Years-Digits	Other-Life Methods	Total
	Percentage Distribution				
3	44.1	14.9	40.9	0.2	100.0
4	66.0	17.3	15.9	0.9	100.0
5	33.3	16.5	50.1	0.1	100.0
6	40.0	27.7	32.2	0.1	100.0
7	38.8	48.8	11.5	1.0	100.0
8	34.4	28.7	36.7	0.2	100.0
9	45.1	26.2	18.3	10.5	100.0
10	49.6	27.6	21.5	1.2	100.0
11 - 14	24.0	40.7	32.7	2.6	100.0
15	26.3	54.0	19.6	0.1	100.0
16 - 19	67.5	20.6	11.0	0.9	100.0
20	33.3	25.6	38.4	2.7	100.0
21 - 24	45.5	38.0	14.9	1.6	100.0
25	24.7	27.2	36.5	11.6	100.0
26 - 29	33.9	46.0	20.0	a	100.0
30	20.0	47.4	30.9	1.7	100.0
31 - 35	50.8	27.7	20.7	.8	100.0
36 - 39	20.2	24.4	55.5	a	100.0
40	21.6	53.5	23.8	1.2	100.0
41 - 49	67.0	15.7	17.2	0.1	100.0
50	41.1	28.2	30.0	0.7	100.0
51 and over	27.6	47.0	25.4	a	100.0
Total	40.8	32.2	25.2	1.8	100.0

Source: Internal Revenue Service, "Life of Depreciable Assets" source book.
[a]Less than 0.05 per cent.

Note: Detail may not add to totals because of rounding. Column totals include small amounts of assets with a service life of 2 years, not shown separately.

TABLE A-12

Cost of Corporations' Depreciable Assets Acquired After 1953, by Industry Division,

Type of Asset, and Method of Depreciation, 1959 (LDA Survey)

Industry Division and Type of Asset	Straight -Line	Declining -Balance	Sum-of-the- Years-Digits	Other-Life Methods	Units-of- Production	Total
	Amount (thousand dollars)					
All Industries						
All asset types	45,655,954	32,242,852	22,116,145	1,548,124	1,245,442	102,808,517
Structure and leasehold improvements	20,882,739	15,712,306	9,432,848	744,787	292,568	47,065,248
Furniture, fixtures, office and store machinery and equipment	2,754,591	1,043,730	1,550,966	3,384	3,449	5,356,120
Transportation vehicles and equipment	4,096,414	3,117,491	1,307,516	182,097	19,645	8,723,163
Production machinery and equipment	17,172,824	11,752,339	9,673,660	617,703	926,322	40,142,848
Agriculture, Forestry, and Fisheries						
All asset types	300,625	56,769	5,538	356	–	363,288
Structure and leasehold improvements	85,175	14,389	990	–	–	100,554
Furniture, fixtures, office and store machinery and equipment	5,538	794	413	–	–	6,745
Transportation vehicles and equipment	45,301	12,745	1,544	356	–	59,946
Production machinery and equipment	97,867	20,938	2,585	–	–	121,390
Livestock, orchards, and vineyards	64,732	7,282	6	–	–	72,020

(continued)

TABLE A-12 *(continued)*

Industry Division and Type of Asset	Straight -Line	Declining -Balance	Sum-of-the- Years-Digits	Other-Life Methods	Units-of- Production	Total
Mining						
All asset types	1,386,563	434,061	52,399	218,424	452,013	2,543,013
Structures and leasehold improvements	662,100	133,276	23,656	67,515	145,084	1,031,631
Furniture, fixtures, office and store machinery and equipment	19,803	3,635	340	-	3,447	27,225
Transportation vehicles and equipment	131,167	46,859	7,403	790	6,582	192,801
Production machinery and equipment	553,821	229,136	15,850	150,119	293,955	1,242,881
Construction						
All asset types	589,745	301,306	53,285	160	-	944,496
Structures and leasehold improvements	71,926	39,269	1,932	-	-	113,127
Furniture, fixtures, office and store machinery and equipment	21,169	5,274	818	-	-	27,261
Transportation vehicles and equipment	201,107	72,541	11,464	101	-	285,213
Production machinery and equipment	288,570	183,151	38,930	59	-	510,710

(continued)

TABLE A-12 *(continued)*

Industry Division and Type of Asset	Straight-Line	Declining-Balance	Sum-of-the-Years-Digits	Other-Life Methods	Units-of-Production	Total
Manufacturing						
All asset types	13,214,503	13,557,109	14,178,378	443,710	705,909	42,099,609
Structures and leasehold improvements	4,398,417	3,803,713	4,403,680	211,512	119,365	12,936,687
Furniture, fixtures, office and store machinery and equipment	745,267	399,436	1,048,201	2,016	-	2,194,920
Transportation vehicles and equipment	820,839	681,392	310,056	2,973	9,484	1,824,744
Production machinery and equipment	6,908,001	8,303,921	8,294,968	227,201	576,556	24,310,647
Transportation, Communication, Electric, Gas, and Sanitary Services						
All asset types	19,115,577	12,787,636	5,874,455	846,424	74,392	38,698,484
Structures and leasehold improvements	8,698,016	8,242,275	4,009,111	444,590	18,433	21,412,425
Furniture, fixtures, office and store machinery and equipment	220,740	45,456	11,596	1,123	2	278,917
Transportation vehicles and equipment	2,015,567	1,954,210	876,821	174,227	3,579	5,024,404
Production machinery and equipment	8,008,140	2,360,912	974,776	226,380	52,369	11,622,577

(continued)

TABLE A-12 *(continued)*

Industry Division and Type of Asset	Straight-Line	Declining-Balance	Sum-of-the-Years-Digits	Other-Life Methods	Units-of-Production	Total
Trade						
All asset types	3,094,919	883,557	940,099	29,150	11,651	4,959,376
Structures and leasehold improvements	1,110,554	216,932	302,462	12,308	9,686	1,651,942
Furniture, fixtures, office and store machinery and equipment	954,988	371,604	365,675	159	-	1,692,426
Transportation vehicles and equipment	470,106	139,009	58,775	3,398	-	671,288
Production machinery and equipment	517,366	146,076	198,922	13,285	1,965	877,614
Finance, Insurance, and Real Estate						
All asset types	6,278,678	3,321,675	749,335	9,090	1,457	10,360,235
Structures and leasehold improvements	5,186,918	2,948,004	593,878	8,155	-	8,736,955
Furniture, fixtures, office and store machinery and equipment	532,423	149,658	80,910	86	-	763,077
Transportation vehicles and equipment	139,743	40,852	6,675	250	-	187,520
Production machinery and equipment	353,803	164,319	61,323	558	1,457	581,460

(continued)

TABLE A-12 *(continued)*

Industry Division and Type of Asset	Straight -Line	Declining -Balance	Sum-of-the- Years-Digits	Other-Life Methods	Units-of- Production	Total
Services						
All asset types	1,652,357	898,764	262,390	719	20	2,814,250
Structures and leasehold improvements	657,031	313,879	97,139	616	-	1,068,665
Furniture, fixtures, office and store machinery and equipment	252,003	67,593	43,012	-	-	362,608
Transportation vehicles and equipment	270,127	169,429	34,593	2	-	474,151
Production machinery and equipment	440,045	343,214	86,226	101	20	869,606
Percentage Distribution						
All Industries						
All asset types	44.4	31.4	21.5	1.5	1.2	100.0
Structures and leasehold improvements	44.4	33.4	20.0	1.6	0.6	100.0
Furniture, fixtures, office and store machinery and equipment	51.4	19.5	29.0	0.1	0.1	100.0
Transportation vehicles and equipment	47.0	35.7	15.0	2.1	0.2	100.0
Production machinery and equipment	42.8	29.3	24.1	1.5	2.3	100.0

(continued)

TABLE A-12 (continued)

Industry Division and Type of Asset	Straight-Line	Declining-Balance	Sum-of-the-Years-Digits	Other-Life Methods	Units-of-Production	Total
Agriculture, Forestry, and Fisheries						
All asset types	82.8	15.6	1.5	0.1	-	100.0
Structures and leasehold improvements	84.7	14.3	1.0	-	-	100.0
Furniture, fixtures, office and store machinery and equipment	82.1	11.8	6.1	-	-	100.0
Transportation vehicles and equipment	75.6	21.3	2.6	0.6	-	100.0
Production machinery and equipment	80.6	17.3	2.1	-	-	100.0
Livestock, orchards, and vineyards	89.9	10.1	a	-	-	100.0
Mining						
All asset types	54.5	17.1	2.1	8.6	17.8	100.0
Structures and leasehold improvements	64.2	12.9	2.3	6.5	14.1	100.0
Furniture, fixtures, office and store machinery and equipment	72.7	13.4	1.3	-	12.7	100.0
Transportation vehicles and equipment	68.0	24.3	3.8	0.4	3.4	100.0
Production machinery and equipment	44.6	18.4	1.3	12.1	23.7	100.0

(continued)

TABLE A-12 *(continued)*

Industry Division and Type of Asset	Straight-Line	Declining-Balance	Sum-of-the-Years-Digits	Other-Life Methods	Units-of-Production	Total
Construction						
All asset types	62.4	31.9	5.6	a	-	100.0
Structures and leasehold improvements	63.6	34.7	1.7	-	-	100.0
Furniture, fixtures, office and store machinery and equipment	77.7	19.4	3.0	-	-	100.0
Transportation vehicles and equipment	70.5	25.4	4.0	a	-	100.0
Production machinery and equipment	56.5	35.9	7.6	a	-	100.0
Manufacturing						
All asset types	31.4	32.2	33.7	1.1	1.7	100.0
Structures and leasehold improvements	34.0	29.4	34.0	1.6	0.9	100.0
Furniture, fixtures, office and store machinery and equipment	34.0	18.2	47.8	0.1	-	100.0
Transportation vehicles and equipment	45.0	37.3	17.0	0.2	0.5	100.0
Production machinery and equipment	28.4	34.2	34.1	0.9	2.4	100.0

(continued)

TABLE A-12 *(continued)*

Industry Division and Type of Asset	Straight-Line	Declining-Balance	Sum-of-the-Years-Digits	Other-Life Methods	Units-of-Production	Total
Transportation, Communication, Electric, Gas, and Sanitary Services						
All asset types	49.4	33.0	15.2	2.2	0.2	100.0
Structures and leasehold improvements	40.6	38.5	18.7	2.1	0.1	100.0
Furniture, fixtures, office and store machinery and equipment	79.1	16.3	4.2	0.4	a	100.0
Transportation vehicles and equipment	40.1	38.9	17.5	3.5	0.1	100.0
Production machinery and equipment	68.9	20.3	8.4	2.0	0.5	100.0
Trade						
All asset types	62.4	17.8	19.0	0.6	0.2	100.0
Structures and leasehold improvements	67.2	13.1	18.3	0.7	0.6	100.0
Furniture, fixtures, office and store machinery and equipment	56.4	22.0	21.6	a	–	100.0
Transportation vehicles and equipment	70.0	20.7	8.8	0.5	–	100.0
Production machinery and equipment	59.0	16.6	22.7	1.5	0.2	100.0

(continued)

TABLE A-12 (concluded)

Industry Division and Type of Asset	Straight-Line	Declining-Balance	Sum-of-the-Years-Digits	Other-Life Methods	Units-of-Production	Total
Finance, Insurance, and Real Estate						
All asset types	60.6	32.1	7.2	0.1	a	100.0
Structures and leasehold improvements	59.4	33.7	6.8	0.1	–	100.0
Furniture, fixtures, office and store machinery and equipment	69.8	19.6	10.6	a	–	100.0
Transportation vehicles and equipment	74.5	21.8	3.6	0.1	–	100.0
Production machinery and equipment	60.9	28.3	10.6	0.1	0.3	100.0
Services						
All asset types	58.7	31.9	9.3	a	a	100.0
Structures and leasehold improvements	61.5	29.4	9.1	0.1	–	100.0
Furniture, fixtures, office and store machinery and equipment	69.5	18.6	11.9	–	–	100.0
Transportation vehicles and equipment	57.0	35.7	7.3	a	–	100.0
Production machinery and equipment	50.6	39.5	9.9	a	a	100.0

Source: Internal Revenue Service, "Life of Depreciable Assets" source book.

aLess than 0.05 per cent.

Note: Column totals in each industrial division include small amounts of livestock, orchards, and vineyards and of intangible and unidentified property not shown separately, except in the case of the agriculture division which does show livestock, orchards, and vineyards. The column totals for all industries include the totals for such property and for the small amounts of each property type of companies not allocable to an industrial division and not shown separately. Row items may not add to totals because of rounding.

APPENDIX B

DATA CHARACTERISTICS

In this survey, we have relied upon data produced in various forms by the Statistics Division of the Internal Revenue Service, primarily in connection with or as adjuncts to its *Statistics of Income* publications. All of the data, therefore, are of a character that would appear on federal income tax returns or supporting schedules. They may differ from those derived from other sources, since the measures of some items of income and expense required or permitted for tax purposes often differ from those the taxpayer would use for nontax accounting purposes. Chief among these items is depreciation. Since our purpose in this survey has been to examine the response of the business community to a change in the tax law governing depreciation, we have focused our attention on data taken from tax returns in order to measure that response.

In the following pages is a description of some of the principal characteristics of the data used in this study.

Number of Businesses Using the Various Depreciation Methods and Amounts of Depreciation Under Each Method

CORPORATIONS

Data on the number of corporation returns on which the various depreciation methods appear and the respective amounts of depreciation are available for each of the taxable years 1954 through 1960. For the years 1954, 1955, 1957, and 1960, the data are derived from large samples of corporation returns, while for the years 1956, 1958, and 1959, they were obtained from small samples of very large corporations. Table B-1 compares the coverage of the large samples for 1954, 1955, 1957, and 1960 with the corresponding *Statistics of Income* estimates.

The sample drawn for the depreciation survey for the taxable year

TABLE B-1

Coverage of Depreciation Survey Samples of Corporation Returns Compared with Statistics of Income *Estimates*

Taxable Year	Special Depreciation Survey[a]	Statistics of Income Estimate
	(amounts in million dollars)	
1954		
Number of returns	414,256	722,805
Amount of depreciation	7,044	11,500
1955		
Number of returns	493,808	807,303
Amount of depreciation	9,582	13,419
1957		
Number of returns	780,734	940,147
Amount of depreciation	17,094	16,968
1960		
Number of returns	816,417	1,140,574[c]
Amount of depreciation	19,293	22,160

Source: Internal Revenue Service; *Statistics of Income, 1959, Supplementary Depreciation Data from Corporation Income Tax Returns* for taxable years 1954 and 1955. For taxable years 1957 and 1960, special tabulations. For all years, *Statistics of Income, Corporation Income Tax Returns,* various years.

[a]Returns showing depreciation methods.

[b]All active corporation returns.

[c]Includes 90,221 Form 1120-S returns of small business corporations electing to be treated as partnerships.

1954 was, as the table clearly indicates, substantially smaller than that upon which *Statistics of Income* for that year was based. Excluded from the depreciation survey sample were returns for life and mutual insurance companies and returns for corporations which did not complete that part of the depreciation schedule showing amounts of depreciation by method. The former exclusion reduced this sample's estimate of the composite return population by only 11,391 returns. The latter constraint accounts for the vast bulk of the difference between the population estimates of the two samples. Since so large a proportion of the *Statistics of Income* sample was not included in the depreciation survey sample for 1954, it should be assumed that the sampling variability of the latter was very high. Essentially the same constraints applied to the depreciation survey sample for the taxable year 1955.

For the taxable year 1957, a much more thorough survey was undertaken. The depreciation survey sample was essentially identical with the sample for *Statistics of Income* for that year. However, the returns in the depreciation survey sample with incomplete depreciation schedules were subsampled and the depreciation schedules of these returns were completed. As a consequence, the depreciation survey produces a slightly larger estimate of the amount of depreciation than is shown in *Statistics of Income* for that year in the main body of tables.[1] The *Statistics of Income* column of Table B-1 shows the total number of returns of active corporations filed in each year and includes returns reporting no depreciation. For 1957, the number of returns with depreciation, as reported in *Statistics of Income,* is 780,734—the same as derived from the depreciation survey sample. For the characteristics of this *Statistics of Income* sample—hence of the depreciation survey sample—see *Statistics of Income, 1957–58, Corporation Income Tax Returns,* pp. 14–15. Relative sampling errors at the 95 per cent level for the depreciation estimates are quite small.

The 1960 depreciation survey sample was somewhat smaller than the *Statistics of Income* sample for that year but is essentially the same in character, accounting for roughly seven-eighths of the *Statistics of Income* estimated amount of depreciation (see *Statistics of Income, 1960–61, Corporation Income Tax Returns,* pp. 12–17). Sampling errors in the depreciation survey sample are deemed to be slightly greater than those indicated for the *Statistics of Income* sample, but nevertheless quite small.

For the taxable years 1956, 1958, and 1959, small samples of very large corporations were drawn to illustrate depreciation patterns among that part of the corporate population which accounted for a substantial proportion of total corporate depreciation allowances. From the *Statistics of Income* samples for the respective years, a selection was made of returns showing total assets of $50 million or more (some real estate

---

[1] A special section of *Statistics of Income, 1957–58, Corporation Income Tax Returns,* presents (p. 115) a brief summary table from the depreciation survey and reports the magnitudes found in that survey.

firms with total assets of $10 million or more were included). The depreciation claimed by these firms were 47.0 per cent, 47.7 per cent, and 47.9 per cent of the total amount of depreciation for the respective years. The number of sampled firms was virtually the same as the total number of firms in the respective populations with total assets of the indicated amounts.

Tables 4 through 10, 15, 16, A-1, and A-4 are based on these depreciation surveys.

UNINCORPORATED BUSINESSES

Data for sole proprietorships and partnerships are limited to the single taxable year 1959, and appear in *Statistics of Income, 1959–60, U.S. Business Tax Returns*.

For sole proprietorships, data were derived from a stratified sample consisting of 141,406 individual income tax returns (Forms 1040) with Schedules C or F, used for reporting income from a business or profession and from farming, respectively. These returns represent slightly more than 1 per cent of the total number of individual returns with such schedules. The sampling rate for returns with Schedules C and F and with various amounts of adjusted gross income is shown in the following table:

Adjusted Gross Income (dollars)	*Sample Rate*
Under 10,000	1/126
10,000 under 50,000	1/34
50,000 under 150,000	1/2
150,000 and over	1/1

A number of adjustments in sample selection were made which had the effect of reducing the number of sole proprietorships represented by the sample from 10,135,293 to 9,142,359. As a result, the basic data file from which our information about depreciation practices of sole proprietorships in 1959 is drawn represents about 90 per cent of the estimated population of such firms in that year.

For partnerships, the data were derived from the information returns, Forms 1065. Although only one such form is required per partnership, duplicate returns are sometimes filed. Elimination of this duplication reduced the estimated number of Forms 1065 filed in 1959 from about one million to 961,247. From these returns, a stratified sample of 76,528 was drawn at the following sample rates:

Business Receipts or Income (dollars)	Sample Rate
Under 200,000	1/19.77
200,000 under 500,000	1/5.25
500,000 under 5,000,000	1/1
5,000,000 or more	1/1

Sampling variability at the 95 per cent level for various frequencies, including numbers of businesses by industrial group, and numbers of businesses with depreciation, by industrial group, is shown in *Statistics of Income, 1959–60, U.S. Business Tax Returns,* pp. 127–135.

From these surveys, we obtained information about the number of sole proprietorships and partnerships using various depreciation methods, as well as the amounts of depreciation under each method in each business receipts size class and in each major industrial division. In the case of partnerships, the same sample also provides information about the number of firms reporting the amount of assets under each depreciation method and the cost of such assets by method. The sampling variability for both of these observations is only slightly higher than for the estimated frequencies of returns showing each method and the amount of depreciation under each method, since the difference between the two population estimates is, in total, less than 2 per cent.

The tables in our study based on these data are Tables 11–14, 17–24, and Tables A-2, A-3, A-5, A-6, A-7.

Cost of Corporations' Depreciable Facilities by Method of Depreciation

Our data concerning the amount of corporations' depreciable property under each depreciation method were derived in large part from the estimates contained in the "Life of Depreciable Assets" survey,[2] part of the source book for *Statistics of Income* for 1959. This survey is also the source of our estimates of the additional depreciation generated by

[2] Our procedures for adjusting the *Statistics of Income* data to incorporate the relationships in the LDA survey are described in Appendix D, below.

TABLE B-2

Comparison of Statistics of Income *Sample and LDA Sample*

Sample Class[a]	Number of Returns Filed	Statistics of Income		LDA	
		Number of Returns	Per Cent of Returns Filed	Number of Returns	Per Cent of Returns Filed
Total, all returns	1,119,700	162,953	14.55	55,248	4.93
Forms 1120,					
1120L, 1120M	1,048,271	154,577	14.75	51,418	4.91
A	11,054	11,054	100.00	3,128	28.30
B	75,961	75,961	100.00	15,693	20.66
C	367,788	36,898	10.03	14,749	4.01
D	546,032	26,028	4.77	16,456	3.01
E	32,702	1,806	5.52	1,392	4.26
F	14,734	2,830	19.21	-	-
Forms 1120S	71,429	8,376	11.73	3,830	5.36
G	8	8	100.00	-	-
H	1,736	1,736	100.00	378	21.77
I	69,685	6,632	9.52	3,452	4.95

[a]*Class A* comprises returns with net income or deficit of $1 million or more, or total assets of $10 million or more. *Class B* comprises special types of returns not included in class A: consolidated returns, returns with personal holding company schedules, life and mutual insurance companies, returns of unincorporated businesses electing to be taxed as corporations, returns with overpayment of tax, other returns with net income or deficit less than $1 million and total assets of $1 million less than $10 million. *Class C* includes returns, other than those in class B, with total assets of $100,000 and under $1 million. *Class D* are returns other than those under class B with assets greater than zero but less than $100,000. *Class E* are active corporation returns not included in class B with zero assets or assets not reported. *Class F* consists of inactive corporations with zero assets or assets not reported. *Class G* are returns of corporations electing to be taxed as partnerships with net income or deficit of $1 million or more, or total assets of $10 million or more. *Class H* are returns of corporations taxed as partnerships with income or deficit under $1 million, and total assets of $1 million but less than $10 million. *Class I* comprises returns of corporations electing to be taxed as partnerships with total assets not reported or less than $1 million.

the use of accelerated methods in lieu of straight-line and of the tax savings resulting therefrom in the taxable year 1959.

The estimates in the LDA survey were based on data from depreciation schedules of 55,248 of the 162,953 corporate returns in the *Statistics of Income* sample. The relationship between the regular *Statistics of Income* sample and the LDA survey sample is shown in Table B-2.

Columns 4 and 5 of Table B-2 reflect a number of limitations in the LDA sample. The extensively detailed information in the depreciation schedules dictated a reduction in sample size in order to keep the data abstraction and processing workload within manageable proportions. At the outset, therefore, the normal sampling rate was reduced by half for returns with total assets of between $1 million and $10 million, except for such returns with net income or deficit of $1 million or more for which the *Statistics of Income* one-for-one rate was initially maintained. A similarly reduced sampling rate was applied to the rest of sample class B, and during the course of processing, efforts to abstract data from life and mutual insurance companies were discontinued. Subsequently, sampling ratios throughout the sample were successively reduced.

It was anticipated that the sample would include returns on which the depreciation schedules would be incomplete or would otherwise be in such a form as to call for a follow up to obtain the desired information. Although it was planned to take a subsample of such returns, the follow up was in fact restricted to the returns showing total assets of $50 million or more.

By virtue of these and other limitations, the LDA sample ultimately afforded the basis for estimates with respect to 556,750 active corporate returns, compared with a population estimate of 1,074,120 active corporations derived from the regular *Statistics of Income* sample. The amount of property in depreciation schedules in the LDA survey, adjusted to put all such amounts on a gross-of-salvage basis [3] is about 69.6 per cent of the estimated amount derived from *Statistics of Income*. The LDA-based estimate of total depreciation allowances in 1959 is roughly 58.0 per cent of that in *Statistics of Income*. As Tables B-3 through B-6 show, however, the relationship of LDA-based estimates to *Statistics of*

---

[3] See Appendix D for the occasion for and the procedures followed in making this adjustment.

Income estimates varies widely from size class to size class and industry to industry. In view of these disparities, it was evident that the LDA could not be relied upon for distributions of amount of assets or depreciation allowances among major industry divisions or among the three size-of-total-asset classes which were set up. On the other hand, we have no basis for assuming that the LDA distributions of assets and depreciation by method *within* any size class in any major industrial division were not adequately representative of the corresponding distributions in *Statistics of Income*.

The tables in this volume based on the LDA survey are Tables 25 through 42, Tables A-8 through A-12, C-1 through C-4 and D-1 through D-9.

TABLE B-3

Percentage Distribution of Cost of Corporations' Depreciable Facilities,

by Size of Total Assets in Each Industry Division, 1959:

"Life of Depreciable Assets" Survey and Statistics of Income

Size of Total Assets (million dollars)	All Facilities on Hand in 1959			Facilities Acquired Since 1953	
	LDA Survey[a]	*Statistics of Income*		LDA Survey[a]	*Statistics of Income*
		Balance Sheets[b]	Depreciation Schedules[c]		Depreciation Schedules[c]
All Industrial Divisions					
Under 1	8.7	14.7	17.0	13.2	24.2
1-25	3.3	16.3	16.2	4.6	19.9
25 and over	88.0	68.9	66.8	82.2	55.8
Agriculture, Forestry, and Fisheries					
Under 1	49.9	55.3	61.9	72.1	75.3
1-25	6.3	24.4	20.3	6.4	17.3
25 and over	43.8	20.3	17.8	21.6	7.4
Mining					
Under 1	6.2	12.2	14.4	9.7	19.1
1-25	3.1	28.5	28.1	4.6	35.1
25 and over	90.7	59.3	57.5	85.7	45.8
Construction					
Under 1	69.1	55.4	57.8	74.2	60.9
1-25	12.8	37.4	32.5	13.0	32.4
25 and over	18.2	7.2	9.7	12.9	6.8
Manufacturing					
Under 1	2.7	8.0	9.5	4.3	14.0
1-25	1.9	17.1	17.2	2.1	18.6
25 and over	95.5	74.9	73.4	93.6	65.4

(continued)

TABLE B-3 *(concluded)*

Size of Total Assets (million dollars)	All Facilities on Hand in 1959			Facilities Acquired Since 1953	
	Statistics of Income			*Statistics of Income*	
	LDA Survey[a]	Balance Sheets[b]	Depreciation Schedules[c]	LDA Survey[a]	Depreciation Schedules[c]
Transportation, Communication, Electric, Gas, and Sanitary Services					
Under 1	0.9	2.9	3.4	1.9	6.8
1-25	0.5	6.0	5.7	1.0	9.9
25 and over	98.6	91.1	90.9	97.1	83.2
Trade					
Under 1	35.6	47.7	48.8	45.0	56.5
1-25	5.0	25.6	22.4	5.2	21.4
25 and over	59.5	26.7	28.9	49.8	22.1
Finance, Insurance, and Real Estate					
Under 1	54.7	46.9	51.4	55.6	50.7
1-25	21.7	33.8	33.6	24.8	37.2
25 and over	23.7	19.3	15.0	19.6	12.1
Services					
Under 1	56.5	55.4	55.9	60.1	59.6
1-25	15.1	32.4	31.9	13.8	29.2
25 and over	28.4	12.3	12.2	26.1	11.2
Not Allocable					
Under 1	89.2	70.2	91.1	87.8	90.0
1-25	10.8	29.8	8.9	12.2	10.0
25 and over	-	-	-	-	-

Source: Internal Revenue Service, "Life of Depreciable Assets" source book, and Appendix, Tables D-1, D-3, and D-4.

Note: Detail may not add to 100.0 due to rounding.

[a]Amounts under straight-line and sum-of-years–digits methods have been grossed up for salvage, assuming salvage value is 15 per cent of an asset's cost. See Appendix D.

[b]Distribution of amounts reported in balance-sheet schedules of corporations' income tax returns, as published in *Statistics of Income*.

[c]Distribution of *Statistics of Income* data adjusted to a depreciation schedule rather than balance-sheet basis. See Appendix D.

TABLE B-4

Percentage Distribution of Cost of Corporations' Depreciable Facilities, by Industry Division in Each Size-of-Total-Assets Class, 1959: "Life of Depreciable Assets" Survey and Statistics of Income

Industry Division	All Facilities on Hand in 1959			Facilities Acquired Since 1953	
	LDA Survey[a]	Statistics of Income		LDA Survey[a]	Statistics of Income
		Balance Sheets[b]	Depreciation Schedules[c]		Depreciation Schedules[c]
All Asset Size-Classes					
Agriculture, forestry, and fisheries	0.3	0.5	0.6	0.4	0.7
Mining	2.0	3.0	2.7	2.4	3.5
Construction	0.5	1.2	1.3	0.9	2.3
Manufacturing	40.4	40.1	39.9	40.9	38.5
Transportation, communication, electric, gas, and sanitary services	43.6	36.4	35.0	37.6	29.0
Trade	3.6	5.9	6.7	4.9	9.0
Finance, insurance, and real estate	8.0	9.6	9.9	10.1	11.5
Services	1.7	3.3	3.7	2.8	5.5
Not allocable[d]					
Under $1,000,000					
Agriculture, forestry, and fisheries	1.8	2.0	2.1	2.0	2.3
Mining	1.4	2.5	2.3	1.8	2.8
Construction	3.8	4.6	4.5	5.2	5.8
Manufacturing	12.5	21.7	22.2	13.2	22.3

(continued)

TABLE B-4 *(continued)*

Industry Division	All Facilities on Hand in 1959			Facilities Acquired Since 1953	
	LDA Survey[a]	*Statistics of Income*		LDA Survey[a]	*Statistics of Income*
		Balance Sheets[b]	Depreciation Schedules[c]		Depreciation Schedules[c]
Under $1,000,000					
Transportation, communication, electric, gas, and sanitary services	4.5	7.2	7.0	5.5	8.2
Trade	14.7	19.1	19.3	16.9	21.0
Finance, insurance, and real estate	50.5	30.5	30.1	42.7	24.0
Services	10.7	12.2	12.3	12.5	13.6
Not allocable	0.1	0.2	0.1	0.2	0.1
$1,000,000 Under $25,000,000					
Agriculture, forestry, and fisheries	0.6	0.8	0.7	0.5	0.6
Mining	1.9	5.3	4.7	2.4	6.1
Construction	1.9	2.8	2.7	2.6	3.8
Manufacturing	22.8	42.0	42.3	18.8	35.8
Transportation, communication, electric, gas, and sanitary services	6.8	13.4	12.2	7.9	14.4
Trade	5.4	9.3	9.3	5.5	9.7
Finance, insurance, and real estate	53.0	19.9	20.6	54.0	21.5
Services	7.6	6.5	7.4	8.2	8.1
Not allocable	d	0.1	d	0.1	d

(continued)

TABLE B-4 *(concluded)*

Industry Division	All Facilities on Hand in 1959			Facilities Acquired Since 1953	
		Statistics of Income			*Statistics of Income*
	LDA Survey[a]	Balance Sheets[b]	Depreciation Schedules[c]	LDA Survey[a]	Depreciation Schedules[c]
	$25,000,000 and Over				
Agriculture, forestry, and fisheries	0.2	0.2	0.2	0.1	0.1
Mining	2.1	2.6	2.4	2.5	2.9
Construction	0.1	0.1	0.2	0.1	0.3
Manufacturing	43.8	43.5	43.8	46.6	44.4
Transportation, communication, electric, gas, and sanitary services	48.8	48.0	47.7	44.4	43.2
Trade	2.4	2.3	2.9	3.0	3.6
Finance, insurance, and real estate	2.2	2.7	2.2	2.4	2.5
Services	0.5	0.6	0.7	0.9	1.1
Not allocable	-	-	-	-	-

For source and notes a through c, see Table B-3.

[d] Less than 0.05 per cent.

TABLE B-5

Percentage Distribution of Corporations' Depreciation Allowances,
by Size of Total Assets in Each Industry Division, 1959:
"Life of Depreciable Assets" Survey and Statistics of Income

Size of Total Assets (million dollars)	All Facilities on Hand in 1959		Facilities Acquired after 1959	
	LDA	Statistics of Income	LDA	Statistics of Income
All Industry Divisions				
Under 1	12.2	23.5	16.5	29.5
1 - 25	3.7	20.3	4.6	22.6
25 and over	84.1	56.2	78.9	47.9
Agriculture, Forestry, and Fisheries				
Under 1	58.9	64.0	70.9	70.4
1 - 25	7.1	22.6	7.1	21.6
25 and over	33.9	13.4	22.0	8.1
Mining				
Under 1	12.9	22.4	17.9	26.5
1 - 25	5.9	36.0	7.6	40.7
25 and over	81.2	41.5	74.4	32.8
Construction				
Under 1	73.4	59.3	75.4	60.2
1 - 25	13.6	35.6	13.9	35.6
25 and over	13.0	5.2	10.7	4.3
Manufacturing				
Under 1	4.0	12.3	5.4	15.9
1 - 25	2.1	19.2	2.3	20.0
25 and over	93.9	68.5	92.3	64.2

(continued)

TABLE B-5 *(concluded)*

Size of Total Assets (million dollars)	All Facilities on Hand in 1959		Facilities Acquired after 1959	
	LDA	*Statistics of Income*	LDA	*Statistics of Income*
Transportation, Communication, Electric, Gas, and Sanitary Services				
Under 1	2.9	8.8	5.2	14.2
1 - 25	1.0	10.8	1.6	15.7
25 and over	96.1	80.4	93.3	70.2
Trade				
Under 1	45.3	54.8	52.9	59.1
1 - 25	5.1	24.0	5.2	23.5
25 and over	49.6	21.2	43.1	17.4
Finance, Insurance, and Real Estate				
Under 1	53.8	45.7	54.1	45.8
1 - 25	20.8	30.0	22.5	32.1
25 and over	25.4	24.3	23.4	22.2
Services				
Under 1	60.4	59.6	61.8	61.6
1 - 25	13.0	29.4	12.1	27.6
25 and over	26.6	11.0	26.0	10.8
Not Allocable				
Under 1	100.0	66.7	90.2	80.0
1 - 25	-	22.2	9.8	20.0
25 and over	-	11.1	-	-

Source: Internal Revenue Service, "Life of Depreciable Assets" source book.

Note: Details may not add to 100.0 due to rounding.

TABLE B-6

Percentage Distribution of Corporations' Depreciation Allowances, by Industry Division in Each Size-of-Total-Assets Class: "Life of Depreciable Assets" Survey and Statistics of Income

Industry Division	All Facilities on Hand in 1959		Facilities Acquired after 1959	
	LDA	Statistics of Income	LDA	Statistics of Income
All Asset Size-Classes				
Agriculture, forestry, and fisheries	0.5	0.8	0.6	0.9
Mining	2.4	3.4	2.6	3.9
Construction	1.3	2.9	2.0	4.1
Manufacturing	49.6	45.0	50.0	43.1
Transportation, communication, electric, gas, and sanitary services	31.4	23.5	26.6	20.0
Trade	5.4	9.6	6.8	11.6
Finance, insurance, and real estate	6.4	8.6	7.0	8.6
Services	3.0	6.2	4.4	7.9
Not allocable	a	a	a	0.1
Under $1,000,000				
Agriculture, forestry, and fisheries	2.3	2.2	2.4	2.2
Mining	2.6	3.2	2.9	3.5
Construction	7.8	7.4	9.0	8.4
Manufacturing	16.3	23.5	16.4	23.2
Transportation, communication, electric, gas, and sanitary services	7.4	8.8	8.3	9.6
Trade	20.2	22.4	21.4	23.2
Finance, insurance, and real estate	28.1	16.7	23.1	13.4
Services	15.1	15.6	16.3	16.5
Not allocable	0.2	0.1	0.2	0.1

(continued)

TABLE B-6 *(concluded)*

Industry Division	All Facilities on Hand in 1959		Facilities Acquired after 1959	
	LDA	*Statistics of Income*	LDA	*Statistics of Income*
$1,000,000 Under $25,000,000				
Agriculture, forestry, and fisheries	0.9	0.9	0.9	0.9
Mining	3.8	6.0	4.4	7.0
Construction	4.8	5.2	6.0	6.4
Manufacturing	28.1	42.5	25.1	38.0
Transportation, communication, electric,				
gas, and sanitary services	8.3	12.4	9.2	13.8
Trade	7.4	11.4	7.8	12.0
Finance, insurance, and real estate	36.0	12.7	34.8	12.2
Services	10.8	8.9	11.6	9.6
Not allocable	0.1	a	0.1	a
$25,000,000 and Over				
Agriculture, forestry, and fisheries	0.2	0.2	0.2	0.2
Mining	2.3	2.5	2.5	2.7
Construction	0.2	0.3	0.3	0.4
Manufacturing	55.3	54.9	58.4	57.7
Transportation, communication, electric,				
gas, and sanitary services	35.9	33.6	31.4	29.2
Trade	3.2	3.6	3.7	4.2
Finance, insurance, and real estate	1.9	3.7	2.1	4.0
Services	1.0	1.2	1.4	1.8
Not allocable	-	-	-	-

Source: Internal Revenue Service, "Life of Depreciable Assets" source book.
Note: Details may not add to 100.0 due to rounding.

[a]Less than 0.05 per cent.

APPENDIX C

SERVICE LIVES OF CORPORATIONS' DEPRECIABLE PROPERTY, 1959

The "Life of Depreciable Assets" study provides a substantial amount of detailed information about the service lives assigned by taxpayers to depreciable assets for purposes of computing depreciation allowances on corporate income tax returns.[1] In fact, two measures of average service life are afforded by these data. One is the weighted arithmetic mean life, derived for any given category (asset size class, industrial division, and so forth) by multiplying the reported service life of each entry in the category by the cost of each entry, summing these products, and dividing by the sum of the costs. The second measure is a harmonic mean service life, computed by dividing the sum of the costs of the entries in a given category by the sum of the quotients of the costs divided by reported lives.[2] The differences between these measures may be substantial.

At first glance, the weighted arithmetic mean may appear to be the superior measure. For example, suppose a group depreciable asset account contains two facilities, each costing $100, one of which has an assumed service life of ten years and the other of twenty years. The average life of the account appears to be fifteen years. But the annual straight-line depreciation with a fifteen-year service life is $6.67 per

---

[1] Service lives for tax purposes may or may not coincide with the actual numbers of years that the properties are retained by the taxpayers. The LDA study affords data on year of purchase by service life, on the basis of which average age may be estimated and compared with service life, only for property acquired after 1953. These data are of little use in making the comparison because of the very few years of purchase, 1954–1959, included.

[2] The weighted arithmetic mean is $\dfrac{\Sigma(C_i \times L_i)}{\Sigma C_i}$, and the harmonic mean is $\dfrac{\Sigma C_i}{\Sigma(C_i/L_i)}$, where C = cost, L = life (in years), and i = the ith entry.

$100.00 of depreciable basis, and over twenty years these annual allowances would aggregate to only $266.67, which would be $33.33 less than the total investment in the account during that period. An annual allowance of $7.50 per $100 depreciable basis is required, which is generated by using a service life of thirteen and one-third years, the harmonic mean life of the account. If the average service life is desired for analyses concerned with the amount of depreciation generated by facilities in group or composite accounts, the harmonic mean life is the superior measure. In fact, a substantial proportion of depreciable assets are in such accounts. We have, therefore, relied primarily on the harmonic mean service life in our analysis. In the following discussion, references to service life are to the harmonic mean, unless otherwise stated.

The average service life of all depreciable property on hand in the taxable year 1959 (as covered in the LDA survey) was 18.5 years. Not surprisingly, a shorter average life—14.7 years—is found for all property on hand in 1959 acquired after 1953.[3]

With respect to the latter facilities, little difference is revealed in the average service life of properties under the straight-line, declining-balance, and SYD methods, although the average service life of the small amount of property under "other" life methods is somewhat higher (Table C-1). The average service life increases with size of total assets, and the difference in each case between companies with total assets less than $1,000,000 and those with assets of $25,000,000 and over is quite substantial (Table C-1).

Substantial differences are also shown in Table C-2 in the average service lives from one industry to another, ranging from a low of 5.3 years in construction to 19.6 years in public utilities. Cross classified with size of total assets, the regular variation of average service life and company size seen in Table C-1 is less observable. In the finance, insurance, and real estate division, the mean service life is lowest in the largest size class, while in the agriculture and construction divisions, the lowest mean life is found among the middle-size companies.

A wide range in mean service lives is also found when the data are

---

[3] On the assumption of a positive correlation between service life and average age of property at retirement, the older the property, the likelier it is to have an older mean service life.

distributed by major asset type, as in Table C-3. For livestock, orchards, and vineyards, the mean life is 6.5 years while for structures and lease-hold improvements a mean life of 22.7 years is found. Here, too, a strong positive association between company size and service life is observable, with the exception of facilities classified as "intangibles" and "not identifiable."

It seems reasonable to suppose that asset type is the principal deter-minant of average service life and that differences in the asset type composition of depreciable facilities accounts chiefly explain differences in average service lives among size classes and industrial divisions. The fact, as shown in Table C-3, that smaller companies had shorter service lives than larger companies for each major type of property appears to challenge this supposition. A distribution by much more detailed asset types shows still more clearly that smaller companies used shorter serv-ice lives than larger companies. Of the 242 asset type classes, only 31 showed shorter service lives for the largest than for the smallest companies.[4] Not all differences from one size class to another in the composition of depreciable facilities are eliminated by this more de-tailed property classification, of course, but such differences must be greatly reduced in frequency. On the other hand, the shorter service lives of the property held by small companies may be accounted for by the fact that a relatively larger amount of this property was secondhand than in the case of bigger concerns and the service life assigned to secondhand facilities is the estimated remaining life. On the whole, how-ever, it appears that the differences in service lives are to be attributed primarily to differences in taxpayers' practices rather than to differences in property characteristics.

In July 1962, the Treasury Department issued Revenue Procedure 62-21, which provides guidelines for service lives of broad classes of depreciable facilities. These guideline lives were, in general, materially less than those set forth in Bulletin "F," which was superseded by the Revenue Procedure. They were also thought to be moderately lower than the service lives widely in use. For all manufacturing corporation facilities, for example, a composite Bulletin "F" life was nineteen years; in the Revenue Procedure, the composite guideline life was thirteen

[4] The distribution is provided in Table Set I of the "Life of Depreciable Assets" source book.

years; the LDA harmonic mean life was fifteen years; and the composite life in actual practice was estimated at about fifteen years.[5]

Bulletin "F" lives are longer than the corresponding lives in the guidelines, as measured by the LDA and as estimated by the Treasury in actual current practice (see Table C-4). The guideline lives, moreover, are in virtually all instances below the LDA and current practice estimates. Guideline lives were not so much intended to reflect average replacement practice as to reflect what was regarded as the replacement patterns of the more progressive companies in an industry subdivision. In combination with the reserve ratio test, these guideline lives are intended to offer inducements for reducing replacement cycles.[6]

It should be emphasized that none of these measures of service life is necessarily deemed to coincide with the actual periods of time, on the average, that the respective groups of assets are held by the taxpayers. These are measures of service lives for use in computing depreciation allowances for tax purposes. The Revenue Procedure 62-21 is intended to induce taxpayers to bring actual service lives in conformity with those assumed for tax purposes, but the guideline lives were not represented by the Treasury as accurate reflections of taxpayers' replacement policies.

[5] U.S. Treasury Department, Office of Tax Analysis, Release, July 10, 1962, and Internal Revenue Service, "Life of Depreciable Assets" source book. The last number appears to be a weighted arithmetic mean, derived in part from the Treasury Department's Depreciation Survey of 1959, in part from the LDA, and in part from industry sources. The Treasury Department survey was similar to the LDA in many important respects; indeed, the LDA relied extensively on these survey data for information which was not available on the tax returns of some of the LDA sample companies. The Treasury depreciation survey, however, was based very heavily on large companies; since these companies had longer service lives, on the average, than the smaller companies, part of the difference between the LDA service lives and those shown as "actual practice" in Table C-4 is undoubtedly attributable to the differing weights of small companies in the respective samples.

[6] See U.S. Treasury Department, Internal Revenue Service, *Depreciation Guidelines and Rules,* Publication No. 456 (7-62), July 1962, pp. 1, 2, 31 ff.

TABLE C-1

Average Service Lives of Corporations' Depreciable Facilities, by

Method of Depreciation and Size of Total Assets, 1959

Method of Depreciation	Size of Total Assets (million dollars)			
	Under 1	1 Under 25	25 and Over	Total
All Facilities on Hand in 1959				
Straight-line	11.4	14.7	21.7	19.6
Declining-balance	10.3	13.5	17.2	15.6
Sum-of-the-years-digits	9.9	14.3	15.6	15.2
Other-life methods	10.1	19.2	22.2	22.2
Total	11.1	14.3	20.0	18.5
Facilities Acquired Since 1953				
Straight-line	9.0	11.8	16.1	13.7
Declining-balance	9.8	12.3	17.2	15.4
Sum-of-the-years-digits	9.8	14.1	15.6	15.2
Other-life methods	10.1	14.9	18.5	18.5
Total	9.3	12.2	16.4	14.7

Source: U.S. Treasury Department, Internal Revenue Service, "Life of Depreciable Assets" source book.

TABLE C-2

Average Service Lives of Corporations' Depreciable Facilities Acquired
After 1953, by Industry Division and Size of Total Assets, 1959

Industry Division	Size of Total Assets (million dollars)			
	Under 1	1 Under 25	25 and Over	Total
Agriculture, forestry, and fisheries	7.2	7.0	8.3	7.4
Mining	5.4	6.4	13.3	10.9
Construction	5.1	4.7	7.3	5.3
Manufacturing	7.4	9.8	14.3	13.5
Transportation, communication, electric, gas, and sanitary services	6.0	9.4	20.8	19.6
Trade	7.0	7.6	12.2	8.9
Finance, insurance, and real estate	17.9	20.0	14.7	17.5
Services	7.5	7.7	8.4	7.8
Total[a]	9.3	12.2	16.4	14.7

Source: Internal Revenue Service, "Life of Depreciable Assets" source book.

[a]Includes facilities of companies not allocable to an industry division. not shown separately.

TABLE C-3

Average Service Lives of Corporations' Depreciable Facilities Acquired After 1953, by Major Asset Type and Size of Total Assets, 1959

Major Asset Type	Size of Total Assets (million dollars)			
	Under 1	1 Under 25	25 and Over	Total
Structures and leasehold improvements	18.2	21.3	23.8	22.7
Furniture, fixtures, office and store machinery and equipment	7.5	8.3	8.9	8.6
Transportation vehicles and equipment	4.2	5.6	9.1	7.1
Production machinery and equipment	6.9	8.2	14.9	13.5
Livestock, orchards, and vineyards	6.2	6.8	6.9	6.5
Not identifiable or intangible	10.3	9.2	13.9	13.2
Total	9.3	12.2	16.4	14.7

Source: Internal Revenue Service, "Life of Depreciable Assets" source book.

TABLE C-4

Service Lives of Depreciable Facilities in Manufacturing Subgroups

Manufacturing Subgroup	Bulletin "F" Composite (years)	Guideline Life	LDA Life[a]	Actual Current Practice[b]
Aerospace	15[c]	8	n.a.	10
Apparel and fabricated textile products	15-30[d]	9	10	15
Chemicals and allied products	15-22	11	14	13
Electrical equipment	17-20	8-12	12	15
Fabricated metal products	14-28	12	13	16
Food and kindred products	12-40	12-18	14	13-19
Lumber, wood products, and furniture	10-25	10	10	16
Machinery except electrical machinery, metalworking machinery, and transportation equipment	10-28	12 ⎫	12	15
Metalworking machinery	17-20	12 ⎭		16
Motor vehicles and parts	15-20[e]	12	13	14
Paper and allied products	15-28	12-16	17	19
Petroleum and natural gas	5-33[d]	6-16	12-17	16-19
Primary metals	17-30[d]	14-18	19	23
Printing and publishing	10-25	11	13	16
Professional, scientific, and controlling instruments, photographic and optical equipment	17-25	12	12	15
Railroad equipment	25-28	12	10	16
Rubber, leather, and plastic products	15-17[f]	11-14	13	15
Ship and boat building	20-25	12	n.a.	19
Stone, clay, and glass products	15-40[d]	14-20	17	19
Textile and mill products	15-25	9-15	17	17
Tobacco and tobacco products	15-20	15	17	17
Other manufacturing	n.a.	12	14	14
All manufacturing	19	13	15	15

Source: U.S. Treasury Department, Office of Tax Analysis, Release of July 10, 1962, and Internal Revenue Service, "Life of Depreciable Assets" source book.

[a]Harmonic means.

[b]Office of Tax Analysis estimates.

[c]Except small tools (4-5 years).

[d]Item lives only.

[e]Special jigs, dies, patterns, which have life of 3-4 years.

[f]Except the mold account (3 years).

APPENDIX D

ESTIMATES OF THE ADDITIONAL DEPRECIATION GENERATED BY ACCELERATED DEPRECIATION METHODS

We estimated the difference between the total amount of depreciation claimed by corporations on their federal income tax returns in 1959, as reported in *Statistics of Income,*[1] and the amount that would have been claimed had the straight-line method been used in lieu of declining-balance and SYD. To make this estimate, it was necessary to determine how much of the depreciable facilities shown in *Statistics of Income* was in accelerated method accounts, the amount of accelerated allowances on these properties, and the amount of straight-line allowances these properties would have generated. Unfortunately, *Statistics of Income* provides only total depreciation allowances for the taxable year 1959. To obtain estimates of the amounts of accelerated depreciation and of the properties generating these allowances, as well as the service lives of these facilities, we have had recourse to ratios derived from LDA data, relying on the assumption that the LDA distributions of property and allowances among depreciation methods, among service lives, and among years of purchase in any given size class and in any given industry were representative of the *Statistics of Income* corporate population. On the other hand, as noted in Appendix B, the LDA distributions of property among size classes and industries are clearly not representative of the *Statistics of Income* population and could not be used to estimate either the industry or size class distribution of the additional depreciation generated by use of accelerated methods.

The initial step is to estimate how much of the depreciable facilities

[1] U.S. Treasury Department, Internal Revenue Service, *Statistics of Income, 1959–60, Corporation Income Tax Returns,* p. 58.

in a given size class in a given industry, shown in *Statistics of Income,* was in declining-balance and SYD accounts in 1959. In essence, our procedure was to apply the LDA ratios of accelerated account properties to total properties in each size class of each industry to the corresponding amounts of property in *Statistics of Income.* A number of adjustments of both LDA and *Statistics of Income* magnitudes were required by this procedure.

The *Statistics of Income* data are abstracted from the balance sheets rather than the depreciation schedules of the income tax returns and therefore show the full cost or other basis of the facilities, whereas the amounts shown in the LDA were taken from depreciation schedules and, in the case of straight-line and SYD accounts, properties are net of salvage. To put the LDA data on a basis comparable to *Statistics of Income,* we "grossed up" the property amounts shown in LDA straight-line and SYD accounts by assuming that the average salvage value of such property was 15 per cent of cost, i.e., we assumed that the LDA magnitudes in these accounts were 85 per cent of the full cost or other basis to the taxpayer. The addition of these grossed up amounts to those shown in LDA in declining-balance and other-method accounts, gave us estimates of the total cost, before salvage, of facilities in each size class in each industrial division (Tables D-1 and D-3).

Because the *Statistics of Income* balance sheets include property which is fully depreciated or valued on a basis different from that used for income tax purposes, it was necessary to adjust these data. To make this adjustment, we derived, for each size class in each industrial division, ratios of the amounts of property taken from depreciation schedules in LDA and grossed up for salvage to the amounts taken from associated balance sheets in the LDA survey.[2] We applied these ratios to the *Statistics of Income* amounts in the corresponding size classes in each industrial division. The products we took to be the total amount of property in each size class in each industrial division, on an income tax depreciation schedule basis rather than balance sheet basis, before deducting estimated salvage in the case of straight-line and SYD properties. To these amounts, we applied the LDA ratios in each size class

---

[2] Table Set VIII in the "Life of Depreciable Assets" source book includes balance sheet data on the amount of depreciable property, by size of total assets and industrial division.

in each industrial division of (1) grossed up SYD amounts of property to grossed up total property and (2) declining-balance amounts of property to grossed up total property. We thus derived estimates of the amounts of property in each size class in each industrial division in the respective accelerated method accounts [3] (Tables D-2 and D-4).

The next step was to estimate the accelerated allowances these properties generated in 1959 and the straight-line depreciation they would have generated if accelerated methods had not been used. The difference between these amounts is the additional depreciation afforded by use of accelerated methods in 1959.

To calculate the amount of accelerated allowances, we distributed by method the depreciation allowances reported in *Statistics of Income* in each size class in each of the major industrial divisions. To effect this distribution, we applied to the amount of depreciation shown in *Statistics of Income* for each size class in each industrial division a ratio derived from the LDA data. The numerator of this ratio is the amount of depreciation on property acquired after 1953 under a given method in that size class in that industrial division; the denominator is the total amount of depreciation on all property on hand in 1959 in that size class in that industry. The products are the estimated amounts of corporate depreciation on property acquired after 1953 under each of the depreciation methods in each size class in each industrial division, the sum of which equals total depreciation allowances for the taxable year 1959 as shown in *Statistics of Income* (see Tables D-5 through D-8). As a rough check on these results, we can compare the amounts of depreciation under each method which we obtain for 1959 with the amounts shown in Table 15 for the taxable years 1957 and 1960.

---

[3] With respect to some of the property in accelerated method accounts in the LDA, the specific year of purchase is not shown. Some of this property, presumably, was acquired in 1959 (or in 1960, in the case of fiscal year companies) and therefore did not generate a full year's allowance in 1959. We allocated the amount of property in accelerated method accounts for which year of purchase was not shown to specific years in the same proportions as the amounts of property in such accounts for which year of purchase was identified. We were then able to derive the ratio of accelerated method properties acquired in 1959 and in 1960 to total accelerated method facilities in each size class in each industrial division. We applied these ratios to the adjusted *Statistics of Income* estimates described above to obtain estimates of the amounts of such property generating only part-year depreciation allowances.

Method of Depreciation	1957	1959	1960	1957	1959	1960
	(million dollars)			*(per cent)*		
Straight-line	11,912	12,469	12,897	70.2	60.8	58.2
Declining-balance	2,630	4,776	5,363	15.5	23.3	24.2
Sum-of-the-years-digits	1,883	2,722	3,280	11.1	13.3	14.8
Other methods	543	526	620	3.2	2.6	2.8
Total	16,968	20,493	22,160	100.0	100.0	100.0

As the table shows, both the amounts and proportions of total allowances under the straight-line, declining-balance, and sum-of-the-years-digits methods for 1959 in relation to the corresponding amounts and proportions for 1957 and 1960 are in line with the trends we have outlined in the text.

From the amounts of accelerated depreciation allowances, so computed, we subtracted our estimates of the straight-line depreciation that would have been allowed on the estimated amounts of property in accelerated method accounts. To compute these straight-line allowances we reduced the estimated amounts of property in declining-balance and SYD accounts in each size class in each industry (Table D-4) by 15 per cent, to allow for estimated salvage.[4] To the remainder, we applied a percentage identified in the LDA as the Computed Depreciation Per Investment (CDPI), which is, in effect, the reciprocal of the harmonic mean service life calculated from the LDA data for the property at each service life.[5] The product is the estimated straight-line allowance which would have been claimed on the property in accelerated method accounts in each size class in each industrial division.[6]

[4] Except in the case of properties with service lives of three and four years for which salvage ratios of 17 per cent and 20 per cent, respectively, were used. These ratios reflect the fact that 19 per cent of three-year property and 50 per cent of four-year property were classified in LDA as Transportation Vehicles and Equipment and were assumed to be automobiles and trucks for which a salvage ratio of 25 per cent was deemed to be appropriate.

[5] The CDPI may be defined notationally as $\dfrac{(C_i/L_i)}{C_i}$, where C = cost, L = life (in years), and i = the ith item. See above, Appendix C, for a discussion of alternative service life measures and of the service life distribution of property in the LDA survey.

[6] With respect to the property in each such cell estimated to have been acquired in 1959 or 1960, for which only a partial year's allowance could have been claimed, we adjusted the full year's straight-line allowances. We applied to it a ratio, the numerator of which was the actual accelerated method allowances shown in LDA for the 1959 and 1960 acquisitions, and the denominator was the calculated amount of a first full year's allowance on such property, given its harmonic mean service life.

Subtracting these estimates of straight-line allowances from our estimated accelerated depreciation allowances, we obtain the estimate of additional allowances generated by use of accelerated methods in lieu of the straight-line depreciation method, in each size class in each major industrial division (Table D-9).

TABLE D-1

Cost of Corporations' Depreciable Assets in "Life of Depreciable Assets" Source Book by Method of Depreciation, Size of Total Assets, and Industry Division, All Facilities on Hand in 1959

A. Thousand Dollars

Size of Total Assets (million dollars)	Straight-Line[a]	Declining-Balance	Sum-of-the-Years-Digits[a]	Other-Life Methods	Units-of-Production	All Methods
All Industry Divisions						
Under 1	17,046,978	4,008,979	884,465	14,575	3,475	21,958,472
1–25	5,758,212	2,047,776	469,569	15,363	284	8,291,204
25 and over	159,584,079	27,811,915	24,798,241	5,767,294	4,217,485	222,179,014
Total	182,389,269	33,868,670	26,152,275	5,797,232	4,221,244	252,428,690
Agriculture, Forestry, and Fisheries						
Under 1	327,840	51,082	5,822	356	–	385,100
1–25	41,512	6,340	693	–	–	48,545
25 and over	337,975	–	–	–	–	337,975
Total	707,327	57,422	6,515	356	–	771,620
Mining						
Under 1	221,615	73,971	15,491	–	2,486	313,563
1–25	103,416	48,066	7,293	22	–	158,797
25 and over	2,994,796	312,870	38,866	218,441	1,055,349	4,620,322
Total	3,319,827	434,907	61,650	218,463	1,057,835	5,092,682

(continued)

TABLE D-1 (*continued*)

Part A. (*continued*)

Size of Total Assets (million dollars)	Straight -Line [a]	Declining -Balance	Sum-of-the- Years-Digits [a]	Other-Life Methods	Units-of- Production	All Methods
Construction						
Under 1	612,859	170,550	55,089	160	-	838,658
1-25	81,795	66,497	6,731	-	-	155,023
25 and over	155,064	64,571	987	-	-	220,622
Total	849,718	301,618	62,807	160	-	1,214,303
Manufacturing						
Under 1	2,145,864	449,268	140,196	857	757	2,736,942
1-25	1,452,425	292,534	141,267	1,141	76	1,887,443
25 and over	59,939,209	13,549,162	16,449,881	4,307,137	2,975,497	97,220,886
Total	63,537,498	14,290,964	16,731,344	4,309,135	2,976,330	101,845,271
Transportation, Communication, Electric, Gas, and Sanitary Services						
Under 1	762,648	174,195	52,360	2,636	2	991,841
1-25	490,249	50,808	19,335	4,594	-	564,986
25 and over	87,476,975	12,717,720	6,839,946	1,205,809	160,613	108,401,063
Total	88,729,872	12,942,723	6,911,641	1,213,039	160,615	109,957,890

(*continued*)

TABLE D-1 (*continued*)

Part A. (*continued*)

Size of Total Assets (million dollars)	Straight-Line [a]	Declining-Balance	Sum-of-the-Years-Digits [a]	Other-Life Methods	Units-of-Production	All Methods
Trade						
Under 1	2,723,651	412,856	84,567	3,952	195	3,225,221
1-25	362,685	63,696	23,549	456	-	450,386
25 and over	3,810,542	464,080	1,061,124	35,176	23,403	5,394,325
Total	6,896,878	940,632	1,169,240	39,584	23,598	9,069,932
Finance, Insurance, and Real Estate						
Under 1	8,532,361	2,147,248	395,713	5,804	-	11,081,126
1-25	2,768,324	1,396,210	218,113	9,150	208	4,392,005
25 and over	4,072,676	446,032	277,432	731	2,623	4,799,494
Total	15,373,361	3,989,490	891,258	15,685	2,831	20,272,625
Services						
Under 1	1,692,359	528,186	134,913	719	35	2,356,212
1-25	454,762	123,054	52,588	-	-	630,404
25 and over	796,840	257,480	130,006	-	-	1,184,326
Total	2,943,961	908,720	317,507	719	35	4,170,942

(*continued*)

TABLE D-1 *(continued)*

Part A. *(concluded)*

Size of Total Assets (million dollars)	Straight -Line [a]	Declining -Balance	Sum-of-the- Years-Digits [a]	Other-Life Methods	Units-of- Production	All Methods
Not Allocable						
Under 1	27,781	1,623	313	91	-	29,808
1-25	3,044	571	-	-	-	3,615
25 and over	-	-	-	-	-	-
Total	30,825	2,194	313	91	-	33,423

B. Per Cent

	Straight -Line [a]	Declining -Balance	Sum-of-the- Years-Digits [a]	Other-Life Methods	Units-of- Production	All Methods
Agriculture, Forestry, and Fisheries						
Under 1	85.13	13.27	1.51	0.09	-	100.0
1-25	85.51	13.06	1.43	-	-	100.0
25 and over	100.00	-	-	-	-	100.0
Mining						
Under 1	70.68	23.59	4.94	-	0.79	100.0
1-25	65.13	30.27	4.59	0.01	-	100.0
25 and over	64.82	6.77	0.84	4.73	22.84	100.0

(continued)

TABLE D-1 *(continued)*

Part B. *(continued)*

Size of Total Assets (million dollars)	Straight -Line [a]	Declining -Balance	Sum-of-the- Years-Digits [a]	Other-Life Methods	Units-of- Production	All Methods
Construction						
Under 1	73.08	20.34	6.57	0.02	—	100.01
1–25	52.76	42.90	4.34	—	—	100.00
25 and over	70.28	29.27	0.45	—	—	100.00
Manufacturing						
Under 1	78.40	16.42	5.12	0.03	0.03	100.00
1–25	76.95	15.50	7.48	0.06	0.01	100.00
25 and over	61.65	13.94	16.92	4.43	3.06	100.00
Transportation, Communication, Electric, Gas, and Sanitary Services						
Under 1	76.89	17.56	5.28	0.27	-	100.00
1–25	86.77	8.99	3.42	0.81	-	99.99
25 and over	80.70	11.73	6.31	1.11	0.15	100.00
Trade						
Under 1	84.45	12.80	2.62	0.12	0.01	100.00
1–25	80.53	14.14	5.23	0.10	-	100.00
25 and over	70.64	8.60	19.67	0.65	0.43	99.99

(continued)

TABLE D-1 (concluded)

Part B. (concluded)

Size of Total Assets (million dollars)	Straight-Line [a]	Declining-Balance	Sum-of-the-Years-Digits [a]	Other-Life Methods	Units-of-Production	All Methods
Finance, Insurance, and Real Estate						
Under 1	77.00	19.38	3.57	0.05	-	100.00
1–25	63.03	31.79	4.97	0.21	-	100.00
25 and over	84.86	9.29	5.78	0.01	0.06	100.00
Services						
Under 1	71.82	22.42	5.73	0.03	-	100.00
1–25	72.14	19.52	8.34	-	-	100.00
25 and over	67.28	21.74	10.98	-	-	100.00
Not Allocable						
Under 1	93.20	5.44	1.05	0.31	-	100.00
1–25	84.20	15.80	-	-	-	100.00
25 and over	-	-	-	-	-	-

Source: Internal Revenue Service, "Life of Depreciable Assets" source book.

[a] Amounts shown are grossed up for salvage, assumed to be equal to 15 per cent of cost, by dividing the amount shown in the corresponding cell in the LDA source book by 85 per cent.

TABLE D-2

Cost of Corporations' Depreciable Assets in Statistics of Income, by Method of Depreciation, Size of Total Assets, and Industry Division, All Facilities on Hand in 1959

(thousand dollars)

Size of Total Assets (million dollars)	Straight-Line	Declining-Balance	Sum-of-the-Years-Digits	Other-Life Methods	Units-of-Production	All Methods[a]
All Industry Divisions[b]						
Under 1	48,045,429	10,902,570	2,611,904	44,202	15,909	61,620,014
1-25	43,542,633	11,541,548	3,558,028	104,441	1,601	58,748,251
25 and over	173,823,667	30,351,054	27,190,779	6,306,175	4,756,807	242,428,482
Total	265,411,729	52,795,172	33,360,711	6,454,818	4,774,317	362,796,747
Agriculture, Forestry, and Fisheries						
Under 1	1,108,868	172,782	19,694	1,198	-	1,302,542
1-25	365,879	55,880	6,110	-	-	427,869
25 and over	375,158	-	-	-	-	375,158
Total	1,849,905	228,662	25,804	1,198	-	2,105,569
Mining						
Under 1	1,006,036	335,806	70,318	-	11,288	1,423,448
1-25	1,811,497	841,953	127,730	389	-	2,781,569
25 and over	3,693,256	385,861	47,919	269,396	1,301,454	5,697,886
Total	6,510,789	1,563,620	245,967	269,785	1,312,742	9,902,903

(continued)

TABLE D-2 *(continued)*

Size of Total Assets (million dollars)	Straight-Line	Declining-Balance	Sum-of-the-Years-Digits	Other-Life Methods	Units-of-Production	All Methods[a]
Construction						
Under 1	2,037,907	567,120	183,193	530	–	2,788,750
1-25	828,621	673,648	68,189	–	–	1,570,458
25 and over	329,209	137,089	2,094	–	–	468,392
Total	3,195,737	1,377,857	253,476	530	–	4,827,600
Manufacturing						
Under 1	10,727,982	2,246,057	700,841	4,242	3,831	13,682,953
1-25	19,142,796	3,855,575	1,861,990	14,926	995	24,876,282
25 and over	65,474,985	14,799,919	17,968,903	4,704,624	3,250,757	106,199,188
Total	95,345,763	20,901,551	20,531,734	4,723,792	3,255,583	144,758,423
Transportation, Communication, Electric, Gas, and Sanitary Services						
Under 1	3,330,742	760,779	228,671	11,522	–	4,331,714
1-25	6,235,642	646,258	245,913	58,424	–	7,186,237
25 and over	93,286,530	13,562,140	7,294,332	1,285,467	171,087	115,599,556
Total	102,852,914	14,969,177	7,768,916	1,355,413	171,087	127,117,507
Trade						
Under 1	10,048,721	1,523,211	311,996	14,517	714	11,899,159
1-25	4,394,939	771,821	285,381	5,512	–	5,457,653
25 and over	4,970,536	605,344	1,384,137	45,878	30,538	7,036,433
Total	19,414,196	2,900,376	1,981,514	65,907	31,252	24,393,245

(continued)

TABLE D-2 (*concluded*)

Size of Total Assets (million dollars)	Straight -Line	Declining -Balance	Sum-of-the- Years-Digits	Other-Life Methods	Units-of- Production	All Methods [a]
Finance, Insurance, and Real Estate						
Under 1	14,272,014	3,591,775	661,896	9,638	-	18,535,323
1-25	7,633,425	3,849,956	601,412	25,190	606	12,110,589
25 and over	4,583,955	502,012	312,292	810	2,971	5,402,040
Total	26,489,394	7,943,743	1,575,600	35,638	3,577	36,047,952
Services						
Under 1	5,451,472	1,701,436	434,600	2,353	76	7,589,937
1-25	3,124,388	845,436	361,303	-	-	4,331,127
25 and over	1,110,038	358,689	181,102	-	-	1,649,829
Total	9,685,898	2,905,561	977,005	2,353	76	13,570,893
Not Allocable						
Under 1	61,687	3,604	695	202	-	66,188
1-25	5,446	1,021	-	-	-	6,467
25 and over	-	-	-	-	-	-
Total	67,133	4,625	695	202	-	72,655

Source: Internal Revenue Service, "Life of Depreciable Assets" source book.

Note: Amounts in each cell were derived by applying ratios in corresponding cells in Table D-1, part B, to row totals (all methods) in this table.

[a]*Statistics of Income* balance sheet amounts were adjusted for differences between the amounts of depreciable facilities included in balance sheets in tax returns and those included in depreciation schedules of these returns for purposes of computing depreciation allowances. See above.

[b]Includes small amounts of property of companies not allocable to any major industrial division.

TABLE D-3

Cost of Corporations' Depreciable Assets Acquired After 1953, in the "Life of Depreciable Assets" Source Book, by Method of Depreciation, Size of Total Assets, and Industrial Division, 1959

(thousand dollars)

Size of Total Assets (million dollars)	Straight-Line[a]	Declining-Balance	Sum-of-the-Years-Digits[a]	Other-Life Methods	Units-of-Production	All Methods
All Industry Divisions[b]						
Under 1	10,597,141	3,627,003	874,442	14,244	3,197	15,116,027
1-25	3,108,322	1,740,006	462,621	7,466	284	5,318,699
25 and over	40,007,424	26,875,843	24,681,931	1,526,414	1,241,961	94,333,573
Total	53,712,887	32,242,852	26,018,994	1,548,124	1,245,442	114,968,299
Agriculture, Forestry, and Fisheries						
Under 1	244,200	50,429	5,822	356	-	300,807
1-25	19,464	6,340	693	-	-	26,497
25 and over	90,013	-	-	-	-	90,013
Total	353,676	56,769	6,515	356	-	417,317
Mining						
Under 1	179,999	73,651	15,491	-	2,418	271,559
1-25	74,033	48,066	7,293	22	-	129,419
25 and over	1,377,219	312,344	38,862	218,402	449,595	2,396,422
Total	1,631,251	434,061	61,646	218,424	452,013	2,797,395

(continued)

TABLE D-3 (continued)

Size of Total Assets (million dollars)	Straight-Line [a]	Declining-Balance	Sum-of-the-Years-Digits [a]	Other-Life Methods	Units-of-Production	All Methods
Construction						
Under 1	559,073	170,305	54,971	160	–	784,509
1–25	63,935	66,430	6,731	–	–	137,096
25 and over	70,809	64,571	987	–	–	136,367
Total	693,818	301,306	62,688	160	–	1,057,972
Manufacturing						
Under 1	1,412,248	445,554	138,221	857	757	1,997,637
1–25	579,019	282,665	138,729	1,141	76	1,001,630
25 and over	13,555,207	12,828,890	16,403,494	441,712	705,076	43,934,379
Total	15,546,474	13,557,109	16,680,445	443,710	705,909	46,933,646
Transportation, Communication, Electric, Gas, and Sanitary Services						
Under 1	609,194	174,110	51,961	2,636	2	837,903
1–25	345,909	50,512	19,335	3,103	–	418,859
25 and over	21,533,811	12,563,014	6,839,827	840,685	74,390	41,851,727
Total	22,488,914	12,787,636	6,911,124	846,424	74,392	43,108,489
Trade						
Under 1	2,065,175	401,245	82,921	3,719	–	2,553,060
1–25	207,048	63,076	23,294	410	–	293,828
25 and over	1,368,858	419,236	999,784	25,021	11,651	2,824,550
Total	3,641,081	883,557	1,105,999	29,150	11,651	5,671,438

(continued)

TABLE D-3 *(concluded)*

Size of Total Assets (million dollars)	Straight-Line [a]	Declining-Balance	Sum-of-the-Years-Digits [a]	Other-Life Methods	Units-of-Production	All Methods
Finance, Insurance, and Real Estate						
Under 1	4,266,792	1,786,782	391,241	5,706	-	6,450,521
1-25	1,548,808	1,103,849	216,239	2,790	208	2,871,894
25 and over	1,571,080	431,044	274,091	594	1,249	2,278,058
Total	7,386,680	3,321,675	881,571	9,090	1,457	11,600,473
Services						
Under 1	1,236,427	523,523	133,501	719	20	1,894,190
1-25	267,095	118,497	50,307	-	-	435,899
25 and over	440,427	256,744	124,886	-	-	822,057
Total	1,943,949	898,764	308,694	719	20	3,152,146
Not Allocable						
Under 1	24,033	1,404	313	91	-	25,841
1-25	3,011	571	-	-	-	3,582
25 and over	-	-	-	-	-	-
Total	27,044	1,975	313	91	-	29,423

Source: Internal Revenue Service, "Life of Depreciable Assets" source book.

[a] Grossed up for salvage.

[b] Includes small amounts of property of companies not allocable to any industry division.

TABLE D-4

Cost of Corporations' Depreciable Assets Acquired After 1953, in Statistics of Income, by Method of Depreciation, Size of Total Assets, and Industry Division, 1959

(thousand dollars)

Size of Total Assets (million dollars)	Straight-Line	Declining-Balance	Sum-of-the-Years-Digits	Other-Life Methods	Units-of-Production	All Methods
All Industry Divisions[a]						
Under 1	32,015,479	10,217,775	2,581,893	43,315	14,835	44,873,297
1-25	22,767,094	10,561,969	3,500,474	67,552	1,576	36,898,665
25 and over	43,887,284	29,322,823	27,048,889	1,689,660	1,420,572	103,361,228
Total	98,669,857	50,102,567	33,131,256	1,792,527	1,436,983	185,133,190
Agriculture, Forestry, and Fisheries						
Under 1	825,969	170,568	19,694	1,204	-	1,017,435
1-25	171,554	55,880	6,110	-	-	233,544
25 and over	99,916	-	-	-	-	99,916
Total	1,097,439	226,448	25,804	1,204	-	1,350,895
Mining						
Under 1	817,116	334,339	70,318	-	10,977	1,232,750
1-25	1,296,795	841,953	127,757	385	-	2,266,890
25 and over	1,698,426	385,177	47,919	269,339	554,450	2,955,311
Total	3,812,337	1,561,469	245,994	269,724	565,427	6,454,951

(continued)

TABLE D-4 *(continued)*

Size of Total Assets (million dollars)	Straight -Line	Declining -Balance	Sum-of-the-Years-Digits	Other-Life Methods	Units-of-Production	All Methods
Construction						
Under 1	1,859,064	566,311	182,803	532	—	2,608,710
1-25	647,689	672,973	68,189	—	—	1,388,851
25 and over	150,330	137,089	2,094	—	—	289,513
Total	2,657,083	1,376,373	253,086	532	—	4,287,074
Manufacturing						
Under 1	7,060,267	2,227,448	690,989	4,284	3,785	9,986,773
1-25	7,631,297	3,725,472	1,828,407	15,038	1,002	13,201,216
25 and over	14,807,353	14,014,045	17,917,927	482,505	770,188	47,992,018
Total	29,498,917	19,966,965	20,437,323	501,827	774,975	71,180,007
Transportation, Communication, Electric, Gas, and Sanitary Services						
Under 1	2,660,583	760,389	226,939	11,512	9	3,659,432
1-25	4,399,702	642,450	245,913	39,468	-	5,327,533
25 and over	22,963,852	13,396,833	7,294,332	896,509	79,330	44,630,856
Total	30,024,137	14,799,672	7,767,184	947,489	79,339	53,617,821
Trade						
Under 1	7,619,269	1,480,374	305,927	13,721	-	9,419,291
1-25	2,508,938	764,344	282,270	4,968	-	3,560,520
25 and over	1,785,565	546,872	1,304,132	32,638	15,198	3,684,405
Total	11,913,772	2,791,590	1,892,329	51,327	15,198	16,664,216

(continued)

TABLE D-4 *(concluded)*

Size of Total Assets (million dollars)	Straight-Line	Declining-Balance	Sum-of-the-Years-Digits	Other-Life Methods	Units-of-Production	All Methods
Finance, Insurance, and Real Estate						
Under 1	7,137,027	2,988,821	654,482	9,544	-	10,789,874
1 - 25	4,270,678	3,043,754	596,204	7,693	574	7,918,903
25 and over	1,768,304	485,157	308,511	669	1,406	2,564,047
Total	13,176,009	6,517,732	1,559,197	17,906	1,980	21,272,824
Services						
Under 1	3,982,819	1,686,408	430,046	2,316	64	6,101,653
1 - 25	1,835,055	814,122	345,624	-	-	2,994,801
25 and over	613,538	357,650	173,974	-	-	1,145,162
Total	6,431,412	2,858,180	949,644	2,316	64	10,241,616
Not Allocable						
Under 1	53,365	3,117	695	202	-	57,379
1 - 25	5,386	1,021	-	-	-	6,407
25 and over	-	-	-	-	-	-
Total	58,751	4,138	695	202	-	63,786

Source: Internal Revenue Service, "Life of Depreciable Assets" source book.
Note: The amount in each cell was computed by applying to the row total in Table D-2 the ratio derived from the LDA survey of the cost of facilities acquired after 1953 to the cost of all facilities on hand in 1959 in the corresponding cell. The numerators of these ratios are in Table D-3 and the denominators are in Table D-1.

a Includes small amounts of property of companies not allocable to any industry division.

TABLE D-5

Amount of Corporations' Depreciation Allowances on All Facilities on Hand in 1959, in "Life of Depreciable Assets"

Source Book, by Method of Depreciation, Size of Total Assets, and Industry Division, 1959

A. Thousand Dollars

Size of Total Assets (million dollars)	Straight -Line	Declining -Balance	Sum-of-the- Years-Digits	Other-Life Methods	Units-of- Production	All Methods
All Industry Divisions						
Under 1	995,237	371,106	80,586	1,310	331	1,448,570
1 - 25	263,567	142,700	32,772	715	83	439,837
25 and over	5,669,734	2,041,133	1,844,562	222,966	222,872	10,001,267
Total	6,928,538	2,554,939	1,957,920	224,991	223,286	11,889,674
Agriculture, Forestry, and Fisheries						
Under 1	25,191	7,342	766	36	–	33,335
1 - 25	2,623	1,176	106	–	–	3,905
25 and over	19,299	–	–	–	–	19,299
Total	47,113	8,518	872	36	–	56,539
Mining						
Under 1	23,055	12,239	2,061	–	234	37,589
1 - 25	8,945	7,176	577	5	–	16,703
25 and over	142,283	25,270	1,968	9,512	53,865	232,898
Total	174,283	44,685	4,606	9,517	54,099	287,190

(continued)

TABLE D-5 (continued)

Part A. (continued)

Size of Total Assets (million dollars)	Straight -Line	Declining -Balance	Sum-of-the- Years-Digits	Other-Life Methods	Units-of- Production	All Methods
Construction						
Under 1	74,499	30,464	8,129	23	-	113,115
1 - 25	8,720	11,839	661	-	-	21,220
25 and over	10,424	8,876	145	-	-	19,445
Total	93,643	51,179	8,935	23	-	153,780
Manufacturing						
Under 1	160,051	60,257	14,944	109	92	235,453
1 - 25	80,432	30,803	12,025	98	76	123,434
25 and over	2,666,550	1,163,606	1,376,745	168,906	157,735	5,533,542
Total	2,907,033	1,254,666	1,403,714	169,115	157,903	5,892,429
Transportation, Communication, Electric, Gas, and Sanitary Services						
Under 1	75,202	26,399	5,866	368	-	107,835
1 - 25	27,586	6,417	2,150	136	-	36,289
25 and over	2,448,355	739,153	347,668	40,822	9,965	3,585,963
Total	2,551,143	771,969	355,684	41,326	9,965	3,730,087
Trade						
Under 1	222,921	59,105	10,349	351	1	292,727
1 - 25	22,423	7,459	2,532	129	-	32,543
25 and over	180,363	47,150	88,701	3,687	1,137	321,038
Total	425,707	113,714	101,582	4,167	1,138	646,308

(continued)

TABLE D-5 *(continued)*

Part A. *(concluded)*

Size of Total Assets (million dollars)	Straight-Line	Declining-Balance	Sum-of-the-Years-Digits	Other-Life Methods	Units-of-Production	All Methods
Finance, Insurance, and Real Estate						
Under 1	280,462	107,108	19,744	377	-	407,691
1-25	85,757	61,730	10,384	347	7	158,225
25 and over	145,842	27,363	19,826	39	170	193,240
Total	512,061	196,201	49,954	763	177	759,156
Services						
Under 1	131,786	67,908	18,676	43	4	218,417
1-25	26,866	16,070	4,337	-	-	47,273
25 and over	56,618	29,715	9,509	-	-	95,842
Total	215,270	113,693	32,522	43	4	361,532
Not Allocable						
Under 1	2,070	284	51	3	-	2,408
1-25	215	30	-	-	-	245
25 and over	-	-	-	-	-	-
Total	2,285	314	51	3	-	2,651

(continued)

TABLE D-5 (continued)

B. Per Cent

Size of Total Assets (million dollars)	Straight -Line	Declining -Balance	Sum-of-the- Years-Digits	Other-Life Methods	Units-of- Production	All Methods
Agriculture, Forestry, and Fisheries						
Under 1	75.57	22.02	2.30	0.11	–	100.00
1 - 25	67.17	30.12	2.71	–	–	100.00
25 and over	100.00	–	–	–	–	100.00
Mining						
Under 1	61.33	32.56	5.48	–	0.62	100.00
1 - 25	53.55	42.96	3.46	0.03	–	100.00
25 and over	61.09	10.85	0.84	4.08	23.13	100.00
Construction						
Under 1	65.86	26.93	7.19	0.02	–	100.00
1 - 25	41.09	55.79	3.12	–	–	100.00
25 and over	53.61	45.65	0.74	–	–	100.00

(continued)

TABLE D-5 *(continued)*

Part B. *(continued)*

Size of Total Assets (million dollars)	Straight-Line	Declining-Balance	Sum-of-the-Years-Digits	Other-Life Methods	Units-of-Production	All Methods
Manufacturing						
Under 1	67.98	25.59	6.35	0.05	0.04	100.00
1-25	65.16	24.96	9.74	0.08	0.06	100.00
25 and over	48.19	21.03	24.88	3.05	2.85	100.00
Transportation, Communication, Electric, Gas, and Sanitary Services						
Under 1	69.74	24.48	5.44	0.34	-	100.00
1-25	76.02	17.68	5.92	0.38	-	100.00
25 and over	68.28	20.61	9.70	1.14	0.28	100.00
Trade						
Under 1	76.15	20.19	3.54	0.12	-	100.00
1-25	68.90	22.92	7.78	0.40	-	100.00
25 and over	56.18	14.69	27.63	1.15	0.36	100.00

(continued)

TABLE D-5 *(concluded)*

Part B. *(concluded)*

Size of Total Assets (million dollars)	Straight -Line	Declining -Balance	Sum-of-the- Years–Digits	Other-Life Methods	Units-of- Production	All Methods
Finance, Insurance, and Real Estate						
Under 1	68.79	26.27	4.84	0.09	-	100.00
1 - 25	54.20	39.01	6.56	0.22	0.01	100.00
25 and over	75.47	14.16	10.26	0.02	0.09	100.00
Services						
Under 1	60.34	31.09	8.55	0.02	-	100.00
1 - 25	56.83	33.99	9.17	-	-	100.00
25 and over	59.07	31.00	9.92	-	-	100.00
Not Allocable						
Under 1	85.96	11.79	2.12	0.12	-	100.00
1 - 25	87.76	12.24	-	-	-	100.00
25 and over	-	-	-	-	-	100.00

Source: Internal Revenue Service, "Life of Depreciable Assets" source book.

TABLE D-6

Amount of Corporations' Depreciation Allowances on All Facilities on Hand in 1959, in Statistics of Income, by Method of Depreciation, Size of Total Assets, and Industry Division, 1959

(thousand dollars)

Size of Total Assets (million dollars)	Straight-Line	Declining-Balance	Sum-of-the-Years-Digits	Other-Life Methods	Units-of-Production	All Methods
All Industry Divisions						
Under 1	3,311,226	1,227,814	273,200	4,343	1,425	4,818,008
1-25	2,617,260	1,211,741	324,837	6,442	-1,123	4,161,403
25 and over	6,540,732	2,336,621	2,123,959	253,619	259,284	11,514,215
Total	12,469,218	4,776,176	2,721,996	264,404	261,832	20,493,626
Agriculture, Forestry, and Fisheries						
Under 1	79,039	23,036	2,404	113	-	104,592
1-25	25,187	11,292	1,018	-	-	37,497
25 and over	22,391	-	-	-	-	22,391
Total	126,617	34,328	3,422	113	-	164,480
Mining						
Under 1	95,006	50,435	8,493	-	965	154,899
1-25	133,468	107,073	8,611	75	-	249,227
25 and over	175,265	31,127	2,424	11,716	66,350	286,882
Total	403,739	188,635	19,528	11,791	67,315	691,008

(continued)

TABLE D-6 (*continued*)

Size of Total Assets (million dollars)	Straight -Line	Declining -Balance	Sum-of-the- Years-Digits	Other-Life Methods	Units-of- Production	All Methods
Construction						
Under 1	235,351	96,240	25,682	72	–	357,345
1-25	88,141	119,668	6,681	–	–	214,490
25 and over	16,436	13,995	229	–	–	30,660
Total	339,928	229,903	32,592	72	–	602,495
Manufacturing						
Under 1	770,323	290,016	71,926	521	442	1,133,228
1-25	1,153,015	441,568	172,381	1,398	1,097	1,769,459
25 and over	3,048,020	1,330,050	1,573,694	193,043	180,330	6,325,137
Total	4,971,358	2,061,634	1,818,001	194,962	181,869	9,227,824
Transportation, Communication, Electric, Gas, and Sanitary Services						
Under 1	296,317	104,020	23,114	1,449	–	424,900
1-25	393,589	91,556	30,678	1,941	–	517,764
25 and over	2,639,225	796,800	374,762	43,990	10,746	3,865,523
Total	3,329,131	992,376	428,554	47,380	10,746	4,808,187
Trade						
Under 1	822,450	218,062	38,186	1,296	3	1,079,997
1-25	325,665	108,330	36,776	1,872	–	472,643
25 and over	234,167	61,217	115,160	4,785	1,480	416,809
Total	1,382,282	387,609	190,122	7,953	1,483	1,969,449

(*continued*)

TABLE D-6 (concluded)

Size of Total Assets (million dollars)	Straight -Line	Declining -Balance	Sum-of-the- Years-Digits	Other-Life Methods	Units-of- Production	All Methods
Finance, Insurance, and Real Estate						
Under 1	554,544	211,780	39,040	742	-	806,106
1 - 25	286,031	205,893	34,636	1,156	26	527,742
25 and over	323,964	60,782	44,041	85	378	429,250
Total	1,164,539	478,455	117,717	1,983	404	1,763,098
Services						
Under 1	453,230	233,544	64,232	143	15	751,164
1 - 25	210,975	126,195	34,056	-	-	371,226
25 and over	81,264	42,650	13,649	-	-	137,563
Total	745,469	402,389	111,937	143	15	1,259,953
Not Allocable						
Under 1	4,966	681	123	7	-	5,777
1 - 25	1,189	166	-	-	-	1,355
25 and over	-	-	-	-	-	-
Total	6,155	847	123	7	-	7,132

Source: Internal Revenue Service, "Life of Depreciable Assets" source book.

Note: The amount in each cell is computed by applying the per cent in the corresponding cell in Table D-5, part B, to the row totals (all methods) in this table.

TABLE D-7

Amount of Corporations' Depreciation Allowance on Facilities Acquired Since 1953 in "Life of Depreciable Assets" Source Book, by Method of Depreciation, Size of Total Assets, and Industry Division, 1959

(thousand dollars)

Size of Total Assets (million dollars)	Straight-Line	Declining-Balance	Sum-of-the-Years-Digits	Other-Life Methods	Units-of-Production	All Methods
All Industry Divisions						
Under 1	779,428	358,718	80,103	1,305	327	1,219,881
1 - 25	169,776	3,206	32,560	485	83	336,110
25 and over	1,833,028	1,996,268	1,839,635	74,403	90,976	5,834,310
Total	2,782,232	2,488,192	1,952,298	76,193	91,386	7,390,301
Agriculture, Forestry, and Fisheries						
Under 1	21,576	7,329	766	36	-	29,707
1 - 25	1,695	1,176	106	-	-	2,977
25 and over	9,199	-	-	-	-	9,199
Total	32,470	8,505	872	36	-	41,883
Mining						
Under 1	20,533	12,226	2,061	-	231	35,051
1 - 25	7,115	7,176	577	5	-	14,873
25 and over	79,894	25,250	1,968	9,508	28,796	145,416
Total	107,542	44,652	4,606	9,513	29,027	195,340

(continued)

TABLE D-7 (continued)

Size of Total Assets (million dollars)	Straight -Line	Declining -Balance	Sum-of-the-Years-Digits	Other-Life Methods	Units-of-Production	All Methods
Construction						
Under 1	71,463	30,434	8,124	23	–	110,044
1 - 25	7,812	11,839	661	–	–	20,312
25 and over	6,560	8,876	145	–	–	15,581
Total	85,835	51,149	8,930	23	–	145,937
Manufacturing						
Under 1	125,168	60,055	14,804	109	92	200,228
1 - 25	42,102	30,288	11,922	98	76	84,486
25 and over	818,422	1,129,508	1,375,282	31,878	54,013	3,409,103
Total	985,692	1,219,851	1,402,008	32,085	54,181	3,693,817
Transportation, Communication, Electric, Gas, and Sanitary Services						
Under 1	68,686	26,391	5,844	368	–	101,289
1 - 25	22,268	6,375	2,150	128	–	30,921
25 and over	715,606	731,776	347,664	29,655	7,428	1,832,129
Total	806,560	764,542	355,658	30,151	7,428	1,964,339
Trade						
Under 1	192,299	58,296	10,284	347	–	261,226
1 - 25	16,293	7,431	2,522	121	–	26,367
25 and over	83,866	44,336	85,703	3,327	656	217,888
Total	292,458	110,063	98,509	3,795	656	505,481

(continued)

TABLE D-7 *(concluded)*

Size of Total Assets (million dollars)	Straight -Line	Declining -Balance	Sum-of-the- Years-Digits	Other-Life Methods	Units-of- Production	All Methods
Finance, Insurance, and Real Estate						
Under 1	165,248	96,025	19,592	376	-	281,241
1 - 25	53,437	52,989	10,337	133	7	116,903
25 and over	74,650	26,870	19,657	35	83	121,295
Total	293,335	175,884	49,586	544	90	519,439
Services						
Under 1	112,539	67,690	18,577	43	4	198,853
1 - 25	18,841	15,902	4,285	-	-	39,028
25 and over	44,831	29,652	9,216	-	-	83,699
Total	176,211	113,244	32,078	43	4	321,580
Not Allocable						
Under 1	1,916	272	51	3	-	2,242
1 - 25	213	30	-	-	-	243
25 and over	-	-	-	-	-	-
Total	2,129	302	51	3	-	2,485

Source: Internal Revenue Service, "Life of Depreciable Assets" source book.

TABLE D-8

Amount of Corporations' Depreciation Allowances on Facilities Acquired Since 1953, in Statistics of Income, by Method of Depreciation, Size of Total Assets, and Industry Division, 1959

(thousand dollars)

Size of Total Assets (million dollars)	Straight-Line	Declining-Balance	Sum-of-the-Years-Digits	Other-Life Methods	Units-of-Production	All Methods
All Industry Divisions						
Under 1	2,678,991	1,200,941	271,522	4,338	1,410	4,157,202
1-25	1,686,663	1,172,886	322,652	5,502	1,118	3,188,821
25 and over	2,165,373	2,284,830	2,117,627	84,507	106,240	6,758,577
Total	6,531,027	4,658,657	2,711,801	94,347	108,768	14,104,600
Agriculture, Forestry, and Fisheries						
Under 1	67,697	22,996	2,404	113	-	93,210
1-25	16,276	11,292	1,018	-	-	28,586
25 and over	10,673	-	-	-	-	10,673
Total	94,646	34,288	3,422	113	-	132,469
Mining						
Under 1	84,614	50,381	8,493	-	953	144,441
1-25	106,163	107,073	8,608	75	-	221,919
25 and over	98,412	31,104	2,424	11,711	35,470	179,121
Total	289,189	188,558	19,525	11,786	36,423	545,481

(continued)

TABLE D-8 (continued)

Size of Total Assets (million dollars)	Straight-Line	Declining-Balance	Sum-of-the-Years-Digits	Other-Life Methods	Units-of-Production	All Methods
Construction						
Under 1	225,760	96,144	25,665	71	–	347,640
1-25	78,962	119,668	6,681	–	–	205,311
25 and over	10,343	13,995	229	–	–	24,567
Total	315,065	229,807	32,575	71	–	577,518
Manufacturing						
Under 1	602,435	289,041	71,246	521	442	963,685
1-25	603,545	434,190	170,912	1,398	1,097	1,211,142
25 and over	935,488	1,291,087	1,572,050	36,433	61,733	3,896,791
Total	2,141,468	2,014,318	1,814,208	38,352	63,272	6,071,618
Transportation, Communication, Electric, Gas, and Sanitary Services						
Under 1	270,640	103,990	23,025	1,449	–	399,104
1-25	317,716	90,956	30,678	1,828	–	441,178
25 and over	771,404	788,837	374,762	31,968	8,002	1,974,973
Total	1,359,760	983,783	428,465	35,245	8,002	2,815,255
Trade						
Under 1	709,472	215,081	37,940	1,285	–	963,778
1-25	236,633	107,923	36,630	1,758	–	382,944
25 and over	108,883	57,561	111,271	4,318	850	282,883
Total	1,054,988	380,565	185,841	7,361	850	1,629,605

(continued)

TABLE D-8 *(concluded)*

Size of Total Assets (million dollars)	Straight-Line	Declining-Balance	Sum-of-the-Years-Digits	Other-Life Methods	Units-of-Production	All Methods
Finance, Insurance, and Real Estate						
Under 1	326,739	189,862	38,741	742	-	556,084
1-25	178,234	176,741	34,477	443	21	389,916
25 and over	165,824	59,687	43,663	77	185	269,436
Total	670,797	426,290	116,881	1,262	206	1,215,436
Services						
Under 1	387,037	232,793	63,886	150	15	683,881
1-25	147,956	124,877	33,648	-	-	306,481
25 and over	64,346	42,559	13,228	-	-	120,133
Total	599,339	400,229	110,762	150	15	1,110,495
Not Allocable						
Under 1	4,597	653	122	7	-	5,379
1-25	1,178	166	-	-	-	1,344
25 and over	-	-	-	-	-	-
Total	5,775	819	122	7	-	6,723

Source: Internal Revenue Service, "Life of Depreciable Assets" source book.

Note: The amount in each cell is computed by applying to the row totals (all methods) in this table the ratios in the corresponding cells of depreciation allowances on post-1953 facilities to the allowances on all facilities on hand in 1959 derived from the LDA source book. The numerators of these ratios are in Table D-5 and the denominators are in Table D-7.

TABLE D-9

Excess of Accelerated Depreciation Over Estimated Straight-Line Allowances on Property in Accelerated Method Accounts, by Size of Total Assets and Industry Division, 1959

(thousand dollars)

Size of Total Assets (million dollars)	Declining-Balance [a]	Estimated Straight-Line [b]	Declining-Balance Minus Straight-Line	Sum-of-the-Years-Digits [a]	Estimated Straight-Line [b]	SYD Minus Estimated Straight-Line	Additional Allowances from Using Accelerated Method
All Industry Divisions							
Under 1	1,200,941	855,607	345,334	271,522	220,116	51,406	396,740
1-25	1,172,886	815,379	357,507	322,652	238,113	84,539	442,046
25 and over	2,284,830	1,366,097	918,733	2,117,627	1,441,666	675,961	1,594,694
Total	4,658,657	3,037,083	1,621,574	2,711,801	1,899,895	811,906	2,433,480
Agriculture, Forestry, and Fisheries							
Under 1	22,996	17,303	5,693	2,404	2,418	–14	5,679
1-25	11,292	6,955	4,337	1,018	670	348	4,685
25 and over	–	–	–	–	–	–	–
Total	34,288	24,258	10,030	3,422	3,088	334	10,364
Mining							
Under 1	50,381	47,400	2,981	8,493	9,294	–801	2,180
1-25	107,073	103,288	3,785	8,608	7,002	1,606	5,391
25 and over	31,104	21,349	9,755	2,424	2,702	–278	9,477
Total	188,558	172,037	16,521	19,525	18,998	527	17,048

(continued)

TABLE D-9 *(continued)*

Size of Total Assets (million dollars)	Declining-Balance [a]	Estimated Straight-Line [b]	Declining-Balance Minus Straight-Line	Sum-of-the-Years-Digits [a]	Estimated Straight-Line [b]	SYD Minus Estimated Straight-Line	Additional Allowances from Using Accelerated Method
Construction							
Under 1	96,144	77,153	18,991	25,665	28,502	-2,837	16,154
1-25	119,668	102,385	17,283	6,681	11,668	-4,987	12,296
25 and over	13,995	13,764	231	229	408	-179	52
Total	229,807	193,302	36,505	32,575	40,578	-8,003	28,502
Manufacturing							
Under 1	289,041	215,842	73,199	71,246	59,873	11,373	84,572
1-25	434,190	283,497	150,693	170,912	126,242	44,670	195,363
25 and over	1,291,087	754,980	536,107	1,572,050	1,054,403	517,647	1,053,754
Total	2,014,318	1,254,319	759,999	1,814,208	1,240,518	573,690	1,333,689
Transportation, Communication, Electric, Gas, and Sanitary Services							
Under 1	103,990	80,094	23,896	23,025	23,159	-134	23,762
1-25	90,956	59,318	31,638	30,678	23,516	7,162	38,800
25 and over	788,837	489,130	299,707	374,762	271,187	103,575	403,282
Total	983,783	628,542	355,241	428,465	317,862	110,603	465,844
Trade							
Under 1	215,081	150,891	64,190	37,940	35,129	2,811	67,001
1-25	107,923	86,254	21,669	36,630	27,971	8,659	30,328
25 and over	57,561	38,635	18,926	111,271	82,997	28,274	47,200
Total	308,565	275,780	104,785	185,841	146,097	39,744	144,529

(continued)

TABLE D-9 *(concluded)*

Size of Total Assets (million dollars)	Declining-Balance[a]	Estimated Straight-Line[b]	Declining-Balance Minus Straight-Line	Sum-of-the-Years-Digits[a]	Estimated Straight-Line[b]	SYD Minus Estimated Straight-Line	Additional Allowances from Using Accelerated Method
Finance, Insurance, and Real Estate							
Under 1	189,862	124,416	65,446	38,741	23,344	15,397	80,843
1 - 25	176,741	98,208	78,533	34,477	19,188	15,289	93,822
25 and over	59,687	20,710	38,977	43,663	16,188	27,475	66,452
Total	426,290	243,334	182,956	116,881	58,720	58,161	241,117
Services							
Under 1	232,793	142,115	90,678	63,886	38,278	25,608	116,286
1 - 25	124,877	75,447	49,430	33,648	21,856	11,792	61,222
25 and over	42,559	27,529	15,030	13,228	13,781	–553	14,477
Total	400,229	245,091	155,138	110,762	73,915	36,847	191,985
Not Allocable							
Under 1	653	393	260	122	119	3	263
1 - 25	166	27	139	-	-	-	139
25 and over	-	-	-	-	-	-	-
Total	819	420	399	122	119	3	402

Source: U.S. Treasury Department, Internal Revenue Service, "Life of Depreciable Assets" source book.

Note: Negative amounts denote the fact that the estimated straight-line allowances exceeded the actual SYD allowances. This resulted generally in those cases where properties with short service lives, which had been acquired relatively early in the period 1954–59, represented large proportions of the total amount of property in SYD accounts.

[a]Table D-8.

[b]See text for estimating procedure.

APPENDIX E

EFFECT OF ACCELERATED DEPRECIATION ON CORPORATIONS' CAPITAL OUTLAYS IN 1959

In estimating the additional capital outlays in 1959 attributable to the use of accelerated depreciation, we have represented the demand for capital goods and the supply of investable funds in the corporate sector by linear functions of the form:

$$r_d = a_d + b_d Q_d \text{ (demand), and}$$

$$Q_s = a_s + b_s r_s \text{ (supply).}[1]$$

These functions are presumed to include the effects of the use of accelerated depreciation: in the demand function, this effect is represented as a higher rate of return with respect to any given amount of capital outlays than would be obtained by using the straight-line method; and in the supply function, the effect is represented as an increase in the amount of investable funds available at any given rate of interest.[2]

In equilibrium, of course,

$$r_s = r_d \text{ and } Q_s = Q_d = \frac{a_s + a_d b_s}{1 - b_s b_d},$$

which is the estimated volume of corporate expenditures for depreciable facilities in 1959. According to a preliminary estimate by the Office of Business Economics, these outlays amounted to $33.8 billion.

Had accelerated depreciation not been available, the functions would have been

$$r'_d = a_d - X + b_d Q'_d \text{ (demand), and}$$

$$Q'_s = a_s - Y + b_s r'_s \text{ (supply),}$$

---

[1] We wish to emphasize the obvious fact that these equations do not imply specific theories of the demand for capital goods nor of the supply of saving. They are consistent, however, with the reasoning advanced to explain the effects of accelerated depreciation on investment, as discussed in Chapter 1.

[2] See Chapter 1 above for a discussion of these effects.

where X and Y are the shifts in the respective functions due to use of accelerated depreciation. In equilibrium, of course, $r'_s = r'_d$ and

$$Q'_s = Q'_d = \frac{a_s - Y + b_s(a_d - X)}{1 - b_s b_d},$$

which is the estimated volume of capital outlays without accelerated depreciation. The difference between this amount and observed outlays for the year is our estimate of the additional outlays attributable to the use of the declining-balance and SYD depreciation methods. This difference may be represented as $Q - Q' = \dfrac{Y + b_s X}{1 - b_s b_d}$.

Determination of $Q - Q'$ in the above equation quite obviously depends on the values of the shift parameters, X and Y, as well as on the slopes b_s and b_d of the supply and demand functions, respectively. We have estimated the shift in the supply function as $Y = \$1.265$ billion, i.e., the reduction in tax liabilities, hence the increase in cash flow, for corporations in 1959 from the use of accelerated depreciation methods. In estimating X, the shift in the demand function, we referred to Table 2, showing percentage point increases in rates of return realized by shifting from straight-line to accelerated depreciation at various service lives and at various rates of return under straight-line depreciation. We assumed an average service life of ten years for corporate depreciable property acquisitions in 1959. If we assume a 10 per cent after-tax rate of return under straight-line for such property, Table 2 shows a 1.1 percentage point increase in rate of return in shifting from straight-line to declining-balance depreciation and a 1.4 percentage point increase in shifting to SYD. The table also shows noticeably lower percentage point increases with respect to ten-year property if the straight-line rate of return were 5 per cent and noticeably higher increases if the corresponding rate of return were 15 per cent. Properly, therefore, the value of X should change with the assumed straight-line rate of return. In the interests of ease of computation, however, we assumed an average increase of 1.2 percentage points in the rate of return on the property added to accelerated method accounts in 1959. Little violence is done by this simplifying assumption, since we are concerned only with a small section of the demand schedule, within which the range of variation in r is likely to be small. We estimate that roughly two-thirds of 1959's property additions were added to accelerated method accounts and one-third to straight-line. Accordingly, with respect to the function representing aggregate corporate demand for depreciable facilities in 1959, we have assumed the shift parameter $X = 0.008$.

Determination of $Q - Q'$ also requires that we find the slopes of the respective functions, i.e., b_s and b_d, which in turn depend on the assumed values of r and the assumed elasticities for the respective functions, given the actual Q observed in 1959. By experiment, we determined that given $Q_{1959} = \$33.81$ billion, we could vary the assumed value of r over a wide range without significant effect on the solution of the equation incorporating the shift parameters. With a given value for Q, differences in r, of course, result in differences in the values of b in the respective functions, for any assumed elasticity, since the elasticities of the functions may be expressed as

$$\eta_d = \frac{r_d}{b_d Q_d} \text{ (demand), and}$$

$$\eta_s = \frac{b_s r_s}{Q_s} \text{ (supply).}$$

In other words, specification of the actual value of r makes relatively little difference for the outcome, given Q_{1959} and the assumed elasticities of the functions.

This is evident in Table E-1. With a demand elasticity of $-.5$, for example, the computed value of $Q - Q'$ (the estimated volume of additional capital outlays due to accelerated depreciation) varies narrowly over a wide range of assumed values of r, for any given elasticity of supply. With a demand elasticity of -1.0, a narrow range of estimate of $Q - Q'$ is also observable. The spread between computed values of $Q - Q'$ from one r to another tends to increase as the demand and supply elasticities increase.

The more significant variance in $Q - Q'$ appears in respect to differences in the assumed elasticities of the demand and supply functions, with any given r. With a low elasticity of demand, the difference in $Q - Q'$ is quite small from one supply elasticity to another. With $\eta_d = -2.5$, however, an appreciable difference appears.

Accordingly, we concluded that precise determination of r would not materially increase the reliability of our estimates. We have, therefore, based these estimates on the assumption that the \$33.81 billion of capital outlays in 1959 involved an after-tax rate of return of 10.0

per cent. As shown in Table E-1, depending on the assumed elasticities of the supply and demand functions, these capital outlays were between $1.3 billion and $5.7 billion more than would have been forthcoming in the absence of accelerated depreciation.

The shift in the demand function resulting from use of accelerated depreciation accounts for a substantial part of the estimated increase in outlays, as seen in Table E-2. Only when the elasticity of supply is very low, e.g., 0.5, is the increase in outlays due to the shift in the supply of investable funds of about the same magnitude as that resulting from the demand shift. Moreover, the greater the elasticity of supply, the greater is the proportion of the total estimated increase attributable to the shift in the demand function.

TABLE E-1

Estimated Additional Corporate Outlays for Depreciable Facilities,
1959, Attributable to the Use of Accelerated Depreciation, at
Selected Rates of Return (r) and Elasticities

(billion dollars)

Elasticity of Supply	Elasticity of Demand		
	−0.5	−1.0	−2.5
	$r = .05$		
0.5	1.43	1.90	2.38
1.0	1.48	2.22	3.17
2.5	1.54	2.63	4.61
5.0	1.56	2.86	5.72
10.0	1.57	3.00	6.61
	$r = .10$		
0.5	1.31	1.75	2.17
1.0	1.32	1.99	2.84
2.5	1.34	2.29	4.01
5.0	1.34	2.47	4.93
10.0	1.35	2.57	5.66
	$r = .15$		
0.5	1.24	1.65	2.06
1.0	1.23	1.84	2.63
2.5	1.22	2.08	3.65
5.0	1.21	2.20	4.44
10.0	1.21	2.31	5.08

TABLE E-2

Estimated Additional Corporate Outlays for Depreciable Facilities,
1959, Attributable to the Shift in the Demand and Supply
Functions, at Selected Elasticities[a]

(billion dollars)

Elasticity of Supply	Elasticity of Demand		
	−0.5	−1.0	−2.5
Supply Shift Only			
0.5	0.63	0.84	1.05
1.0	0.42	0.63	0.90
2.5	0.21	0.36	0.63
5.0	0.12	0.21	0.42
10.0	0.06	0.12	0.25
Demand Shift Only			
0.5	0.68	0.90	1.13
1.0	0.90	1.35	1.93
2.5	1.13	1.93	3.38
5.0	1.23	2.25	4.51
10.0	1.29	2.46	5.41

[a] $r = .10.$

INDEX

LDA study-defined -pg 7